Food and Drink in Antiquity

Bloomsbury Sources in Ancient History

The Bloomsbury Sources in Ancient History series presents a definitive collection of source material in translation, combined with expert contextual commentary and annotation to provide a comprehensive survey of each volume's subject. Material is drawn from literary, as well as epigraphic, legal, and religious sources. Aimed primarily at undergraduate students, the series will also be invaluable for researchers, and faculty devising and teaching courses.

Greek and Roman Sexualities: A Sourcebook, Jennifer Larson
Women in Ancient Rome, Bonnie MacLachlan

Food and Drink in Antiquity

Readings from the Graeco-Roman World

A Sourcebook

John F. Donahue

Bloomsbury Sources in Ancient History

B L O O M S B U R Y
LONDON • NEW DELHI • NEW YORK • SYDNEY

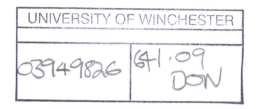
Bloomsbury Academic

An imprint of Bloomsbury Publishing Plc

50 Bedford Square	1385 Broadway
London	New York
WC1B 3DP	NY 10018
UK	USA

www.bloomsbury.com

Bloomsbury is a registered trade mark of Bloomsbury Publishing Plc

First published 2015

© John F. Donahue 2015

British Library Cataloguing-in-Publication Data

A catalogue record for this book is available from the British Library.

ISBN: PB: 978-1-44113-345-8
      HB: 978-1-44119-680-4
      ePDF: 978-1-44112-223-0
      ePub: 978-1-44113-098-3

Library of Congress Cataloging-in-Publication Data

A catalog record for this book is available from the Library of Congress.

Typeset by Fakenham Prepress Solutions, Fakenham, Norfolk NR21 8NN
Printed and bound in India

Contents

Acknowledgments

I am grateful to Michael Greenwood, now of Ashgate Publishing, for his encouragement and assistance in the critical early stages of this book; to Charlotte Loveridge and Chloe Shuttlewood of Bloomsbury Press for their cheerful expertise; and to the anonymous readers of the original manuscript, whose comments and suggestions have greatly improved this volume.

I would also like to thank the College of William and Mary for its support, especially the Plumeri Award for Faculty Excellence and the Craig W. Broderick/ Goldman Sachs Faculty Research Investment Fund, both of which provided welcomed financial assistance to complete this project. I would be remiss as well if I did not thank the many students at William and Mary who have put up with my teaching for the past 15 years and who have patiently endured while I formulated many of the ideas that have now found their way into the pages to follow. For my colleagues, too, who make our department such a pleasant place to work each day, I owe a great debt of gratitude.

Finally, this book simply would not have been possible without the continuing support of my wife Jaime and my two children, Catherine and Jack … *Familiae carissimae*.

Translations Used by Permission

Beck L. 2005. *Pedanius Dioscorides of Anazarbus, De Materia Medica*. Hildesheim: Georg Olms, 70 (7.20), 129–30 (7.18), 140–1 (7.19).

Powell, O. 2003. *Galen: On the Properties of Foodstuffs*. Cambridge: Cambridge University Press, 56 (3.14), 76 (7.10).

Grant, M. 2000. *Galen on Food and Diet*. London: Routledge Press, 78–9 (3.7), 152 (7.8), 155 (5.53), 157 (7.9).

Figure List

Figure 7. Mosaic from the "House of the Gladiators" of two gladiators facing each other and ready for fight. Their names, Hellenikos and Margareites, appear in Greek above their heads. The composition was probably commissioned after gladiatorial games, which took place in the Kourion theatre. Kourion, Cyprus, third century CE. Photo Credit: Edgar Knobloch/Art Resource, NY.   144

Figure 8. Detail of the Marriage at Cana, the blessing of water and changing it into wine. From the back of the pulpit of Archbishop Maximian. Carved ivory plaque, sixth century CE. Museo Arcivescovile, Ravenna, Italy. Photo Credit: Erich Lessing/Art Resource, NY.   152

Chapter 5

Figure 9. Terracotta kylix (drinking cup) of a Greek drinking party (symposium) featuring reclining male drinkers with musical and female accompaniment. Signed by Hieronas potter, attributed to Makron, c. 480 BCE. Metropolitan Museum of Art, Images for Academic Publishing.   163

Figure 10. Banquet scene depicting people eating and drinking at a *convivium* (feast) beneath a portico. Roman fresco from House of Triclinium, Pompeii, first century CE. Museo Archeologico Nazionale, Naples, Italy. Photo Credit: Erich Lessing/Art Resource, NY.   173

Figure 11. Mosaic of the Unswept Floor. Roman copy of a Greek original depicting the remains of a feast, second century CE. Museo Lateranense, Vatican Museums, Vatican State. Photo Credit: Alinari/Art Resource, NY.   185

Figure 12. Roman wine bar/café (*thermopolium*), Via dell'Abbondanza (Street of Abundance), Pompeii, Italy. Photo Credit: Gianni Dagli Orti/ The Art Archive at Art Resource, NY.   190

Chapter 6

Figure 13. Writing-tablet with a letter from Octavius, an entrepreneur supplying goods on a considerable scale to the army at the fort in Vindolanda, Roman Britain. Food items typically would have been among these supplies, late first or early second century CE. © The Trustees of the British Museum/Art Resource, NY.   212

Chapter 7

1

Introduction

The purpose of this volume is to present a reasonably representative selection of literary and documentary sources illustrating food and drink in the Graeco-Roman world from the earliest surviving literature of the eighth/seventh century BCE to the fourth/fifth century CE. In recent years we have witnessed an explosion of interest in the social world of the Greeks and Romans. This is partly the result of viewing antiquity less as the great deeds of great men and more as an era with much to tell us about the remarkably varied life of the everyday world. Food and drink comprised an essential part of such a world, and it is my hope that by gathering a selection of relevant sources into a single volume, the reader, whether he or she has interests in ancient history, anthropology, sociology, or food studies, will come to recognize the topic both as a unified whole and as one that has much to tell us about how the Greeks and Romans understood themselves and others.

A work of this nature can never be truly comprehensive. Inevitably, I have had to make decisions on what material to include and what to exclude within the space available. The result is some 340 extracts derived from more than 100 sources. As the reader will discover, most of the passages derive from ancient literature. At the same time, literature cannot tell the entire story; as a result, inscriptions, papyri, and legal codes also make valuable contributions to this study.

In selecting this material my guiding principle has been to provide as broad and varied a spectrum as possible for understanding this essential topic. At times, the choices have been clear; at other times it has meant choosing a passage that is perhaps less obvious than other possibilities but ultimately more engaging and illuminating for the topic at hand. Furthermore, it does not seem appropriate in this space to offer a comprehensive treatment of ancient food and drink. Instead, I have tried to place the selections in their social and historical context through careful explanation wherever necessary, with the expectation that readers will be encouraged to make their own syntheses and draw their own conclusions from the material assembled. In order to assist in this process I have included "Suggestions for Further Reading" at the end of each chapter. These are not specialist works but readings accessible to an English-speaking audience that may not necessarily possess a detailed understanding of the ancient Mediterranean world. The works of those modern authors cited in each chapter can also be found in "Suggestions for Further Reading."

The volume begins in Chapter 2 with food and drink as it appeared in ancient Greek and Roman literature. This chapter, organized by traditional literary genres, will introduce the reader to many of the authors and texts found elsewhere in the volume. Chapter 3 treats the foodstuffs available and utilized by the Greeks and Romans, with special focus on wine, oil, and bread, the foundational foodstuffs of the ancient Mediterranean diet. From there, the chapters unfold by topic, including selections and their interpretation on religion (Chapter 4), social context (Chapter 5), the military (Chapter 6), and health and medicine (Chapter 7). A list of "Works Cited," which provides the reader with additional information about the authors and works appearing in the chapters, follows Chapter 7.

Here it is worth making a point that is perhaps obvious but nonetheless important: none of these selections was originally written with their inclusion in a volume such as this in mind. As a result, context becomes important. In some of the selections, the context might be reasonably clear but in most instances we cannot fully recapture the conditions in which these writings were produced. A good example is ancient inscriptions. An inscription will usually be helpful on certain particulars—for instance, the name of a person who provides a feast for the community and the honors that the community will provide in response to this gift—but we know much less about who may have been invited, the expectations linked to such a gift (both on the part of the donor and the beneficiaries), and more generally how such a feast fitted into the social fabric of the typical ancient town. Many, if not all, of these features would have been apparent to the attendees but we must remain somewhat at a loss, since inscriptions do not typically record qualitative data of this sort.

Closely related to this point is the reality that the values and emphases of a particular passage tend to reflect those of the genre they represent. As we shall see, food and drink will often be treated quite farcically in Greek comedy where social criticism may be the ultimate goal, but quite sycophantically in poetry that is meant to flatter a Roman emperor. In the same way, agricultural writers will necessarily treat food differently from those who produce the symposiatic literature associated with the Greek drinking party. We cannot escape the reality, therefore, that there was always an agenda in the writings we will encounter and this volume will attempt to assist readers in recognizing this aspect in order that they may understand a given passage in its fullest terms.

Finally, all of the translations are my own, unless otherwise noted, with the citations keyed to the texts of the Loeb Classical Library. These translations are meant to be workable and accurate renderings that remain as true as possible to the original Greek and Latin. Difficulties or obscurities in particular texts will receive attention as needed but such commentary can never be the final word on such matters, and the reader is encouraged to consult the appropriate texts and commentaries for a more complete interpretation of the evidence. Any errors and infelicities, of course, remain my responsibility.

Eating, Drinking, and Reading: Food and Drink in Ancient Literature

For this is living like the gods – when you get the chance to eat someone else's food and you don't have to worry about paying for it.
Antiphanes, fr. 252 at Athenaeus, Sophists at Dinner 1.8d

Antiphanes, a prolific Athenian playwright whose works survive only in fragments, begins this chapter with a sentiment that was surely as common in his own time during the fourth century BCE as it was throughout antiquity—the simple joy of the meal. And so much the better if one did not have to cook the dinner or pay for it himself. The play from which this quote survives is lost, yet we know that Antiphanes wrote comedy, a genre that was especially amenable to presenting food and drink in lively and colorful ways. We shall have more to say about this in due course.

In the meantime, Antiphanes offers a useful starting point for considering the ways in which eating and drinking appear in the literature of ancient Greece and Rome. In fact, Graeco-Roman literature is a remarkably rich source for exploring customs and attitudes relating to food and drink. Most amenable to the topic were epic, considered a high genre by the ancients along with comedy and satire, both regarded as low genres. Equally useful contributions come from elsewhere: lyric poetry, which often offers intensely personal views of ancient life; historical writings, which provide critical insight into dining habits and character, especially of Roman emperors and foreign peoples; philosophical literature and ancient letter writing, both quite important for personal perspectives on diet and behavior; and a robust technical literature of agricultural treatises and cookbooks, which tell us how the ancients grew, gathered, stored, and cooked their food.

Before we begin, however, two points must be made. First, the term "literature" is not as tidy as it seems, especially when we consider that there are all sorts of additional texts such as law codes, curses, and inscriptions on graves, statues and buildings, which, despite their value as evidence of literary activity, have typically been excluded from ancient and modern surveys of Graeco-Roman literature (Braund). The reality is that any survey of literature must be arbitrary in what it chooses to include and exclude and this study is no different in this regard. My method, therefore, has been to organize this chapter around many of the traditional literary genres that the reader would expect to find in works such as the *Cambridge History of Classical Literature* and in the more recent Oxford and Blackwell handbooks, all of which can be found in the "Suggested Readings" at the end of this chapter. The other kinds of texts mentioned above will appear in the book's thematic chapters. This method offers the advantage of providing at the outset an introduction to many of the authors who will appear in the later thematic chapters while still ensuring that the reader engages with the widest variety of textual material possible. Second, we must recognize the evidence not only for what it is but also for what it is not. With a few exceptions, the reality is that food and drink tend not to be in the forefront of most ancient writings. Instead, as John Wilkins has noted, food often serves to explain situations or characters, not to indicate larger trends (Wilkins 2006). This was due partly to an ancient belief that eating and drinking was not always dignified enough to merit sustained literary attention (Gowers), and partly to the very nature of this activity as common and ephemeral, and therefore easy to overlook (Donahue). Furthermore, we must always recognize that every source represents the point of view of a particular author and that recognizing such "filters" is a critical step in making sense of the ancient evidence.

While we must remain mindful of these considerations, there is no denying that the ancient evidence is remarkably rich and diverse. The passages to follow will help to emphasize this reality while confirming the importance of food and drink as a tool for illuminating a broad array of cultural beliefs in ancient society.

Epic

As a long narrative poem in hexameters that treated the deeds of gods, heroes, and men, epic drew much of its literary and cultural authority from Homer, to whom are attributed the *Iliad* and the *Odyssey* in Greek, and from Vergil, author of the *Aeneid* in Latin (Haubold, in Boys-Stones et al.; Hardie, in Harrison). The consumption of food and drink in epic poetry was typically tied to the social status of the characters portrayed, a convention that reflected contemporary practice. Of central importance was the noble warrior, whose heroic stature required that he eat well. Hence, we find a strong emphasis on the consumption of roasted meat, the foodstuff most closely associated with elite status in the ancient world. We see this clearly in Homer's portrayal of Achilles, the mercurial warrior who led the Greeks to victory in the Trojan War as portrayed in the *Iliad*.

2.1. Homer, *Iliad* 24.621–7

> At that, the swift Achilles sprang to his feet and slaughtered a white sheep, and his companions flayed it, and prepared it well and in good order. Skillfully they cut the meat into pieces, pierced the morsels with spits, roasted them with great care and pulled everything off the fire. Automedon brought the bread and set it out on a table in ample baskets, but Achilles served the meat. So they reached out for the good things that lay ready before them.

At the same time, epic poetry provides insight into how the ancients connected political stability with the larger notion of food security. Here, in Homer's *Odyssey*, Odysseus is disguised as a beggar in a ruse ultimately aimed at removing the suitors who have taken over his kingdom during his long absence while fighting in the Trojan War. His faithful wife Penelope asks Odysseus who he is and where he is from. In his reply, Odysseus compares Penelope's reputation to that of a king whose wise rule ensures a plentiful prosperity, and hence the political stability of Homer's Dark Age community of Greece in the eighth century BCE.

2.2. Homer, *Odyssey* 19.108–14

> … your fame goes up into the wide heavens, as of some blameless king who, as a god-fearing man, upholds justice as he lords over many powerful men; and the black earth yields him wheat and barley, his trees are heavy with fruit, his sheep flocks continue to bear young, the sea provides fish because of his good leadership, and his people prosper under him.

At the same time, Odysseus' appearance as a beggar raises an equally significant Dark Age reality, that of food shortage. This theme resonates powerfully and ironically when Odysseus is forced to compete with another beggar for table scraps from his own house.

2.3. Homer, *Odyssey* 18.1–22

Now there arrived a public beggar, who used to go begging through the town of
Ithaka and, well known for his greedy belly, he ate and drank without end. He
possessed no strength or might, but his build was big indeed to look upon. His
name was Arnaios, the name his honored mother called him from birth; but all
the young men called him Iros,[1] because he would run and give messages when
anyone told him. This man came to chase Odysseus out of his own house and,
insulting him, he addressed him in winged words: "Give way, old man, from the
doorway, so that you are not soon dragged out by the foot. Don't you see that all
of the men are giving me a sign by winking and telling me to drag you? Still, as
for myself, I am ashamed to do it. So get up, before our quarrel quickly comes
to blows." Then, the wily Odysseus, looking fiercely at him, replied: "My good
man, I am doing you no harm nor speaking any, nor am I jealous, if someone
takes a large portion and gives it to you. This threshold is large enough for both
of us, nor is it necessary that you be jealous of others. You seem to me to be a
beggar, as am I too; but as to good fortune, the gods are fated to bestow that. But
do not provoke me too much with your fists, lest you make me angry, so that,
even though I am an old man, I bloody your chest and mouth."

Epic poetry also preserves much about peoples or creatures portrayed as obstacles
to the intended mission and personal growth of the main protagonist, who
must struggle against these forces as part of humankind's wider challenge to
overcome nature. As he continues on his difficult journey home after the Trojan
War, Odysseus' encounter in Book Ten with the Lastrygonians, a tribe of giant
cannibals who eat many of the Greeks and destroy almost all of their ships, represents one such obstacle. Another involves Vergil's account of the Harpies, a flock of
foul and ravenous birds typically associated with death in ancient mythology. Here
they defile and steal the food of Phineas and his men at the Strophades Islands
during the Trojans' journey to found a new homeland in Italy in the *Aeneid*.

2.4. Vergil, *Aeneid* 3.219–34

When we were carried away to this place and pulled into the harbor, lo and
behold we see fattened herds of cattle scattered in the fields and flocks of goats, no
one attending them. We rush upon them with our swords, and we call upon the
gods and Jove himself to share the windfall with us; then on the curving beach
we set out couches and feast upon a most savory banquet. But instantly, in a terri-
fying swoop from the mountains, the Harpies are upon us, and they shake their
wings with loud clanging, and they snatch away our feast and defile everything

Figure 1. Banquet of Dido and Aeneas. Faience plate on stem, ordered by Isabella d'Este. Nicola da Urbino (fl. 1520–37/38). Musée du Louvre, Paris, France. © RMN-Grand Palais/Art Resource, NY.

with their foul contagion; then, amid the foul stench comes a hideous scream. In a deep recess beneath a hollowed rock, closely encircled by trees and dreadful shadows, we spread out our tables once again and relight our altars; again from a different quarter of the sky and from hidden retreats the noisy horde flies around its prey with hooked talons and spoils our feast with their lips.

Lyric poetry

Lyric poetry was poetry of a certain meter sung to the accompaniment of the lyre. Originating in the seventh century BCE, lyric was especially associated with eastern Greece. This was intensely personal poetry whose themes, often deriving from the life of the poet, might include love, war, politics, or the abuse of a rival (Capra, in Boys-Stones et al.; Harrison, in Harrison). Wine and drinking was also a common topic, owing to the fact that lyric was often sung as part of the entertainment provided at the Greek drinking party, the symposium (see Chapter 5).

By the third century BCE scholars at the famed library at Alexandria in Egypt had compiled a list of nine of the best-known lyric poets who lived during the period 650–450 BCE. Included in this list were Alceaeus and Anacreon. Alcaeus (born c. 625–620 BCE) produced lyric poetry known for its vitality and vivid descriptive power, features on display in the first excerpt below, an invitation to drink in order to forget one's troubles. Anacreon (born c. 575–570 BCE) wrote especially of wine and love (both homosexual and heterosexual) in poetry that was often epigrammatic, witty, and ironical. The second excerpt below, on the ideal drinking buddy, nicely preserves these features. Both of these passages are preserved by Athenaeus, a very important figure in ancient food studies. He wrote in the third century CE a fictitious account of a banquet of learned men, which preserves much important information about food, table manners, and literary genres.

2.5. Athenaeus, *Sophists at Dinner* 10.430c–d

For Alcaeus says:

Let's drink! Why do we wait for the lamps? There's only a finger's breadth of day left. Friend, bring down the large decorated cups. The son of Semele and Zeus[2] gave men wine to make them forget their cares. Mix one part of water with two of wine,[3] pour it up to the top, and let one cup jostle with another.

2.6. Athenaeus, *Sophists at Dinner* 11.463a

And the elegant Anacreon says:

I am not fond of the man who, while drinking his wine beside the full mixing bowl, speaks of strife and tearful war, but I do like him, who, by mixing the beautiful gifts of the Muses and Aphrodite,[4] remembers the lovely good cheer of the banquet.

Latin lyric favored meter over the Greek emphasis on musical accompaniment. Its greatest practitioner was Horace (65–8 BCE), who considered himself to be the first Latin lyric poet, and even asked to be added to the Alexandrian canon of Nine Greek Lyricists. His *Odes* in four books combine a technical refinement of meter with the spirit of Greek lyric that have made them the crowning achievement of Latin lyric poetry. *Ode* 1.20, the poet's call to drink simple wine (Caecuban and Calenian) amongst good friends (in this instance his famed literary patron Maecenas) instead of the choicest vintages (Falernian

Figure 2. Shell of an Attic red figure kylix (drinking cup) depicting drunken revelers, some with musical instruments, including the lyre, which was closely associated with drinking. Capua, Dokimasia Painter, c. 490 BCE. Antikensammlung, Staatliche Museen, Berlin, Germany. Credit: Art Resource, NY.

and Formian) is part literary conceit but also evidence of a poet and a reading audience intimately familiar with Roman drinking culture during the early Empire.

2.7. Horace, *Ode* 1.20

Maecenas, beloved knight, in small cups you will drink common Sabine wine, which I myself sealed up and stored in a Grecian jar when you received applause in the amphitheater, so that the banks of your paternal river,[5] and at the same time the playful echo of the Vatican hill, repeated your praises.[6] You will drink Caecuban wine and the wine of the grape crushed in a Calenian press; neither the Falernian vines nor the Formian hills season my drinking cups.

Comedy

Because it largely ignored the great themes of epic and tragedy, comedy, along with satire and epigram, was considered a "low" genre among ancient commentators. Its predilection for spoofing all aspects of ancient society, however, provided ample opportunity for exploiting food and drink. To be sure, the tradition of exaggerated costuming and the celebratory atmosphere of the large public festivals in which these plays were produced only served to enhance the comic experience (Konstan, in Boys-Stones et al.; Panayotakis, in Harrison).

Comedy was especially fond of lampooning the gods, as well as championing the cause of the common man over the more powerful. Aristophanes treats these themes brilliantly in *Wealth*, a comic meditation on the consequences that would follow from equalizing wealth and eradicating poverty from the playwright's home of Athens in the early fourth century BCE. Here, Wealth, in human form, is brought to a healing sanctuary in order to be cured through incubation, a process that involved the suppliant bringing a food offering to the temple and waiting for the god to offer advice and perform his cures through a dream. Upon waking the next morning, the suppliant had to pay a fee to the temple treasury. Note especially the kinds of foods mentioned for propitiatory and medical purposes, especially the punishment cure for the politician Neocleides, and the corruption associated with the stealing of food in these temples. In this way, comedy utilizes food for insight into religion, medicine, and social relations that is unequalled in other genres of ancient literature.

2.8. Aristophanes, *Wealth* 658–763

CARIO: Then, we went to the precinct of the god. After the cakes and first offerings were burnt on the altar—a mixture for Hephaestus' flame—we put Wealth to bed properly and each of us set up beds for ourselves.

WIFE: Were there any other patients of the god?

CARIO: One was Neocleides, who is blind but who, when it comes to stealing, surpasses those who can see; and there were many others with all kinds of afflictions. Then the temple servant extinguished the lamps and ordered us to go to sleep, saying that, if anyone heard any noise, to be silent; and we all lay there, well behaved. But I could not fall asleep. A certain pot of porridge next to the head of an old hag was driving me nuts; I had a supernatural longing to grab it. Then I looked up and saw the temple slave snatch the pastries and figs from the sacred table, and next he circled about all the altars looking for any left over cakes; then he "dedicated" these into a sack. Recognizing the full lawfulness of this procedure, I got up from my bed for that pot of porridge.

WIFE: You completely foolish man, didn't you fear the god?

CARIO: Yes, I was certainly fearful—that he'd come out wearing his garlands and beat me to the pot! His own priest had taught me that one. Now when the old hag heard the noise I was making, she stuck her hand into the pot; then I grabbed it by my teeth with a hiss, like Ascleipius' sacred snake. Straightway she pulled back her hand, and she lay there all wrapped up peacefully in the blanket, farting in fear, smellier than a weasel. That's when I took a big gulp of that porridge, and when I was full, I stopped.

WIFE: But didn't the god approach you?

CARIO: Not yet; after this, I now did one more amusing thing. As he was approaching, I let go a really big fart; my stomach had bloated on me.

WIFE: I'll bet because of this he felt an immediate disgust for you.

CARIO: No, but Iaso, who followed him in, blushed at once, and Panacea turned away, holding her nose. I don't fart incense!

WIFE: And the god himself?

CARIO: By god, he paid no attention at all.

WIFE: Are you saying that the god is a hick?

CARIO: Good lord, certainly not, but a shit eater.

WIFE: Ugh, you're disgusting!

CARIO: Well, after that I got scared and immediately covered up, while the god made his rounds in a very orderly way, examining everyone's illness. Then his attendant brought him a stone mortar, a pestle, and a box.

WIFE: Made of stone?

CARIO: No, the mortar only, not the box.

WIFE: But you say you were covered up—you thoroughly wretched man—so how did you manage to see?

CARIO: Through my cloak; it certainly had its share of holes! His first job was to grind a poultice for Neocleides. He threw in three heads of Tenian garlic. Then he mixed together in the mortar fig juice and squill, soaked all of it with Sphettian vinegar, turned out his eyelids, and smeared it in, to make it sting more. Neocleides screamed and yelled, and he tried to escape but the god laughed and said, "Now you sit right here, all poulticed up, so that I'll put an end to your swearing oaths in the assemblies."

WIFE: That god loves his city, and he is clever too!

CARIO: Next, he sat beside Wealth, and felt his head first, and then took a clean linen cloth and daubed around his eyelids; Panacea wrapped his head and whole face in crimson cloth. Then the god whistled, and two snakes rushed out from the temple, immense in size.

WIFE: Oh dear gods!

CARIO: They slipped quietly beneath the crimson cloth and started licking around his eyelids, as it seemed to me. And before you could drink five pints of wine, lady, Wealth stood up and could see. I clapped my hands in sheer happiness and woke up my master, and the god immediately disappeared into the temple, the snakes too. You can imagine how those who were lying down in the temple embraced Wealth, and stayed up the whole night long, hugging him until daylight dawned. I was quite excessive in my praise of the god, for quickly giving Wealth his sight, and for making Neocleides more blind!

WIFE: You have such great power, my sovereign lord! But tell me, where is Wealth now?

CARIO: He's coming. But an enormous crowd has gathered around him. The people who formerly lived upright but meager lives have welcomed him and everybody has received him kindly out of sheer joy; but all who were wealthy and had many possessions, who had acquired their living by unjust means, they knit their brows and frowned at the same time. The others followed behind wearing garlands, laughing and proclaiming their blessings. The old men's shoes beat out a nice rhythm for the procession. (to the Chorus) Come on now, everyone start leaping, skipping, and dancing at the same time, because no one will ever announce to you as you return home that there's no more grain in your sack.

Food and drink could also be cleverly brought to bear on politics and war, as Aristophanes displays in another play, the *Acharnians*. Produced in 425 BCE during the Peloponnesian War between Athens and Sparta, the play centers on the protagonist, Dicaeopolis ("Just City"), who obtains a private peace treaty with the Spartans, despite opposition from some of his fellow Athenians. The humor in the following excerpt derives from the double meaning of treaties (*spondai* in Greek), which means "treaties" but also the "libations of wine poured to celebrate treaties." The reference to pitch, or resin, is also significant, as it was widely utilized to caulk ships but also as a flavoring agent in inferior table wines.

2.9. Aristophanes, *Acharnians* 186–200

DICAEOPOLIS: Well, let them cry out. Do you have the treaties?

AMPHITHEUS: Indeed, I do. I have three varieties for sipping. This one's a five-year treaty. Try a sip.

DICAEOPOLIS: Uggh!

AMPHITHEUS: What's the problem?

DICAEOPOLIS: I don't care for this one; it reeks of pitch and battleships being built.

AMPHITHEUS: Well then, here's a ten-year treaty for you to sip.

DICAEOPOLIS: This one also stinks, of embassies to the allies. It's a sour smell, like someone being beaten up.

AMPHITHEUS: Well, here's a thirty-year treaty by land and sea.

DICAEOPOLIS: Holy Dionysia! This treaty smells of nectar and ambrosia,[7] and never waiting to hear "Time for three days' rations," and it says to my taste buds, "Go wherever you wish." I accept it; I pour it in libation; I drink it off! And I tell the Acharnians to go to hell!

Through its skewering of foibles both human and divine comedy was also able to offer alternative versions of reality—in exaggeratedly comic terms, of course. This fragment below, the largest of those surviving from the comedies of Teleclides, a contemporary of Aristophanes in Athens, describes an extravagant Golden Age utopia, made all the more memorable by fish that cook themselves and streams of soups and meat that flow abundantly past the diners' couches. As we shall see in more detail in Chapter 3, such accounts also reflect an anxiety about food security in a world where the threat of shortages, and even famine, remained very real.

2.10. Athenaeus, *Sophists at Dinner* 6.268b–d

I will speak now of the life I first provided for mortals. In the first place there was peace like water over the hands.[8] The earth produced neither fear nor diseases but all the things necessary for living were automatically present. Every torrent flowed with wine, and barley cakes fought with bread at the mouths of men, begging them to devour them if they loved the whitest loaf. Fish came to the house, baked themselves, and presented themselves at the dinner tables. A river of soup flowed past the couches, whirling with steaming meats. Channels of rich sauces were available for those who were interested, so that there was plenty for moistening a mouthful and gulping it down. Cakes[9] sprinkled with tasty flavorings were on dishes; roast thrushes served with milk cakes flew into the throat. There was calamity as flat cakes jostled for position with each other at the jaw; slaves could play dice with slices of sow's womb and intestines. Men were fat in those days and they were a great host of giants.

Finally, stock characters—the greedy pimp, the scheming parasite, the hapless young lover, and the harsh but gullible father—all helped to drive the chaos of the conventional comic plot to its happy resolution. Included among these *dramatis personae* was the cheeky cook for hire, a character who has much to tell us not only about dining habits and food preparation but also, on a larger scale, about the social disparity between those who did the hiring and those who did the cooking. Cooks are significant for another reason as well: the elites who hired them were interested in their services as an opportunity for competitive display. This aspect is easy to overlook but it was significant nonetheless and likely had its roots in the cooks from Sicily and elsewhere, who began to appear in Athens for hire in the fourth century BCE (Wilkins, 2006). The cook in the *Pseudolus* in the first excerpt below is typical of what this character had become in Latin comedy of the second century BCE as depicted by Plautus, the first playwright to write plays in Latin that have survived completely. Here the cook is a highly amusing and ever-confident self-promoter with the ability to bring much comic energy to the plot. Cooks would continue to be a source of abuse in later literature as well, as Petronius' *Satyricon* (no. 32 below) confirms. The portraits of the sausage seller, fishmonger, and butcher in the second and third passages preserve a similar tone of humorous derision aimed at those who occupied these lowly professions in the ancient food industry.

2.11. Plautus, *Pseudolus* 790–892

> BALLIO: Those who call it Cooks' Square speak foolishly because it's not Cooks' Square but Crooks' Square. Why, even if I had sworn to find a man worse than this cook, I wouldn't be able to deliver one worse than I'm delivering—blathering, arrogant, foolish, useless! The only reason that Pluto has not wanted to take him back to Hell is so that there would be someone here to cook the dinners honoring the dead. Why, he's the only one who can cook what they like.
>
> COOK: If you've been thinking of me as the sort that you say, why did you hire me?

BALLIO: A shortage. There was no one else. But if you were a cook, why were you sitting in the square alone and apart from the rest?

COOK: I'll tell you. I have been made a less desirable cook by a defect of human nature, not by a fault of my own.

BALLIO: How did you figure that out?

COOK: I'll tell you. This is how it goes, once people come to hire a cook, no one looks for the best and the most expensive one but hires instead the cheapest. That explains why I was sitting alone today hanging around the forum. Those wretched buyers are penny pinchers. No one can get me off my ass for less than two drachmas. I do not spice up a dinner the same way as other cooks, who, it seems to me, season entire fields and bring them out on platters, who turn the dinner guests into cattle and pile on the fodder, and then season that fodder with more fodder: they serve sorrel, cabbage, beets and spinach, flavored with coriander, fennel, garlic and parsley; they pour in a pound of assafoetida, and grind in a wicked mustard, which makes the eyes of the graters water before they have grated it. When these guys season the dinners they cook, they do not use seasonings but screech owls, which disembowel the living guests. For sure, this explains why men here live such a short life, filling their bellies with fodder of this kind, dreadful to mention, not just to eat. The fodder that cattle don't eat, men do.

BALLIO: What about you? Do you use celestial seasonings that can prolong the lives of man, you who criticize these seasonings?

COOK: Damn right, I do. Why, men who eat the food I spice up actually live for two hundred years. When I season dishes with a bit of ciciliander or cipoliander or macarosis or secatopsis,[10] they immediately get spiced up. These, of course, are seasonings for seafood; for beef I use chicimandrium, halitosis, or cataracticum.[11]

BALLIO: May Jupiter and all the gods blast you to Hell with your seasonings and all those lies!

COOK: Please allow me to finish.

BALLIO: Speak, and go to hell!

COOK: When all my dishes are heated, I open all of them up and the fragrance flies to heaven with outstretched arms.

BALLIO: A fragrance with outstretched arms?

COOK: I made a careless mistake.

BALLIO: How so?

COOK: I meant to say, with outstretched feet.

BALLIO: What if you don't get hired—how does Jupiter dine?

COOK: He goes to bed without his dinner.

BALLIO: And you can go to hell. Do you think that I'm going to pay you for that sort of nonsense?

COOK: For sure, I admit that my cooking is very expensive, but whoever hires me gets a bang for his buck.

BALLIO: For robbery, you mean.

COOK [still smiling]: Ah well, are you demanding to find a cook anywhere who has not got claws like a bird of prey?

BALLIO: Do you expect to be allowed to cook anywhere without having your claws tied up? [To his slave] Here, you boy—you who belongs to me—I tell you now, hurry inside and move away all our stuff; and then, keep your eyes fixed on this man's eyes: wherever he looks, you look that way too; wherever he goes, go with him; if he puts out his hand, stick yours out too; if he picks up something that belongs to him, let him keep it; if it's something of ours, get hold of the other end of it. If he moves, you move; if he stands still, you stand near him; if he stoops down, you stoop down. And, I'll provide private watchmen for these assistants of his.

COOK: There's nothing to worry about.

BALLIO: I'm begging you, tell me how I can have nothing to worry about when I'm giving you the run of my house?

COOK: Wait till you see what my broth does for you today—just like Medea cooked up old Pelias and with her potions and her poisons made the old man young again—I'll do the same for you.

BALLIO: Eh? Are you a poisoner, too?

COOK: Ah no, good heavens, no—I'm a life preserver.

BALLIO: Hmm, how much would you charge to teach me your recipe for that?

COOK: For what?

BALLIO: For saving you from stealing from me.

COOK: If you trust me, two drachmas; if not, nothing less than a hundred. But tell me whether you are giving this dinner today for your friends or your enemies?

BALLIO: Good lord, for friends, of course.

COOK: Why not invite your enemies rather than your friends? For I'll be serving your guests such a delicious dinner today, and so sweetly and delicately seasoned, that whoever tastes such a dish seasoned by me, I'll have him biting off his own fingers.

BALLIO: Then for God's sake, before you serve a single guest, take a taste of it yourself, and give your helpers some, so that you bite off your own thieving fingers first.

COOK: I think perhaps that you don't believe what I' m saying.

BALLIO: Stop being a nuisance, you cackle too much. Can't you shut up? That's my house there. Get inside and cook the dinner. Hurry up.

2.12. Aristophanes, *Knights* 211–19

SAUSAGEMAN: …but I am amazed that someone like me is fit to manage the people.

FIRST SLAVE: It's the easiest task. Do what you are doing now: stir up and make mince meat of state affairs and always keep the people on your side, sweetening them up with culinary bon mots. You have everything else a demagogue requires: a coarse voice, low birth, market place manners. You have everything needed for public life.

2.13. Plautus, *Captives* 813–22

ERGASILUS: Next, the fish sellers, who offer the people stinking fish, who are conveyed here on a gelding, a tormented nag, whose stench drives all the arcade slackers out into the market, I'll smack their faces with their fish baskets so that they know what a nuisance they are to the public nose. Next, moreover, the butchers who arrange for sheep to be bereft of their children, who arrange for the lambs to be slaughtered and then sell the meat for double the price, who cloak the gelded sheep with the name of Petro;[12] if I set my eyes on this Petro in a public street, I'll make Petro and its master the most wretched of mortals.

Tragedy

Along with epic poetry, tragedy was one of the most significant literary forms to originate in antiquity. It is particularly associated with Athens of the fifth century BCE, where the Athenian spring festival of Dionysius Eleuthereus, the City Dionysia, took place. This festival included tragic performances and sacrifices in the theater, as well as libations and other public activities. Typically, three tragedians competed, each producing three tragedies and a lighter fourth piece, the so-called satyr play, which would come to form the basis of Greek comedy. Ten judges, one from each of the city's tribes, were chosen to evaluate the plays, with the winner receiving a crown of ivy in the theater. The three most notable playwrights of this time were Aeschylus, Sophocles, and Euripides.

The subject matter of Greek tragedy was almost exclusively heroic myths, which would have been familiar to the audience from the well-established tradition of oral renditions by itinerant singers, who recited epic narratives for public entertainment. While these epic stories were well known, tragedians presented them in such a way as to resonate in the Athenian *polis*; it is not surprising, therefore, to find tragedies that deal with issues such as Greeks vs foreigners, male vs female, or the individual vs the city–state (Taplin, in Boys-Stones et al.).

When it came to food and drink, tragedy did not treat the topic in the exaggerated and playful manner of comedy. On the contrary, food and drink tend to appear more sparingly and, when they do, it is often in a negative context, emphasizing the themes of murder or corrupt sacrifice. Both of these features appear in the *Electra* of Euripides, which dramatizes the murder of Clytemnestra by her children, Electra and Orestes, in retribution for their mother's murder of their father, Agamemnon. In this passage, a slave tells Electra of the murder of Aegisthus, Clytemnestra's new husband and king of Mycenae, by his master, Orestes. Food appears in two interesting ways. First, Orestes declines Aegisthus' offer of purifying waters, an invitation to hospitality, which would have included food, drink, and shelter. Aegisthus' offer is a good example of *xenia*, the hospitality a host provided for a guest who was far from home. This social convention, best known from Homeric epic, is often translated as "guest–host friendship" or "ritualized friendship." It helped to ensure the safety of travelers and created an obligation for the guest to return the favor in the future. By cleverly declining Aegisthus' invitation, Orestes avoids becoming a guest of the new king, which would have made him a violator of the *xenia* ritual through his killing of a host. Second, the sacrifice of the bull would have provided a meal for the celebrants. The fact that its entrails are corrupt, however, signifies that the house of the king is polluted, thereby providing a dramatic setting for Orestes to reveal his true identity and to kill the usurper of his father's throne.

2.14. Euripides, *Electra* 798–843

Now the king's bodyguard put aside their spears and all the slaves put forth their hands to work. Some brought the bowl used to catch the blood of the sacrificial victims; others brought baskets for the sacred barley; still others lit the fire and set cauldrons upright around the hearth. The whole house echoed with activity.

Then your mother's lover took the barley cakes and threw them on the altar as he spoke these words: "Nymphs of the rocks, I have offered sacrificial bulls many times, and my wife, Tyndareus' daughter, has sacrificed at home. Preserve our present fortune, but may my enemies fare badly"—he was speaking of you and Orestes. But my master, not speaking his words aloud, prayed for the opposite—to get back his father's house. Aegisthus raised from the basket a straight-bladed sacrificial knife, cut off a hair of the calf, placed it on the sacred fire with his right hand and cut its throat, as his servants lifted up the animal upon their shoulders. Then he said to your brother: "There is a boast among the Thessalians that one of their fine accomplishments is this—to cut up a bull well and to tame horses. Take the knife, stranger, and display the true reputation of the Thessalians."

Orestes took the finely wrought Doric blade in his hand, stripped his fine cloak from his shoulders, chose Pylades as his attendant in this task, and pushed back the slaves. Taking the animal by its foot, he laid bare the white flesh, stretching it out with his hand. And he stripped away the hide, faster than a runner could have finished both legs of a hippodrome course, and he loosened the flanks. Aegisthus took the sacred portions in his hands and inspected them. The liver lobe was missing among the viscera and the portal vein and sac of the gall bladder showed that dark evils were advancing toward the observer.

Aegisthus became sullen, and my master asked, "Why are you despondent over these things?" "Stranger, I am afraid of some treachery from abroad. The son of Agamemnon is my most hated enemy and he is a hostile toward my house." But Orestes said, "Do you really fear the treachery of a fugitive when you are in charge of the city? Now will someone bring me a Phthian knife instead of this Doric one to split open the breast bone so that we may feast on the sacrificial meat?" After he received it, he struck. Aegisthus took the innards and began to divide and inspect them. While he was stooping down, your brother, standing on his tiptoes, struck his backbone and smashed his vertebrae. His whole body convulsed from head to toe and he shook, dying in his bloody gore.

Another of Euripides' tragedies, *Ion*, treats the story of Creusa, who bore a son with the god Apollo. Fearing her father's anger, she abandoned the child in a cave, where he was rescued by Hermes and raised as a servant of the temple at Delphi. Remaining childless, Creusa went to the temple at Delphi to pray for offspring. Meanwhile, Apollo had ordered her husband to adopt the first child he came upon at the temple; this happened to be Ion, the very boy whom Creusa had given up years earlier. Thinking the child to be the bastard son of her husband, Creusa attempted to poison the boy, as described in the passage below, but she failed. Eventually, the boy's true identity is revealed and the family is reunited. This excerpt is important for its excellent depiction, rare in tragedy, of a community feast according to the standard ritual of a Greek meal. Note that the guests occupy a large outdoor tent erected for the occasion; that they eat first, then sing a hymn to the accompaniment of the reed pipe; and finally, that they conclude with the drinking party (symposium), where they consume wine mixed with water from large mixing bowls. The occasion is festive, with plenty of food and drink. It also served to enhance the status and reputation of Xuthus as a generous benefactor of the community.

2.15. Euripides, *Ion* 1132–40; 1165–216

SERVANT: ... The young man (Ion) solemnly raised on poles the sides of the tent, as yet unwalled, taking good account of the sun's rays so as to avoid the midday and the setting beams of the sun's blaze, and measured off the length of a *plethron*[13] into a square with an interior area (so the experts say) of ten thousand feet, so that he might invite the whole population of Delphi to a banquet ...

In the middle of the dining hall he set up golden mixing bowls. A herald drew himself up to his full height and invited to the feast all who wished to come. When the hall was filled, the guests wreathed their heads with garland and took their heart's fill of the rich food. And when they had satisfied their desire for food, an old man came forward and stood in the middle of the floor, and he incited much laughter among the banqueters by his eager bustling about. From the water jars he brought water for the guests to wash their hands, burned myrrh resin as incense, and took charge of the golden drinking cups, having assigned this task to himself.

When the time came for singing to the reed pipe and the common mixing bowl of wine, the old man said, "We must remove these small wine vessels and bring in large ones, so that these guests may find their pleasure more quickly." There was the toil of silver and gold cups being brought in. Then he took a special cup, as if offering thanks to his new master, and gave him the vessel filled with wine, slipping into the drink the efficacious drug they say my mistress gave him, in order to kill this newfound son. No one paid attention to this. But as the boy held it in his hand, [holding the drink along with others, this newly appeared boy] one of the slaves uttered an ill-omened word. The boy, since he had been raised in the temple and among noble seers, took it as an omen and ordered that another new mixing bowl be filled. He poured out upon the ground the first libations to the god and told everyone to do the same. Silence came over the crowd. We filled the holy mixing bowls with water and Bibline[14] wine. While we were involved in this task, a riotous band of doves rushed in upon the tents (these dwell without fear in the temple of Loxias[15]). Since drink had fallen to the floor, they put their beaks down into it, as they were thirsty, and drew it up into their well-feathered throats. For most of them the holy libation was not harmful. But one bird perched itself where the newfound son had poured out his drink and tasted it; immediately her feathered body shook and raved with Bacchic frenzy, and she shrieked out, crying utterances difficult to understand. The whole assembly of feasters was astonished at the bird's agony. Struggling amid convulsions, it died, as its red legs and feet went limp. Then the son ordained by the god bared his arms from his cloak as he brought them over the table and shouted, "Who has been attempting to kill me? Tell me, old man. You were the one eager to serve, and I received the drink from your hand." Immediately he searched the old man, taking him by the forearm, expecting to capture him in the act with <some small vial of deadly poison>[16]. It was discovered, and under compulsion he confessed Creusa's bold act and the drink plot.

In the Roman world, tragic performances began in the third century BCE and continued perhaps as late as the first century CE. Adaptation of the better-known works of the three most famous Attic tragedians remained popular, although themes from Roman legend and history are also known. By the first century, some men preferred to read aloud literary works to small groups in private, a literary practice known as the *recitatio*; this was most likely the setting for the tragedies of Seneca, a first-century philosopher whose Greek-inspired plots were characterized by excessive mythological emphasis and moralizing but also by vivid description and clever epigrams (Fantham, in Harrison). In this excerpt, the curse associated with the legendary house of Pelops comes down upon Thyestes, whose children have been murdered, cooked, and served by his own brother Atreus, the king of Mycenae, in revenge for Thyestes' seduction of the king's wife. The passage is lurid in a way that is typical of much of literature in first-century Rome. Especially striking are the ways in which both the natural world and Thyestes himself react to this gruesome feast. Here the speaker is a messenger, responding to the inquiries of the Chorus.

2.16. Seneca, *Thyestes*, 753–84

Oh, no age could believe in such a crime. The future would deny it! The organs, ripped from the boy's living breasts, throb, the veins pulse, and the heart still beats in terror; but Atreus handles the entrails and examines the signs and inspects the still-hot veins of the viscera. After the victims proved satisfactory, free from care, he takes time for his brother's feast. He himself cuts and separates the body limb by limb; he cuts away the broad shoulders and resisting arms, working back to the trunk; coldly, he lays bare the joints and chops away the bones; he keeps only the faces and the hands given in trust. Some of the flesh clings to spits and, given over to slow flames, drips; boiling liquid tosses about other parts in a seething cauldron. The fire leapt across the feast above it, and forced two and three times upon the trembling hearth and ordered to stay in place, it burns unwillingly. The liver on the spits hisses. I could not easily say whether it was the bodies or the flames that groaned more. The fire turns into pitch-black smoke; but the smoke itself, a gloomy and heavy cloud, does not go straight up and raise itself into the air: it settles around the very household gods in a hideous cloud.

Oh Apollo, allowing too much! Though you have fled backward and have sunken the day snatched from the mid-sky, you have set too late! A father is ripping to pieces his sons and he chews his own limbs with a grisly mouth. He glistens, his hair soaked in flowing perfume; often his throat, blocked up, held the food. Amid your troubles, Thyestes, there is one good—that you are ignorant of your troubles. But this too, will perish.

Satire

Satire was a literary form that the Romans claimed as their own. The word itself conveys notions of "fullness" or "mixed stuffings," meanings that find confirmation in the mixture and variety of literary techniques and authorial personae typical of this genre. At its essence, satire allowed the author to expose pretension and hypocrisy in a humorous or scathing manner, while often posing as a cynic or as an outsider. While it was the Romans who especially embraced this genre (Freudenburg), satire displayed Greek precedents too, most notably seen in lyric poetry of iambic meter from as early as the seventh century BCE. Later, the diatribe, a form of philosophical rant, which relied upon fables, philosophy, jokes, and split dialogue to make its point, was also an important vehicle for satire. The Roman claim upon this form was linked to the belief that satire could criticize life in Rome more effectively than any of the genres inherited from the Greeks. In Roman hands, satire extends from the fragments of the late third century BCE to the emperor Julian's character assessments of his imperial predecessors written in Greek in the fourth century CE.

The authors gathered here represent a sampling of the most influential voices of ancient satire from this time period. Among many features, they all share one thing in common: the ability to utilize food and drink in order to sharpen social distinctions between classes, often by exposing the culinary pretensions of the rich in contrast to the meager existence of the poor. We see this in Lucilius' fragments, with their emphasis on luxury items like oysters and fattened fowl. Satire reaches its fullest potential, however, under Juvenal. His biting and unrelenting assessment of Rome's moral depravity during the first and second centuries finds expression in *Satire One* below, where the social distancing between patron and client is made all the more palpable by qualitative differences in the food available to members of each class. While we must always be careful to recognize a certain level of hyperbole and exaggeration in Juvenal's indignation, his deft ability to convey meaning through the short but powerful character sketch remains one of his greatest attributes. Horace, on the other hand, dishes out a slightly different flavor of satire. His *sermones* ("conversations") are more restrained and erudite than those of Lucilius or Juvenal, as evident in *Satire* 2.4. Here the poet convinces a certain Catius to let him in on new philosophical precepts that surpass those of Pythagoras, Plato, and Socrates. The reader finds out, however, that the precepts are gastronomic ones, a mixed list of simple and extravagant foodstuffs that the poet invests with fake importance as part of a larger parody of poetic principles (Gowers). Furthermore, while *Satire* 2.4 is a clever parody, it is nevertheless one that Horace hands over to a pundit. This strategy allows him to treat controversial topics like gastronomy in a less direct way, an indication of the more restrictive environment under Augustus, Rome's first emperor. The final excerpt provides evidence of satire from Greek literature during the Roman imperial era, in this instance from Lucian, a Syrian Greek who operated as a rhetorician, philosopher, and humorist during the second century CE. This excerpt on mourning is typical of his wit, religious skepticism, and belief in simple, commonsense living.

2.17. Lucilius, 13.465–6

This same thing happens at a dinner; you will provide oysters purchased for a thousand sesterces.

2.18. Lucilius, 20.601–3

Furthermore, he ordered to be brought to the table and arranged what each one wanted. Pigs' paps and a dish of fattened fowl pleased one man, a licker-fish[17] caught between the two bridges of the Tiber pleased the other.

2.19. Horace, *Satire* 2.4.1–58

HORACE: Where are you coming from, and where are you going, Catius?

CATIUS: I haven't a minute, I'm anxious to impress upon my memory such precepts that surpass Pythagoras, and the man accused by Anytus,[18] and erudite Plato.

HORACE: Oh, my fault, since I have interrupted you at such a poor time. I beg you, do pardon me. If something has slipped your mind now, you will remember it soon. Whether because of your training or because of some native power, you are wondrous in both.

CATIUS: I was anxious as to how I might retain all these precepts, especially since they were of a delicate nature and treated in a delicate style.

HORACE: Do tell me the man's name. A Roman or a stranger?

CATIUS: I shall repeat the precepts themselves from memory; the name of the author shall be concealed.

"Remember to serve oval eggs: their flavor is better, their whites are whiter than round eggs; they're tough-shelled, and contain a male yolk. Cabbages grown in dry fields are sweeter than those raised on farms near the city: nothing is more insipid than a watered garden. If all of a sudden a guest has surprised you for evening dinner, in order to ensure that your tough old hen should not prove disagreeable to his palate, you'll be smart to plunge it alive in the dregs of Falernian wine: this will make it tender. Mushrooms from meadowlands are by far the best; it is unwise to trust other kinds. A man will spend his summers in good health if he finishes off his lunch with the black mulberries he has picked from the tree before the sun becomes oppressive. Aufidius[19] injudiciously used to mix his honey with strong Falernian—it is proper to entrust nothing but the mildest of things to empty veins. You'd do better to wash out your bowels with a mild honey wine. If you are constipated, the mussel and cheap shellfish will remove the obstructions, and the short leaf of sorrel, but not without white Coan wine.[20] New moons fill out the flesh of slippery shellfish, but not every sea produces the best varieties: the Lucrine mussel is better than the Baian cockle; the best oysters come from Circei, crayfish from Cape Misenum; the well-heeled town of Tarentum prides herself on her fat scallops ..."

2.20. Juvenal, *Satire* 1. 127–46

The day itself is marked out by a fine round of business: the dole, then the forum and Apollo learned in the law, and the triumphal statues, among which some Egyptian and Arabarch has dared to display his titles,[21] at whose statue to take a piss is not the only right! The old and wearied clients depart from the doorways and put aside their desires, although the deepest hope for a man is for a dinner; the poor wretches have to buy their cabbage and fuel. Meanwhile, their kingly patron will devour the best of the forests and the sea, and will lie alone on empty dining couches. And certainly from so many beautiful, grand and ancient rounded tables they devour whole inheritances at a single sitting. Soon the parasite will not exist! But who can stand to witness luxury so mean? How huge is the gullet that has a whole boar served for itself, an animal created for dinner parties! But soon you will pay the penalty when, with your bloated belly, you take off your cloak and carry your undigested peacock into the baths. The result—a sudden death and old age without a will; a new and happy tale makes the circuit through all the dinners: enraged friends have to cheer at the funeral as it is led past.

2.21. Lucian, *On Mourning* 24

Then to add to all of this, there's the funeral feast. The relatives are all in attendance and they console the parents over the loss of the departed and persuade them to eat (nor, by Zeus, are they compelling the mourners in an unwelcome way, since already they're weak with hunger after three days of fasting). How long, man, are we going to mourn? Let the soul of the dead man have a break! And even if you have resolved to keep up the weeping altogether, for this very reason you must not starve yourself; you must stay at full strength to match the magnitude of your mourning.

At this point everyone breaks out two lines from Homer, as if they were rhapsodes:

Even fair-haired Niobe reminded herself to eat.[22]

and:

The Achaeans should not mourn the dead with their bellies.[23]

And so they grasp for the food, but they are ashamed at first and afraid to appear still bound by human necessity after the death of their loved ones.

One will discover these and much more ridiculous things happening at funerals because many people regard death as the greatest of evils.

Historiography

For the ancient Greeks and Romans history was essentially the study of the memorable deeds of men, in other words, a record of *res gestae*, accomplishments, of a particular kind, especially military and political (Fornara). As a result, we find a historiographical tradition that is open to myth and moralizing, for example, in ways that are at odds with our modern notions of history as being critical, accurate, objective, and explanatory (Cartledge). Indeed, as Paul Veyne has noted, "ancient history was as complete a means of creating belief as is our journalism of today, which it resembles a great deal" (Veyne).

Given these features, we might ask what role food and drink played in the historical writings of Greece and Rome. The answer is similar to our earlier findings, namely, that while eating and drinking were not necessarily at the forefront of historical thought, they nevertheless provide significant insight into a range of important issues, including ancient perceptions of social relations, foreigners, and even the nature of political organization. This last issue is preserved in the first reading below, Livy's account of the speech delivered in the early fifth century BCE by the consul Agrippa Menenius Lanatus to Rome's soldiers, whom he must convince to rejoin the community after their secession over oppressive debt laws and, more generally, the inequity in power during the early Republic. Menenius, who later appears in the first act of Shakespeare's *Coriolanus*, tells the soldiers a (Greek) political parable about how the body decides to stop nourishing the stomach because it feels the latter is getting all the nourishment while doing little of the work. Soon, the other parts grow fatigued and realize that not only does the stomach do important work but also that they cannot function without it. In this metaphor, the stomach represents the wealthy patrician class and the other body parts represent the plebeians. Livy concludes by recording that the soldiers return to the city once the patricians make certain concessions to the plebs. The metaphor underscores how easily the biological processes of eating and digestion could be appropriated for illuminating larger political concerns. As we shall see below, when the emperor himself essentially became the state, his body and eating habits would attract even more scrutiny.

2.22. Livy, 2.32.8–12

The senatorial party therefore decided to send Menenius Agrippa as their spokesman to the plebeians. He was an eloquent man, and dear to the plebeians, since he was one of them by birth. After he was admitted to the deserters' camp, he is said to have told them in that old-fashioned and rough way of speaking nothing other than this: "In the time when man's bodily parts did not, as now they do, agree among themselves, but each had its own means of expression and intentions, the other parts were indignant and complained of their own pains in providing out of their own labor and attendance everything for the belly, which remained idle in their midst, with nothing to do but to enjoy the pleasant things they gave it. So they conspired that the hand should carry no food to the mouth, nor that the mouth should take anything that was offered it, nor that the teeth should accept anything to chew. While they wished in their anger to subdue the belly by starvation, the parts themselves and the whole body wasted away together to nothing. By this it was apparent, too, that the belly had no idle task to fulfill, and it was no more nourished than it nourished the rest, restoring to all parts of the body that by which we live and thrive, when it has been divided equally among the veins and is enriched by digested food, that is, the blood." By comparing from this analogy how the internal dissension of the body was similar to the anger of the plebeians against the senators, he changed the minds of the listeners.

Historians also relied on food to underscore prosperity, most notably in their accounts aimed at establishing identity of a people or nation. This is especially true of Dionysius of Halicarnassus, whose history, *Roman Antiquities*, often reads as an eloquent tribute to Roman virtue. Some of that sentiment is apparent here, where he praises the fertility and abundance of Italy in a way that marks out Rome as a place of special significance.

2.23. Dionysius of Halicarnassus, *Roman Antiquities* 1.36.2–3

For, in comparing one country with another of the same extent, in my opinion, Italy is the best, not only of Europe but also of all the rest of the lands. And yet it has not escaped my notice that for many people I will not seem to speak credibly when they reflect on Egypt, Libya, Babylonia and any other fertile countries that may exist. But I do not assign the wealth derived from the soil to a singular sort of produce, nor does a strong passion come upon me to dwell where there are only rich arable lands and little or nothing else that is useful; but I consider that country the best that is the most self sufficient and stands least in need of imported goods. And I am persuaded that Italy enjoys this universal fertility and useful advantages beyond any other land.

For while it has a great deal of good arable land, Italy does not lack trees, as does a grain-bearing country; nor, on the other hand, while suitable for growing all kinds of trees, does it produce scanty crops when sown, as does a tree-rich country. Nor, while producing both of these things abundantly, is it unsuitable for the grazing of cattle; nor can anyone say that, while it is rich in crops, timber, and herds, it is nevertheless disagreeable for men to live in. On the contrary, it abounds, so to speak, in everything that provides either pleasure or profit.

At the same time, the threat of cultural corruption over time through luxurious dining practices was another important theme in ancient historical writing. Livy conveys this concern when he cites the influx of Greek luxury as particularly problematic in the early decades of the second century BCE.

2.24. Livy, 39.6.7–9

Indeed, the origin of foreign luxury was introduced into the city by the army from Asia. For the first time they imported into Rome bronze couches, valuable robes for coverlets, tapestries, and other textiles, and what at that time was considered luxurious furniture—tables with one pedestal and sideboards. At that time female players of the lute and the harp and other festal delights of entertainments were added to the banquets; and also the feasts themselves began to be planned with both greater care and expense. At that time the cook, to the ancient Romans the most worthless of slaves, both in value and in usefulness, became a prized possession, and what had been merely a necessary service came to be regarded as an art. Nevertheless, those things that were looked upon as remarkable at that time were hardly even the seeds of luxury to come.

We find yet another important theme connected to food and drink in the way in which historians typically viewed peoples from elsewhere as barbarians, effectively rendering them as "other" in relation to the inhabitants of Italy and Greece. Eating and drinking habits frequently entered into this cultural assessment of foreigners, as we see in the remaining excerpts in the portrayal of the North Africans by Herodotus, the famed Greek historian of the fifth century BCE (2.25); of the Huns by Ammianus Marcellinus, who wrote an important history of the later Roman Empire in Latin (2.26); and of the Germans by Tacitus, one of the foremost historians of antiquity, who wrote of Rome during the first century CE (2.27).

2.25. Herodotus, 4.194

Their neighbors are the Gyzantes, whose land is very well supplied with honey—much of it produced by bees but even more by some method the people have discovered. Everybody here paints himself red and eats monkeys, of which there is a bountiful supply in the hills. Off the coast, the Carthaginians say, lies an island called Cyrauis, about 25 miles long but narrow, which can be reached on foot from the mainland and is rich in olive trees and vines.

2.26. Ammianus Marcellinus, 31.2.3

But although they have the form of men, however ugly, they are so severe in their mode of life that they require neither fire nor flavorful food, but they feed on the roots of wild plants and the half-raw flesh of any kind of animal whatever, which they insert between their thighs and the backs of their horses and heat up by a little warmth.

2.27. Tacitus, *Gemany and its Tribes* 21–3

No other people indulge in feasting and hospitality more lavishly: to close the house against any human being is considered a crime. Everyone receives a feast according to his level of wealth. When it comes to an end, he who has been your host points out your entertainment and accompanies you. You go next door uninvited. It doesn't matter: you are welcomed with the same courtesy. No one distinguishes between stranger or acquaintance where the right of hospitality is concerned … On waking from sleep, which they generally stretch into the day, they wash, more often in warm water, since winter looms large in their lives. After washing, they take a meal, seated apart, each at his own table: then, arms in hand, they proceed to business or, no less often, to revelry. It is a reproach to no man to make day and night run together by heavy drinking. Brawls are frequent, naturally, among heavy drinkers: rarely are they settled with abuse, more often by bloodshed and wounds. But for the most part they deliberate at these banquets about the mutual reconciliation of enemies, the forming of family alliances, the appointment of chiefs, and even the matter of war and peace, as if at no other time were the mind more open to obvious thoughts, or better warmed to greater ones. The people are neither crafty nor clever, and expose in the freedom of the occasion the heart's previous secrets; and thus everyone's mind is laid bare and naked. On the next day the matter is revisited and the principle of each debating time is preserved: they deliberate while incapable of pretence, they decide when they are incapable of illusion.

For drink they use the liquid from barley or wheat, fermented to a certain semblance of wine. Those closest to the riverbank also buy wine.[24] Their diet is simple: wild fruit, fresh game, or curdled milk. They banish hunger without preparation, without appetizing sauces. They do not display the same temperance toward thirst. If you humor their drunkenness by supplying as much drink as they covet, no less easily will they be overcome by their vices than by war[25]

Finally, it is important to note that, with its impulse to focus on single actors, including poets, politicians, grammarians, and sometimes even women, ancient biographical writing was a literary form closely connected to history. It is not entirely accurate, however, to characterize it as a well-defined genre, as it embodied a mixture of literary genres in both the Greek and Roman traditions. In this regard we would do well to see biography and history as *genera proxima*—closely related genres—which were difficult to distinguish in antiquity and remain hard to distinguish even now (Kraus, in Harrison). Even so, biography is a very important source for eating and drinking habits, and we will have the opportunity to examine this evidence in more detail in the chapters to follow.

Letter writing

Owing to its frequent references to daily living, epistolary literature must be rightfully included among the ancient literary genres that provide insight into food and drink. In the Greek world, private letters preserved on papyrus tell us much about economic and social life in Egypt and in the Roman provinces from the third century BCE onwards. The letter also provided a medium for philosophical and moral instruction and for advancing or attacking certain beliefs and/or individuals. Among these possibilities, an important category was the fictitious letter. The passage below comes from Alciphron, who wrote about 100 of these letters, supposedly from Athenians of low social stature, such as fishermen, farmers and prostitutes during the fourth century BCE. This letter describes the escapades of the parasite, a stock character from contemporary comedy, who typically attached himself to his social superiors for gain, especially for a free meal. The term itself originally meant "fellow eater" in a religious context but became generalized over time to mean a "sponger" of any sort (for more, see 5.32–4).

2.28. Alciphron, *Letters of Parasites* 17

Acratolymas to Chonocrates[26]

Yesterday, while Carion[27] was busy at the well, I made my way to the kitchen; then, having discovered a platter dressed with rich and very savory sauce, and a roast hen, and a pot containing anchovies and Megarian sprats, I snatched them up and, setting off, considered where I might land and opportunely devour my meal by myself. For lack of a better place, I ran over to the Painted Porch (and not a single one of those babbling philosophers were disturbing it)[28] and there I began to enjoy the fruits of my labors. But as I looked up from my dish, I saw some of the young men from the gaming tables coming towards me; frightened, I set the food behind me and lay down on the ground myself, hiding the stolen goods and praying to the Averting Gods that the storm cloud might pass by, I vowed an offering of a sufficient number of grains of frank-incense—good and moldy—which I had gathered up from sacrifices and keep at home. And I didn't miss the mark; for the gods turned them off by another road. Hastily gulping down all the contents of the dishes, I gave as a gift to an innkeeper friend of mine the pot and the platter—all that remained of the spoils—and I departed, having shone forth as a kind and clever fellow as the result of my gifts.

Without question, the most prolific letter writer of antiquity was the famed Roman orator, Marcus Tullius Cicero (Edwards, in Harrison). As a result of his more than 900 letters to various friends and family members and nearly 60 speeches, we often have more information about a single week during the first century BCE than we possess for vast stretches of time during the later imperial period. Not surprisingly, Cicero tended to be less guarded in his letters than he was in his public speeches, a feature that we observe in the first excerpt, a call to frequent and pleasurable dining with friends and a declaration of the superiority of Roman dining over Greek. The second letter is interesting on two counts. First, the sumptuary law of this period refers to one of many attempts by the Roman government from the second century BCE onwards to place limits on public ostentation—from the display of female clothing and jewelry to fancy foods, dinners, and tableware—in order to shrink the gap between rich and poor and to discourage the growing demand for luxury items from the East. Second, these measures were seldom successful. Rome discovered, as did America with Prohibition, that efforts to legislate behavior were ultimately doomed to fail.

2.29. Cicero, *Letters to his Friends* 9.24.2–3

To L. Papirius Paetus, Rome, October, 46 BCE

I am distressed that you have ceased going out to dinner. Indeed, you have deprived yourself of a great deal of amusement and pleasure. In the next place, I fear (for I need not mince words) that you will unlearn and forget to some extent what you were accustomed to doing—to give little dinners yourself. For if, at the time when you had plenty of hosts to imitate, you did not show much proficiency, what am I to think that you will do now? Indeed, when I pointed out the issue to Spurinna, and described your previous life, he indicated that the republic was in great danger unless you reverted to your previous habits when Favonius began to blow;[29] for the present, he said that such conduct might be tolerated, if by chance you could not endure the cold.

But by god, my dear Paetus, joking aside, I advise you to do what I think has a direct bearing on living happily—that you live with men who are good and pleasant and fond of you. Nothing is better suited to life, nothing is better adapted to living well. I am not referring to the pleasure of the palate, but to the fellowship of life and of food, and that relaxation of mind that is most effectively brought about by familiar conversation, and assumes its most charming form in *convivia*, as our fellow countrymen, who are wiser than the Greeks, call them; the Greeks call them *sumposia* or *sumdeipna*, which is to say "drinking together" or "dining together;" we call them *convivia*, "livings together," for then, more than ever, do our lives coincide. Do you see how I am trying to win you back to our dinners by philosophizing? Take care to remain healthy. The easiest way to ensure this is to make a practice of dining out.

2.30. Cicero, *Letters to his Friends* 7.26.2

To M. Fadius Gallus, Tusculanum, 57(?) BCE

But anyway, in case you should wonder what caused this illness, or how I brought it upon myself, the sumptuary law,[30] which seems to have inaugurated "plain living,"—this was my downfall. For while those gourmets wish to bring into favor the fruits of the earth, which are exempted under that law, they season their mushrooms, pot herbs, and greens of every kind to such an extent that nothing is able to be more delicious. When I happened upon that sort of food at an augural banquet at Lentulus' house,[31] so great an attack of diarrhea seized me, that today for the first time it seems to have begun to stop. And thus I, who used to abstain with ease from oysters and lampreys, have been done in by the beet and by the mallow. After this incident I will be more cautious. As for you, however, since you had heard about it from Anicius (in fact he saw me when I was ill), you not only had a just reason for sending an inquiry about me but also of visiting me. I am thinking of staying on here until I am well, for I have lost both strength and weight. But if I beat off this attack, easily, I hope, will I regain both.

Fables and the novel

Ancient fables were fictitious short stories that typically had several features in common: the presence of a conflict, which usually, but not always, involved the speaking and action of an animal; a victory of some kind, typically of the strong over the weak or vice versa; and a comic element (Finkelpearl, in Barchiesi and Scheidel; Nimis, in Boys-Stones et al.). In antiquity many of these fables were attributed to Aesop, a figure as obscure as Homer, who dates perhaps to the sixth century BCE. The sample below is a burlesque animal epic. Note the spoofing of epic in the names of the mice, all of which are connected to foods; observe also how the mouse affirms the simplicity of the traditional grain-based Mediterranean diet. This repurposing in a comic context of everyday items such as food and drink helped to contribute to the popularity of fables in ancient times and beyond.

2.31. *Homeric Apocrypha, The Battle of the Frogs and the Mice 24–39*

> Then Crumb-snatcher answered him and said: "Why do you ask my race? It is well known to all men, gods, and birds of the heavens. I am called Crumb-Snatcher. I am the son of Bread-Nibbler, my stout hearted father. My mother was Quern-Licker,[32] the daughter of Ham-Gnawer, the king. She gave birth to me in the mouse hole and nourished me with food, figs and nuts, and all kinds of dainties. But how are you to make me your friend, since I am different by nature? For you get your living in the water, but as for me I am used to eating such foods as men have. The loaf kneaded three times does not forget me in its neat, round basket, nor the thinly wrapped flat cake full of sesame and cheese, nor the slice of ham, nor liver dressed in white fat, nor cheese newly curdled from sweet milk, nor delicious honey cake, which even the blessed gods long for …"

Defined as extended prose narrative fiction, the ancient novel is best known to us through the Latin authors Petronius and Apuleius. Both took the basic plot of the Greek novel, which involved faithful young lovers, and parodied it by emphasizing sex, humor, and low-life sensibilities. The next three passages all belong to arguably the most famous episode in Petronius' novel, the *Satyricon* – the over-the-top dinner offered by a wealthy ex-slave, Trimalchio. The dinner, known as the "dinner of Trimalchio" (*cena Trimalchionis*), is served to a male couple (one of whom is the narrator) as part of their comic adventures in southern Italy. The dinner and conversation are meant to show wit and learning but instead reveal the pretentiousness and ignorance of the bombastic host. The first passage highlights the main course, a stuffed pig, whose presentation is clever but vulgar at the same time. The second excerpt lampoons banquet entertainment, while the final selection spoofs the food habits and mores of a boorish but harmless municipal official who bursts on to the scene after having participated in a funeral feast. He is the sort of person who must have been common in municipal Italy of the first century CE. This novel remains a rich source for dining customs and gastronomy under the early empire.

2.32. Petronius, *Satyricon* 49–50

He had not yet puffed out all of his talk, when a dish holding a huge pig filled the table. We began to marvel at the speed, and swore an oath that not even a fowl could have been cooked so quickly, especially since the pig seemed to us to be much bigger than the boar had been a little while earlier. Then Trimalchio, looking at it more and more closely, said, "What, what, has this pig not been gutted? I swear it has not. Call the cook, call the cook up here to us." When the poor cook stood by the table and said that he had forgotten to gut it, "What? Forgotten?" shouts Trimalchio. "You would think that he had not seasoned it with pepper and cumin. "Strip him!" There was no delay; the cook was stripped and stood gloomily between two executioners. Nevertheless, we all began to intercede on the cook's behalf and say: "These things will happen. We ask that you let him off; if he does it again, none of us will say a word for him." I, very cruel in my severity, was unable to hold myself, but leaned over and said in Agamemnon's ear: "Clearly, this must be the most worthless slave; how could anyone forget to gut a pig? By god, I would not have forgiven him if he had passed over a fish like that." But not Trimalchio, who, with his face softened into a smile, said. "And so, if your memory is so bad, clean him here in front of us." The cook put on his shirt, seized a knife, and carved the pig's belly in this place and that with a trembling hand. At once, from the slits that had grown from the pressure within, sausages and black puddings tumbled out. After this, the household slaves offered spontaneous applause and shouted together, "God bless Gaius!" The cook too was rewarded with a drink and a silver crown, and received a drinking cup on a Corinthian dish.

2.33. Petronius, *Satyricon* 53–4

At last, however, the acrobats came in. A very dull blockhead stood there with a ladder and commanded a boy to dance from rung to rung and at the very top to dance to songs, and then he made him hop through burning hoops, and to hold a wine jar with his teeth. Trimalchio alone was in awe of these things and he kept saying that it was a thankless profession. Moreover, he said that there were only two things in the world that he could watch most pleasantly, acrobats and trumpeters; the rest of the entertainments were pure nonsense. "Why," he said, "I once bought a Greek comedy company, but I preferred them to do Atellane plays,[33] and I told my pipe player to play Latin songs."

Just as he was speaking, a boy slipped [against the arm][34] of Trimalchio. The household slaves raised a cry, no less the guests, not on account of such a stinking man, whose very neck they would have been glad to see broken, but because it would have been a gloomy finish to the dinner to have to mourn the death of a stranger. Trimalchio himself groaned aloud in pain, and hung over his arm as if it were hurt; the doctors rushed up, and among the first Fortunata,[35] with her hair down and a cup in her hand, proclaimed what a poor unhappy woman she was. The boy who had fallen down at this time was crawling around at our feet, and begging to be let off. I very much feared by these petitions that he was seeking [some sort of ridiculous comic turn].[36] For not yet had the cook who had forgotten to gut the pig faded from my memory. And so I began to look around the whole dining room, in case some self-propelled toy should jump out of the wall, especially after the slave, who had wrapped the bruised arm of his master with white wool instead of purple, began to be beaten. And my suspicion was not far off; for instead of punishment there came Trimalchio's decree, which ordered the boy to become a free man, so that someone might not be able to say that so great a man had been injured by a slave.

2.34. Petronius, *Satyricon* 65–6

Relieved by this news, I lay down in my place again, and I watched Habinnas' entrance with great astonishment. He was already drunk, however, and had put his hands on his wife's shoulders; he was wearing several wreaths, and ointment was running down his forehead into his eyes.[37] He sat down in the chief magistrate's place, and immediately requested wine and hot water. Trimalchio was delighted at this cheerfulness; he asked for a larger cup for himself, and inquired how Habinnas had been received. "We had everything there except you," he said, "for my eyes were here with you. By god, it was terrific. Scissa was having a funeral feast on the ninth day[38] for her poor dear slave, whom she had set free on his deathbed. And I think that she will have a hefty profit to record with the five-percent tax collectors,[39] for they estimate that the dead man was worth fifty thousand sesterces. Anyways, it was a pleasant occasion, even if we were compelled to pour half of our drinks over his insignificant bones." "Ah," said Trimalchio, "but what did you have for dinner?" "I shall tell you if I can," he said, "but I am of such a fine memory that I frequently forget my own name. Well, first we had a pig crowned with a wine cup, with honey cakes placed around it, and giblets very well done, and beetroot, of course, and pure whole meal bread, which I prefer to white myself; it makes you strong, and when I move my bowels, I don't groan. The next dish was a cold tart, with excellent Spanish wine poured over warm honey. Indeed, I ate a lot of the tart, and soaked myself through and through with the honey. Chickpeas and lupines were passed around, a choice of nuts and an apple each. I took two myself, and look, I have them tied up in my napkin; for if I do not bring some gift back to my pet slave-boy, I'll be in trouble. Oh! My wife is offering a timely reminder. We had a piece of bear in our sights. When Scintilla had the poor sense to taste it, she almost vomited her own insides; on the other hand, I ate more than a pound myself, for it had the very taste of wild boar. And I say this, since the bear eats up a poor little man, how much better is it for the poor little man to devour a bear? To complete the meal, we had cheese mellowed in new wine, and single snails, and pieces of intestines, and liver in little dishes, and eggs in caps, and turnip, and mustard …"

Apuleius' *Metamorphoses*, written about a century after the *Satyricon* but no less picaresque than its predecessor, chronicles the changing of a young man into an ass and his comic adventures until he is re-transformed by the goddess Isis. In this passage Lucius, the narrator and man turned into the ass, eats and drinks human fare with a sense of gusto that thoroughly amuses his captors. This is especially welcome for Lucius' owner, who now uniquely owns as companion and dinner guest, an ass who can wrestle, dance, understand language, and say what he wants by nods. Ultimately, the humor lies in Apuleius' ability to blur the boundaries that traditionally separate the cuisine and eating habits of humans and animals.

2.35. Apuleius, *Metamorphoses* 10.15–16

Finally, such loud and unrestrained laughter had overtaken the slaves that the noise even reached their master's ears as he was passing by. He inquired what amusement the household slaves were laughing at, and when he discovered what it was, the master too peeped through the same hole and he also was exceedingly amused. He laughed so hard and long that his stomach hurt. Then, after the door to the room was opened, he stood close by and watched in the open. Since I finally saw fortune's face shining somewhat more kindly upon me, and with the joy of those present bolstering my confidence, I was not agitated in the least and kept right on eating, free from care. Soon the master of the house, delighted by the novelty of the spectacle, ordered me to be taken—or rather he conducted me himself with his own hands—to the dining room; he had a table set up and he ordered every kind of solid food and untasted dishes put before me. But I, although already splendidly stuffed, nevertheless wanted to make myself pleasing and more commendable to him, and so I hungrily attacked the foods laid out before me. Calculating precisely what would be especially abhorrent to an ass, they kept offering these items to me to test my tameness: meats spiced with silphium, fowl sprinkled with pepper, and fish soaked in exotic sauce. Meanwhile, the banquet rang with uproarious laughter.

Then one blockhead who was present said, "Give this comrade a little wine." The master followed this suggestion and said, "That is not such a ridiculous joke, you scoundrel. It is quite possible that our messmate would be glad to have a cup of honey wine to go with his food." Then he turned to a slave and said, "Hey there, boy, rinse this golden cup carefully, mix in some honey wine and offer it to my sponger here. Impress upon him at the same time that I have drunk to his health."

Thereupon, a mighty sense of expectation arose among the banqueters. Not in the least perturbed, I leisurely and cheerfully curled the edges of my lips like a ladle and I swallowed down in one gulp that very large draught. A shout arose, as they all wished me good health with a single voice.

Food for thought

Food and drink lent themselves quite easily to philosophical inquiry, given that they were both life sustaining and easily abused. One tradition that was especially popular in the Greek world was writings connected with wise men (*sophoi*). The earliest *sophoi* date from the sixth century CE, and the list typically included four men from eastern cities (Thales of Miletus, Bias of Priene, Cleobulus of Rhodes, and Pittacus of Mytilene) and three from the mainland (Solon of Athens, Chilon of Sparta, and Periander of Corinth)—the canonical Seven Sages. Poets and historians alike cited them for their wisdom about statecraft and other critical issues. Especially noteworthy is Plutarch's engaging account in the first excerpt of a dinner at which all seven supposedly gathered to eat but also to discuss, among other things, the need to avoid becoming a slave to filling one's belly with the riches of land and sea. It is Solon, the wise man of Athens, who speaks here. The second excerpt, from Plato's *Republic*, broadens the scope by considering how one might provision the ideal city as described by Socrates in his exchange with Glaucon. As we see, this city relied on a host of producers. It was Plato's vision that these producers work in harmony with the rulers to create and distribute goods and services within a system where all classes subordinated their desires for the common good (Sedley).

2.36. Plutarch, *On Mores (Moralia), Dinner of the Seven Wise Men* 160a–c

> For food is taken as a remedy for hunger, and all who eat food in a prescribed way are said to be providing themselves treatment, not thinking that they are doing something pleasant and grateful, but that this is a necessity by nature. Indeed, it is possible to count more pains than pleasures derived from food; or rather, pleasure affects a limited area in the body, and lasts for a short time; but as for the ugly and painful experiences that fill us up by the bother and discomfort of digestion, why is it necessary to speak of their number? I think that Homer had this in mind when he makes an argument to show that, in the case of the gods, they do not die in that they do not live by food:

> " ... since they do not eat bread, nor drink sparkling wine. For this reason, they are bloodless and are called immortals,

> so that food is not only an element conducive to life, but also to death. For it is from this source that illnesses emerge, thriving on the very same food as men's bodies, which find no less disadvantage in satiety than in fasting. For frequently it is a greater task to use up food and to distribute it again, once the body has received it, than it was to acquire it and to get it together in the first place. But just as the Danaids[40] would be at a loss to know how to live and what to do, if freed from the enslavement of trying to fill the great jar, so we are at a loss to know, if we should have the chance to cease from piling the plentiful products of land and sea into this relentless flesh of ours, what we shall do, since, by our inexperience with things of beauty, we now content ourselves with the necessities of life. Just as men who are slaves, once emancipated, do for themselves and by themselves those very things which they used to do in service to their masters, so the soul now supports the body with many toils and hardships; but if it be relieved of its enslavement, it will doubtless maintain its newly established freedom and live with a view to itself and the truth, since there will be nothing to distract or divert it."

2.37. Plato, *Republic* 2.372A–373E

"First, therefore, let us examine how the men provided for in this way will live. Will they not make bread, wine, clothing and shoes, and build houses for themselves, doing their work in summer, naked for the most part and without shoes, but in winter clothed and shod sufficiently? And will they provide meal from their barley and flour from their wheat for nourishment and, once they have kneaded and cooked these, serve noble barley cakes and loaves upon some reeds or clean leaves and, reclining on a litter spread with yew and myrtle, feast with their children, drinking their wine, wearing garlands and singing hymns to the gods in sweet companionship with each other, and not producing children beyond their means, mindful of poverty or war?"

Here Glaucon replied: "You are describing these men," he said, as feasting without relish, it seems." "You are right," I said. "I forgot that they will also have relishes— salt, clearly, and olives and cheese. And they will boil together onions and garden herbs, the kind of things they boil in the country. But for dessert we will serve them figs, chickpeas and beans, and they will roast myrtle berries and acorns on the fire, washing them down moderately with drinks. And so, living in peace and health, it is likely that they will die in old age and hand on a similar kind of life to their descendants." And he said, "If you were founding a city of pigs, Socrates, what else would you provide other then these things?" "Why, what would you have, Glaucon?" I said. "The typical things," he replied; "they should recline on couches, I suppose, if they intend to be comfortable, and dine from tables and have the relishes and sweetmeats such as they now have." "Good," I said, "I understand. It is not only how a city alone comes into being, but a luxurious city. Indeed, that's not such a bad idea. For by observing such a city, perhaps we could discern the source of justice and injustice in cities. The true city seems to me to be the one I have described—the healthy city, as it were. But if, on the other hand, you wish that we also contemplate a fevered city, there is nothing to prevent it. For there are some, it appears, who will not be satisfied with this sort of fare or with this way of life; but couches will have to be added and tables and other equipment, and also relishes, myrrh, incense, girls, and cakes—each of these of every kind. And the houses, garments and shoes we spoke of must no longer be considered necessities, but we must set painting and embroidery in motion, and we must acquire gold and ivory and all such similar things, don't you agree?" "Yes," he said. "Then won't we have to make the city larger again? For that healthy city is no longer sufficient, but already we must swell its bulky mass with things that are unnecessary, such as all the huntsmen, and the imitators, many of them concerned with figures and colors and many with music—the poets and their assistants, rhapsodists, actors, chorus dancers, theater managers—and producers of all kinds of articles, especially those who have to do with women's cosmetics. We'll want more servants. And doesn't it seem that we'll need tutors, wet and dry nurses, beauticians, barbers and, yet again, cooks and chefs? Additionally, we shall need swineherds. These were not a part of our former city; we had no need for them. But in this city there will be this further need; and we shall also require other herds of cattle in large numbers, if one is to eat them. Don't you agree?" "Yes." "Then will we be much more likely to need the services of doctors, if we live in this way rather than as before?" "Very much."

"And the land, I suppose, that was sufficient at that time to feed the then population, will it go from being sufficient to insufficient? Is this so or not?" "It is so." "Then we'll have to cut out a piece of our neighbor's land, if we are intending to have enough for pasture and plowing, and they in turn will have to cut out a piece of ours, if they too give themselves over to the unlimited acquisition of wealth, exceeding the limit of our necessary wants?" "Inevitably, Socrates," he said. "After this, shall we go to war, Glaucon? Or what will happen?" "What you say," he said.

Food and drink also figure prominently in the two major philosophical systems of antiquity—Stoicism and Epicureanism (Sedley). Epicureanism promoted human pleasure—not hedonism, as the modern connotation of the word can suggest—but freedom from pain and disturbance in order to achieve a life of harmonious balance. For Epicureans, this was the ultimate goal, especially given that the gods showed indifference at best to the plight of man and that of the world itself. Lucretius had the difficult task of presenting these ideas as earlier developed by Greek philosophers to a Roman audience. He recognized this challenge, telling his elite male Roman readers that he must beguile them with poetry in order to get them to accept difficult doctrines, much like a doctor must trick a child into taking unpleasant medicine by coating the cup with sweetener (*On the Nature of Things* 4.11–25). For additional excerpts from Lucretius, see 3.2 and 7.30.

For Stoics, Epictetus, a former slave who wrote in Greek and is known to us through the preservation of his doctrines by the historian Arrian, underscored the importance of mastering key principles, a process that he likens to digestion in the first excerpt. As we saw earlier in the case of historians (see 2.22), philosophers too could analogize in bodily terms. Seneca, the great Roman master of the moral epistle, provides a similar view in the second passage, where, in offering advice to his friend Lucilius, he equates reading with digestion, which in turn becomes intellectual nourishment for readers. Food became a handy sort of dialect for Seneca that allowed him to expose the moral and philosophical shortcomings of his audience. To be sure, the most important principle for the Stoic adherent was virtue, which alone was sufficient for happiness. This meant avoiding emotion and extravagant living by assuming the kind of "Stoic demeanor" that the emperor Marcus Aurelius exudes in the third reading. Note especially the emperor's satisfaction with his meager lunch compared to that of others. In the final excerpt, Persius, a poet connected to the Stoic opposition of the emperor Nero in the first century CE, ridicules the rich man who prays for additional wealth while dissipating his resources through constant sacrificing and luxurious eating. Thus does the poet hope to expose the hypocrisy of those who sacrifice to the gods for material gain, not for moral virtue.

2.38. Arrian, *Discourses of Epictetus* 3.21.1–6

Those who have learned principles without supporting arguments wish to throw them up immediately, just as persons with an upset stomach throw up their food. First, digest your principles, and then you will surely not vomit them up in this way. If you do not do this, they are mere vomit—foul stuff and inedible. But once you have digested these principles, show us some change in your governing principle that is due to them, just as athletes display their shoulders as a result of their training and eating, and as those who have mastered the arts can show the results of their learning. The builder does not come forward and say, "Listen to me as I lecture about the art of building," but after he has taken a contract for a house and has built it, he demonstrates that he possesses the art. Do something of the same sort yourself, too. Eat as a man, drink as a man, adorn yourself, marry, have children, be an involved citizen. Tolerate criticism, be patient with an uncooperative brother, father, son, neighbor and fellow traveler. Show us these things, so we can observe that in all truth you have learned something of the philosophers.

2.39. Seneca, *Epistle* 2

I am forming a good opinion of your future, judging by what you write me and by what I hear. You do not run here and there nor distract yourself by changing your residence. That kind of restlessness is the sign of a disordered spirit. I think that the first proof of a well-ordered mind is one's ability to stay in one place and to linger in one's own company. See to it, however, that the reading of many authors and of all kinds of books does not make you discursive and unsteady. You must linger among dependable master thinkers, and digest their works, if you wish to draw upon ideas that will faithfully abide in your mind. Everywhere is nowhere; for the person who spends his life in foreign travel ends up having many acquaintances but no friends. And the same thing must apply to men who devote themselves intimately to the talent of no single author, but pass through everything in a hasty and hurried manner. Food does no good nor is it assimilated into the body if it is dispersed as soon as it is eaten; a wound does not heal if the salve is changed; a plant that is often moved does not grow strong. Nothing is so efficacious that it can be helpful while it is being moved about. Reading many books causes distraction.

Accordingly, since you cannot read all the books that you may have, it is enough to possess as many that you can read. "But," you say, "I wish to unroll this book first and then another."[41] It is the sign of an over nice appetite to sample many dishes; for when they are manifold and different, they offer slight taste but they do not nourish. And so, always read the standard authors, and when you crave a change, go back to those whom you read before. Each day acquire something that will help you against poverty, against death, no less against the remaining misfortunes; and after you have run through many thoughts, select one that you thoroughly digest that day. I myself do this as well; from the many things that I have read, I claim some part for myself …

2.40. Marcus Aurelius, *Letter to Fronto* 4.6.1

Marcus Aurelius to Fronto (144–145 CE?)

Hail, my sweetest of masters.

Then we went to lunch. What do you think that I ate? A small portion of bread, although I witnessed others devouring beans, onions, and herrings full of roe. We then diligently gathered grapes, working up a good sweat, and we were happy; and, as the poet says, we "still left some clusters hanging high as gleanings of the vintage." After six o'clock, we came home.

2.41. Persius, *Satire* 2.41–51

You pray for the help of strength and for a body reliable in old age. Good, let it be so! But your elaborate dishes and rich sauces forbid the gods from listening to you, and they stay the hand of Jupiter. Longing to pile up riches, you slay an ox and summon Mercury with a liver. "Grant that my household gods may prosper me, grant me a flock and offspring for the herds!" But how can that happen, poor fool, when the entrails of so many heifers of yours melt away in the flames? Yet on the fellow goes with his entrails and his rich sacrificial cakes, intent upon winning: "Now my field is growing, now my sheepfold increases, now it will be granted, now, now"—until deceived and out of hope, the coin at the bottom of his purse sighs in vain.

Specialized literature

We conclude this survey with a brief consideration of food and drink in technical or specialized literature. By technical or specialized literature I mean agricultural treatises and the literary form most closely related to eating and drinking, the cookbook. Two other categories, encyclopedic works and medical literature belong to this rubric as well. The former, treated primarily by the great Roman polymath Pliny the Elder, who, for example, devoted an entire chapter to wine making and the wine trade, will appear throughout this source book; medical literature, owing to its vastness and complexity, will receive its own treatment in Chapter Seven.

In the area of technical literature, farming was especially critical, given its role as the primary industry of the ancient Mediterranean basin. As early as the eighth century BCE, the Greek poet Hesiod was providing practical instruction about primitive rustic life in his poem, *Works and Days*, a genre of wisdom literature that was common in Greece and in the rest of the ancient world. In the first passage below the poet describes the summertime bounty that awaits the farmer who has worked diligently and lived properly throughout the year. Roman writers were equally invested in this tradition. In his *Georgics* ("agricultural poems") Vergil celebrated simple living and a return to the land, values that were important to the political program of Augustus, Rome's first emperor. These emphases are beautifully captured in the second passage, the poet's account of the care with which one had to prepare the land for bee-keeping. The honey produced from this activity was put to use in various medical remedies and as the most popular sweetener in the ancient world. A similar respect for farming combined with careful attention to detail is present in the final excerpt as well. It belongs to Columella, whose 12-book treatise *On Agriculture*, written in the first century CE, marked the high point of this genre.

2.42. Hesiod, *Works and Days* 582–96

When the golden thistle blooms and the chirping cicada, sitting in a tree, incessantly pours down its clear sounding song from beneath its wings in the season of toilsome summer, it is then that goats are fattest, and wine is best, and women are most lascivious, but the men are weakest, since Sirius parches their head and knees, and their skin is dry from the heat. At that time, let there be a rock's shadow and Bibline wine,[42] barley bread made with milk, cheese from goats that are just drying up, and the meat of a cow fed in the forest that has not yet calved and of newly born kids. Drink too some sparkling wine, sitting in the shade, when you have eaten to your heart's content, your face turned toward the fresh blowing West wind. Pour three measures from the water of an ever flowing spring, running and undisturbed, then put in a fourth part of wine.

2.43. Vergil, *Georgics* 4.8–32

First, you must find a settled home for your bees, where the winds may find no access—for winds prevent the bees from carrying home their food—where no sheep or frisky young goats may trample the flowers, nor straying heifer brush off the dew from the fields and rub away the springing blade. Let the spangled lizards with their scaly backs also be strangers to the rich stalls, and the bird that devours bees, and other birds, and Procne,[43] with breast marked by her blood-stained hands. For these destroy everything far and wide, and carry off in their mouths the very bees as they fly along, a sweet snack for their cruel nestlings. But let clear springs be near, and moss-green pools, and a tiny brook that disappears through the grass; and let a palm or huge wild olive shade the porch, so that, when the new kings lead forth the first swarms of springtime, and the young bees revel in their freedom from the combs, a nearby riverbank may tempt them to quit the heat, and a tree in their path may hold them in leafy shelter. Into the midst of the water, whether it stands idle or flows onward, bring together willows and large rocks, so that they might have many bridges to halt upon and spread their wings to the summer sun, if by chance the East wind has scattered them or has plunged them headlong into the water. All around these things let green cassia bloom, and wild thyme with its wafting fragrance, and a wealth of strong-scented savory, and let violet beds drink of the trickling spring.

2.44. Columella, *On Agriculture* 12.14

At this same season, or even at the beginning of August, apples and pears of the sweetest flavor are picked when they are moderately ripe, and, after they have been cut in two or three parts with a reed or small bone knife, they are placed in the sun until they become dry. If there is a large supply of them, they provide the country folk not the least part of their winter food; for they serve in the place of relish, just like the fig, which, when dried and stored away, helps to feed the country folk in wintertime.

Once considered a simple how-to guide of the kitchen, the cookbook is now recognized as an important source for understanding cultural values and the past. These features are characteristic of the ancient cookbook as well. Although few survive from antiquity, we do possess one notable work, the *De re coquinaria* (*On Cookery*), attributed to the proverbial gourmand, M. Gavius Apicius of the first century CE (but actually produced by a compiler in the fourth century CE). This cookbook consists of more than 450 recipes organized into ten chapters. Included are topics on kitchen management, sausages, vegetables and stews, as well as pulses, poultry, meat, and seafood. In the selections that follow, it is helpful to bear in mind three general features: first, Apicius' recipes often do not include proportions of ingredients or details of cooking procedure, information that is considered essential in modern cookery; second, products now closely associated with modern Italian cuisine, such as tomatoes, peppers, and eggplant, are New World imports that were not part of the ancient diet—still, there is a preference for foodstuffs such as breads and sausages, which remain important in Italian cookery today; third, the Romans typically did not consume items like meat and fish in their pure form, a preference that is evident in their wide use of sauces to add flavor and also to mask any undesirable tastes.

2.45. Apicius, *On Cookery* 2.5.2=Grocock and Grainger 154–5

Sausages

Another method. Make a mixture of boiled spelt-grits and coarsely chopped meat that has been pounded with pepper, *liquamen*[44] and pine kernels. Stuff in a sausage skin and boil. Then grill with salt and serve with mustard, or serve boiled, cut up on a round dish.

2.46. Apicius, *On Cookery* 7.6.4=Grocock and Grainger 244–5

White sauce for boiled meat.

Pepper, *liquamen*, wine, rue, onion, pine-kernels, spiced wine, a little soaked bread for thickening, oil. When it is cooked, pour over the meat.

2.47. Apicius, *On Cookery* 8.9.1=Grocock and Grainger 284–5

Dormice[45]

Stuff the dormice with minced pork, the minced meat of whole dormice, pounded with pepper, pine-kernels, asafoetida,[46] and *liquamen*. Sew up, place on a tile, put in the oven, or cook, stuffed, in a small oven.

Suggestions for Further Reading

Useful essays on the genres discussed in this chapter along with the most recent scholarship can be found in Boys-Stones et al. (2009) *The Oxford Handbook of Hellenic Studies*; Barchiesi and Scheidel, eds. (2010) *The Oxford Handbook of Roman Studies*; Harrison, ed. (2005) *A Companion to Latin Literature*; and the *Cambridge Companion* Series on various Graeco-Roman authors and genres. The following works are meant to provide additional background.

Bober, P. P. 1999. *Art, Culture, and Cuisine: Ancient and Medieval Gastronomy.* Chicago.

Braund, S. H. 1989. *Satire and Society in Ancient Rome.* Exeter.

—2002. *Latin Literature.* London.

Cartledge, P. 1993. *The Greeks: A Portrait of Self and Others.* Oxford.

Dalby, A. 1996. *Siren Feasts: A History of Food and Gastronomy in Greece.* London.

—2003. *Food in the Ancient World from A to Z.* London.

Davidson, A., ed. 1999. *Oxford Companion to Food.* Oxford.

Donahue J. 2004. *The Roman Community at Table during the Principate.* Ann Arbor.

Flower, B. and Rosenbaum, E., trans. 1958. *The Roman Cookery Book: A Critical Translation of The Art of Cooking by Apicius.* London.

Fornara, C. 1983. *The Nature of History in Ancient Greece and Rome.* Berkeley.

Freudenburg, K. 2005. *Cambridge Companion to Roman Satire.* Cambridge.

Gagarin, M. 2010. *Oxford Encyclopedia of Ancient Greece and Rome.* 7 vols. Oxford.

Gowers, E. 1993. *The Loaded Table: Representations of Food in Roman Literature.* Oxford.

Grocock, C. and Grainger, S., text, comm. and trans. 2006. *Apicius: A Critical Edition with an Introduction and an English Translation.* Devon.

Katz, S. and Weaver, W. W., eds. 2003. *Encyclopedia of Food and Culture.* 3 vols. New York.

Leigh, M. L. 2004. *Comedy and the Rise of Rome.* Oxford.

Morley, N. 2000. *Ancient History: Key Themes and Approaches.* London.

Motto, A. L. 2001. "Seneca's Culinary Satire." In Motto, A. L. *Further Essays on Seneca*, 169–83. Frankfurt-am-Mein.

Richardson-Hay, C. 2009. "Dinner at Seneca's Table: The Philosophy of Food." *Greece and Rome* 56: 71–96.

Sedley, D. N. 2003. *Cambridge Companion to Greek and Roman Philosophy.* Cambridge.

Sherratt, S. 2004. "Feasting in Homeric Epic." *Hesperia* 73: 301–37.

Veyne, P. 1988. *Did the Greeks Believe in Their Myths? An Essay on the Constitutive Imagination*, trans. P. Wissing. Chicago.

Wilkins, J., Harvey, D., and Dobson, M., eds. 1995. *Food in Antiquity*. Exeter.

Wilkins, J. and Hill, S. 2000. *The Boastful Chef: The Discourse of Food in Ancient Greek Comedy*. Oxford.

—2006. *Food in the Ancient World*. Oxford.

3

Grain, Grapes, and Olives:
The Mediterranean Triad and More

And wine to gladden the heart of man, oil to make his face shine and bread to strengthen man's heart.

Psalm 104:15

This chapter begins at the most sensible point of departure—with the food and drink actually consumed by the ancient Greeks and Romans. The evidence is plentiful, thereby allowing us to develop a rich account of what people ate and drank from the second millennium BCE to the fifth century CE. At the outset, it is important to emphasize that there was no single monolithic diet; differences by region, custom, climate, and belief helped to guarantee a certain level of variety across the Mediterranean. Additionally, the choice of what to eat made an important statement about a society's given identity, as did the context in which one ate without committing a social blunder (Nadeau, in Erdkamp). The latter concern was especially critical. Much like we would not serve a birthday cake at a funeral, so too were the Greeks and Romans careful to make food choices according to generally held cultural beliefs, as in the instance of sacrificing only those animals that fit a recognizable paradigm.

Within this framework of food availability and cultural choice, three foodstuffs—grain, olive oil, and grapes—defined the ancient diet more than any other commodities. Furthermore, the Greeks and Romans regarded the bread and wine that emerged from this triad as symbols of a civilized people, since these items required complex preparation. A rich variety of fruits and vegetables, both native and imported, provided additional dietary balance and choice, while a strong preference for sauces, relishes, and spices provided texture while also helping to mask flavors that were less than agreeable to the ancient palate. As we shall see, these were the typical items of consumption—nutritious staples accompanied by condiments and sauces along with wine of various vintage and quality. Those with access to these items enjoyed a diet that was generally healthier than many modern regimens, which tend to feature processed foods traditionally heavy in fats and salt. This surely helps to explain the popularity in recent years of health plans like the so-called "Mediterranean diet," with its emphasis on simplicity and healthy, or "good" fats.

In addition to these items, we shall also explore the place of beef and fish in the ancient diet. Issues of status and availability had much to do with limiting their popularity among a wider audience, yet these commodities retained their value as important markers of rank and status among those able to afford them. That the sources preserve so much testimony about beef and fish points to a literary agenda dominated by elites who were concerned with developing a "high cuisine" while reinforcing their own status. At the same time, a strong tradition of criticizing the value system of the upper class, found especially in comedy and satire, serves as a colorful counterbalance to this evidence, while often providing valuable insight into the dietary habits of the ordinary citizen.

A final section of the chapter will briefly examine food supply and distribution in the Graeco-Roman world. The food for most citizens came from local sources; hence, self-sufficiency was the norm—and much revered as a virtue. Only by exception did powerful city-states like Athens and Rome possess the military resources and political will to obtain foodstuffs from beyond their borders in order to feed their citizens. This power had important consequences for social relations, as elites could control the distribution of foodstuffs to reinforce class distinctions, win votes, or enhance their own reputation. We shall also observe that food shortages did sometimes occur, although famine was much less common. Before considering all of this evidence we must appreciate the role of myth in preserving the cultural importance of food and drink for the Greeks and Romans.

Food, drink and myth

Myth served many functions in antiquity: it provided entertainment; it helped the ancients to define the world and their place in it; and it provided explanations for various features of ancient life such as rituals and monuments (aetiology). A classic definition of myth describes it as a "traditional tale with secondary, partial reference to something of collective importance" (Burkert). It could be argued that nothing was more collectively important in antiquity than food security. We witness this concern in some of the earliest myths of the Graeco-Roman world, where a common motif was that of a Golden Age.

This was an imagined time of peace and prosperity, free from toil and trouble, where the plentiful earth freely and generously provided sustenance for her inhabitants (Wilkins 2006). In the first passage Hesiod, a Greek poet of the seventh century BCE who wrote about the gods and farming, captures what this was like for the immortals. In the second excerpt Lucretius, who attempted to introduce Epicurean philosophy to a Roman audience, describes in vivid terms the abundance of the primitive earth within the larger context of his famous description of the birth of human civilization in the fifth book of his poem.

3.1. Hesiod, *Works and Days* 107–19

Golden was the first race of men made by the gods who reside on Olympus. They lived in the time of Kronos,[1] when he ruled the heavens; and they lived like gods with carefree hearts, strangers to labor and misery. Miserable old age did not affect them either, but with hands and feet ever the same, they delighted in feasting, in living apart from all evils. They died as if overtaken by sleep. All good things belonged to them, and the grain-giving earth bore fruits of its own accord, abundant and provoking no envy. Willingly and at peace did they manage their affairs amid many good things.

3.2. Lucretius, *On the Nature of Things* 5.933–47

There was no sturdy driver of the curving plow, no one knew how to till the fields with iron, nor to dig new shoots into the ground, nor to cut down old branches from tall trees with a sickle. What the sun and the rains had given, what the earth had created of its own accord, that gift was pleasing enough to their hearts. Amid the acorn-bearing oaks they refreshed their bodies for the most part; and wild strawberries, which now you see ripen with crimson color in wintertime, at that time the earth bore in abundance, and even larger than now. And at that time the flowering infancy of the world produced many other foods besides—harsh nourishment but sufficient for poor mortals. But rivers and springs summoned them to quench their thirst, as now the waters running down from great mountains re-gather far and wide the thirsting breeds of wild animals.

At the same time, the notion of change, especially in the form of decline from earlier times, was an equally prominent feature of the ancient worldview, and thus a topic well suited to myth. Here Vergil in his early poem on various forms of rural industry signals the end of the Golden Age due to the progress of man and his many innovations, from the plow and ships to fishing nets and snares. As Vergil indicates, however, with progress came toil and poverty.

3.3. Vergil, *Georgics* 1.125–46

Before the time of Jupiter,[2] no tillers subdued the fields; it was not even legal to mark a field or divide it with a boundary; man sought things for the common good, and the earth herself gave things more freely when no one begged for them. Man brought deadly venom to black serpents and commanded wolves to plunder and the seas to be moved; and he shook honey from the leaves, and he hid fire, and held in check the wine that ran everywhere in the streams, so that, by taking thought, practice might hammer out various arts little by little, might seek out the stalk of grain in furrows, and might strike forth the hidden fire from veins of flint. Then did rivers first feel the hollowed alder tree; then the sailor numbered the stars and gave them names—Pleiades, Hyades, and Arctos, shining offspring of Lycaon; then man discovered how to capture wild game in traps, to cheat with bird lime,[3] and to circle great marshes with hunting dogs. And now he lashes the broad stream with a fishing net, seeking the depths, and another drags his dripping net in the sea. Then came the stiffness of iron and the shrill blade of the saw (for early man cut the split wood with wedges); then came diverse arts. Relentless toil conquered everything, and poverty that presses down hard in tough times.

Myth was also important in that it provided explanations for the introduction of various critical foods such as wine, grain and beef to mortals through the intervention of the gods (Wilkins 2006). That these foodstuffs were linked with the divine and preserved in myth is powerful proof of their wider cultural significance in the Mediterranean world. Of these accounts one of the most entertaining is how beef came to Italy, in this instance through the cattle of Geryon, which Hercules brought to Italy as one of his famous 12 labors. Our source for this story, Dionysius of Halicarnassus, was especially interested in Roman religious tradition, and so we find in his account an instance of early animal sacrifice as well as the foundation by Hercules of what came to be known as the Forum Boarium (Cattle Market) near the Porta Trigemina[4] in Rome.

3.4. Dionysius of Halicarnassus, *Roman Antiquities* 1.39

Of the stories told concerning this god, some are more legendary and some are closer to the truth. The legendary story of his arrival is as follows. Commanded by Eurystheus to drive Geryon's cattle from Erytheia to Argos, Hercules performed the task among other labors and, having passed through many parts of Italy on his way home, he came also to the district of Pallantium in the country of the Aborigines; and finding much excellent grass for his cattle, he let them graze there and, overcome with weariness, he lay down and gave himself over to sleep. Thereupon, a certain robber of that region by the name of Cacus chanced upon the unguarded cattle as they were feeding and he longed to possess them. But observing Hercules lying there asleep, he imagined he could not drive them all away undetected and at the same time he realized that the task was not an easy one. So he hid a few of them in the cave nearby in which he lived, dragging each of them backwards by the tail to that place. This might have destroyed all evidence of his theft, as the direction in which the oxen had gone would not correspond to their tracks. Hercules, then, awakening soon afterwards, and having counted the cattle and found some were missing, was for a time at a loss to know where they had gone; and supposing them to have wandered from their pasture, he looked for them up and down the countryside. Then, when he had failed to find them, he came to the cave and, although he was deceived by the tracks, he believed, nevertheless, that he ought to investigate the place. But Cacus stood in front of the entrance and, when Hercules inquired about the cattle, denied that he had ever seen them; and when the other desired to search the cave, Cacus would not allow him to do so, but called upon his neighbors to help him, complaining of the violence offered him by the stranger. And while Hercules was puzzled to know how to act in the matter, he hit upon the idea of driving the rest of the cattle to the cave. In this way, when those inside heard the lowing and sensed the smell of their companions outside, they bellowed to them in turn and thus their lowing brought the theft to light. Cacus, therefore, when his evil deed was thus detected, turned toward his defense and began to call out to his fellow herdsmen. But Hercules killed him by striking him with his club and he drove out the cattle; and when he saw that the place was well suited to the harboring of criminals, he brought the cave down upon the robber. Then, having purified himself of the murder through the waters of a river, he set up an altar near the site to Jupiter Inventor, which is now in Rome near the Porta Trigemina, and he sacrificed a calf to the god as a thank-offering for the finding of his cattle. Even down to my day the city of Rome continued to celebrate this sacrifice, observing in it all the ceremonies of the Greeks, just as he had established them.

Cereals

Cereals were generally well suited to the ancient Mediterranean ecosystem, largely because of their variety and flexibility in adapting to the topographical and climatic variations of that environment (Horden and Purcell; Margaritis and Jones, in Oleson). Together with beans and pulses, cereals formed the staples (*sitos*) of the ancient diet, providing the majority of the body's energy requirements as the principal source of carbohydrates. Meat, fish, vegetables, or fruit (*opsa* in Greek; in Latin, *pulmentaria*) provided critical supplements of protein (Garnsey 1999). These energy needs varied, depending, for example, on whether one worked on a farm or lived in a city. Furthermore, it is difficult to know how frequently the ancients failed to obtain their annual energy requirements, although modern ethnographic studies suggest that this diet would have been sufficient in most cases (Wilkins 2006; Garnsey 1999).

The range of cereals in antiquity was wide. The Greeks and Romans cultivated wheat, barley, oats, rye, and millets. Of these, barley and wheat were the most popular. Galen, a prominent physician and medical writer of the second century CE, provides a hierarchy of cereal and other food plants in Books 1 and 2 of his *On the Powers of Foods*, in which he places wheat and barley at top of list of human nutrients. At the same time, there is plentiful evidence for wheaten breads of all sorts. Athenaeus describes over 70 varieties, while Pliny and Galen provide much additional information. These varieties were typically ranked on the basis of quality and style, suggesting that the popularity of wheat was just as much cultural as it was ecological (Oleson). At the same time, ancient bread was coarser than modern varieties and it is likely that only the wealthy could afford fine "white" bread. Equally prominent were cakes. As with breads, there were many varieties involving different cooking methods and ingredients. Galen and Cato, an important agricultural writer of the second century BCE, both provide recipes for cakes, which appear frequently in the sources in both religious and non-religious contexts.

Before examining the sources, two additional points are important. First, although the ancients looked upon grain eating as an essential activity of a civilized people, the transformation of grain into bread was a laborious and time-consuming process, with much of this labor falling to women and slaves. It is a reminder that the hard work of food preparation was inexorably linked to gender and status in the ancient world. Second, the predilection for the hierarchical ordering of breads that we find in the sources, a practice also found for vintages of wine, reveals that ancient writers were ever aware of the importance of rankings and status. At the same time, these authors—elite, educated, and urban—had attained a level of sophistication that was not widely shared in Greece and Italy. As a result, their point of view would have been quite different from that of the farmers who grew these cereals or from the largely poor population that consumed them. Regrettably, we do not have the opinions of such ordinary folk; nevertheless, we must always keep this distinction in mind, especially since the sources are not as complete as we would like (Wilkins 2006).

Wheat

Wheat was the most popular and expensive cereal in antiquity, partly because it was better able to raise a loaf due to higher gluten content than that of other cereals. An important distinction was between free-threshing or "naked" wheat (club wheat, durum wheat, and bread wheat), in which the grain was easily removed from its glumes by threshing and winnowing, and husked wheat (emmer and spelt), in which the glumes could not be separated from the grains by threshing. Club wheat (*Triticum aestivum compactum*) and durum wheat (*Triticum turgidum durum*) were utilized for flat bread and flat cakes and later for pasta, while bread wheat (*Triticum aestivum*) was for raised breads. Emmer and barley were more suited to biscuits, broths and gruels.

Husked wheat required much labor, yet was more popular than free-threshing wheat in many regions of the Mediterranean because of its high productivity. Over time, however, free-threshing wheat became ascendant, a development that stands as one of the most important in the history of cereals in antiquity. Furthermore, this preference for wheat had consequences for terminology, as the original Greek and Latin words for wheat, *puros* and *triticum*, respectively, came to be replaced by *sitos* and *frumentum*, the terms for "grain" in general. Finally, wheat appeared in forms other than baked loaves: as archaic groats, perhaps the equivalent of modern cracked or bulgar wheat; as grainy in texture, like semolina; and as porridge, especially among rural inhabitants, who boiled wheat flour in milk and, in a more coarse version, boiled it in water and ate it with a wine and honey mixture, among many possible mix-ins (Wilkins 2006).

The following passages confirm the popularity of wheat. Note, especially in Pliny and Galen, the propensity toward ranking, as noted earlier, while Galen also emphasizes the healthful qualities of certain kinds of wheat.

3.5. Athenaeus, *Sophists at Dinner* 3.112c–d

Antiphanes in the *Omphale* recalls the high quality of Athenian bread in the following passage: "How could any well-bred man ever be able to leave this abode, when he sees these white-bodied loaves crowding the oven in close ranks, and when he sees, too, how they have changed their shape by baking pans—the creation of an Attic hand ..."

3.6. Pliny, *Natural History* 18.12

There are several kinds of wheat that have taken their names from the countries where they were first produced. For my own part, however, I should not rate any of them to that of Italy, either for whiteness or weight, qualities for which it is more especially known. Indeed, foreign wheat can only be compared with that of the mountainous regions of Italy; among foreign kinds, the wheat of Boeotia has reached the first rank, then Sicily and, after that, Africa. The third place for weight used to belong to Thracian and Syrian wheat and later also to Egyptian, by the vote of athletes in those times, whose power to consume cereals, resembling that of cattle, had established the order of rank as already stated.

3.7. Galen, *On the Powers of Foods* 1 (trans. Grant, 78–9)

I think it quite reasonable that most doctors should begin what they propose to explain with wheat, since this grain is the most useful and the most used by far among all the Greeks and most foreigners. The wheats that are hulled and whose whole substance is dense and compressed are the most nourishing; consequently, these can only be broken by the teeth with difficulty. These wheats furnish the body with nourishment from just a little volume. The opposite of these wheats can be broken up by the teeth easily, appears loose in texture and spongy after chewing, and provides little nourishment from a large volume. If you wish to compare an equal volume of each wheat, you will discover that the compact wheat far heavier … Among the Roman, as among nearly all the peoples over whom they rule, the whitest bread is called *silignites*, while that which is a bit less white is called *semidalites*. Yet *semidalis* is an ancient Greek term, but *silignis* is not Greek, although I am unable to think of another term. The most nutritious bread is *silignites*, followed by *semidalites*; bread from partially unbolted flour comes in third place, while fourth place belongs to bread made from unsifted flour, of which bran bread is the most extreme, and this provides no nutrition and is more cleansing of the bowels than other breads.

Barley, emmer, and spelt

Barley was one of the oldest grains known in antiquity. Relatively tolerant of drought and salinity, it was especially suited to Greece, although it was to be found in Italy as well. Barley was commonly utilized in Roman rituals of sacrifice, especially as a salted cake (*mola salsa*), which was poured with wine over the head of the sacrificial animal upon the altar. A law of Solon from the sixth century BCE requiring Athenian brides to bring to their weddings a *phrygetron*, a barley-roaster, points to the importance of this cereal in the domestic sphere too. Because it could not easily produce a well-risen loaf, barley was frequently transformed into porridge, a product that was associated with simple poverty. More palatable was barley that was roasted as a preliminary to making *alphita*, barley meal, which, when kneaded with water, milk or oil and eaten without baking, produced a barley cake known as ancient *maza* (Braun, in Wilkins et al. 1995). This cake was not much leavened, if at all, and could be eaten both wet and dry. While these cakes could not compete with wheat in taste and quality, they nevertheless are well represented in Greek literature. Surely, part of the appeal lay in convenience, as barley cakes did not require the time, skill, and heat needed to produce fresh leavened wheaten bread. Telemachus took barley, not wheaten flour, on board his ship when setting off to obtain news of his father Odysseus (Homer, *Odyssey* 2.349–55). Here, Pliny provides information on the various ways that Greeks and Romans made barley porridge.

3.8. Pliny, *Natural History* 18.14

There are various ways of making barley porridge: the Greeks first soak barley in water and then leave it for a night to dry, and next day they parch it by the fire and then grind it in the mill. Some people roast it more thoroughly, and then sprinkle it again with a bit of water and dry it before grinding. Others, however, shake the grain out of the ears while green, clean it, and soak it in water, and pound it in a mortar. Then they wash it of husks in baskets and leave it to dry it in the sun; and again pound it, clean it, and grind it. But whatever kind of preparation is used, the proportions are always twenty pounds of barley to three pounds of flax seed, half a pound of coriander seed, and an eighth of a pint of salt: the ingredients are roasted first and then ground in the mill. Those who wish to keep it for some time store it away in new earthenware jars with fine flour and bran. The Italians parch it without steeping it in water and grind it into fine meal, with the addition of the ingredients previously mentioned and millet also.

Despite its appeal and ancient lineage, barley never escaped its reputation as a cereal of the poor and the enslaved. The helots of Sparta were known to pay their rent in barley, and there is little indication in the sources that the Romans ever embraced barley with enthusiasm. In fact, Pliny characterized barley bread as fodder for animals (*HN* 18.74); furthermore, it was common for Roman soldiers to be punished with rations of barley instead of wheat (see Chapter 6, no. 44).

Much like barley for the Greeks, the traditional Roman staple was emmer (*alica*), a hulled wheat commonly referred to as *far*. A related species was spelt (*triticum spelta*), popular today as a pasta and high-fiber cereal. Similar to the barley-based *mola salsa*, these hulled wheats were common to the most ancient sacrifices of the Romans, primarily because they were uncorrupted by yeast and thus remained pure. Plutarch elaborates further on this point:

3.9. Plutarch, *On Mores* (*Moralia*), *The Roman Questions* 109–10=289e–290a

> Why is the priest of Jupiter, whom they call the *Flamen Dialis*, not allowed to touch either flour or yeast? Is it because flour is an incomplete and crude foodstuff? For wheat has neither remained what it was, nor has it become what it must become, bread; but it has lost both the germinative power of the seed and at the same time it has not attained the advantage of food … Yeast itself is also the result of corruption, and produces corruption in the dough with which it is mixed; for the dough becomes slack and inert, and on the whole the process of leavening seems to be one of putrefaction; at any rate, if it goes too far, it sours and ruins the flour completely.

Emmer was also the basis of *puls*, porridge or pottage, a time-honored Roman dish that was easier to prepare than bread. In the next selections Varro, Juvenal and Pliny all attest to its simplicity and ancient status, while the fourth-century Roman cookbook attributed to Apicius underscores its popularity. The recipe of Apicius would not be familiar to the modern taste palette, yet it was filling and relied on common ingredients that would have been accessible to the humble consumer. Note too the lack of precise measurements for many of the ingredients, a feature typical of ancient recipes.

3.10. Varro, *On the Latin Language* 5.105

> Concerning foods, the most ancient is *puls*, "porridge." This received its name either because the Greeks called it thus, or from the fact that Apollodorus[5] records that it makes a sound like *puls* when it is thrown into boiling water.

3.11. Juvenal, *Satire* 11.56–9

> Persicus, you will find out today in actuality, in my lifestyle, and behavior whether I live up to these most noble maxims that I preach, or whether I praise beans but am secretly a glutton, asking my slave for porridge when others are present, but whispering "cheesecakes" in his ear.

3.12. Pliny, *Natural History* 18.19

Emmer, however, is the most hardy of all the grains and the one that best resists the harshness of winter. It will grow in the coldest localities and those that are poorly cultivated or in soils that are very hot and dry. It was the first food of ancient Latium, a strong proof of this is the offerings of *adorea*, as already mentioned.[6] It is clear, too, that for a long time the Romans lived on pottage,[7] not on bread; for we find that from its name of "puls," certain kinds of foods are called "pulmentaria,"[8] even in present times. Ennius, too, the oldest of our poets, in describing a famine during a siege, recalls how fathers snatched away pottage from their crying children.[9] Even today, sacrifices that are made according to ancient rites and those made upon birthdays are performed with parched pottage.

3.13. Apicius, *On Cookery* 5.1.1=Grocock and Grainger 206–7

Pottage: Hull the emmer, soak it and cook. When boiling, add oil. When it thickens, add two brains previously cooked and a half-pound of meat minced as if for rissoles, pound with the brains and place in a saucepan. Then pound pepper, herbs, fennel seed, moisten with fish sauce and a bit of wine, and place in the saucepan over the brains and the meat. When this has cooked enough, mix it with stock. Slowly add this mixture to the spelt and stir until smooth, to the consistency of a thick soup.

Two other aspects are significant. First, the Latin word for flour, *farina*, derives from *far* (Pliny, *HN* 18.88), revealing that pounded emmer was capable of producing flour as much as naked wheats. Second, Roman bakers were called *pistores* or "pounders," which confirms that bread was initially made from emmer rather than from naked wheat. Before the appearance of the bakeshop, women had done this work at home (Braun, in Wilkins et al. 1995).

Rye, millet, and oats

These were inferior cereals that receive far less positive treatment in the sources than wheat and barley. Like barley, these grains were associated with poverty. Galen informs us that millet seeds were made into bread only in times of famine, as was the case with oats:

3.14. Galen, *On the Properties of Foodstuffs* 1.14.523 (trans. Powell, 56)

It is food for draught animals, not for men, unless perhaps at some time when, being at the extreme of hunger, they are forced to make bread from this grain.

Famine aside, when it has been boiled with water, it is eaten with sweet wine, boiled must or honeyed wine …

Athenaeus (*Sophists at Dinner* 3.109b–c) speaks of breads made of rye but he ranks them as inferior to both raised and unleavened breads and those made with fine flour. Rye bread was known to be dense and heavy, of some texture but lacking the subtlety of wheaten breads. Galen found it to be malodorous (*Powers of Foods* 1.13).

Cakes

The varieties of ancient cakes are too numerous to receive anything but brief treatment here. Several monographs on the subject were written in antiquity and they are well summarized in the modern literature (Dalby 2003; Wilkins 2000, 2006). Essentially, cakes consisted of baked cereal flour to which a broad range of ingredients might be added to alter the flavor and texture, either before or after baking. Cakes were an important feature of religious ceremonies, although it is difficult to know whether the participants actually ate them on these occasions, in what ways they might have differed from non-religious cakes, or even if they were edible at all. In a private context, they might be consumed as dessert and at symposia along with wine, nuts, and dried fruits. Greek vase paintings and images of sacrifice often depict cakes as a supplement to the literary sources. General terms in Greek included *plakous* and *pemma*, in Latin, *libum* (Dalby 2003).

In his treatise *On Farming*, Cato includes a section on cakes. This has raised questions as to whether he utilized cakes for religious purposes or for retail sale to supplement his farm income. As Wilkins has noted, the terminology was diverse and the boundaries between sacred and secular not always clear (Wilkins 2006). What follows is a sample recipe that utilized cheese.

3.15. Cato, *On Farming* 75

Recipe for *libum*. Break up two pounds of cheese thoroughly in a mortar. When it has been broken up well, add one pound of wheat flour or, if you wish the cake to be more delicate, a half-pound of fine flour and mix well with the cheese. Add one egg and mix everything together completely. Next, shape a loaf, place it on leaves, and bake it slowly on a warm hearth under a crock pot.

Cereal processing and baking

As already mentioned, barley and emmer were husked cereals, which meant that they required processing before consumption. This typically involved either pounding these cereals with a wooden pestle in a stone mortar or roasting or parching to render them brittle before pounding to release the kernel. On the other hand, free-threshing cereals, such as bread wheat, did not require this extra work, but once threshed and sieved could be ground directly. This helped to account for the popularity of wheat cereals, especially among the Romans (Curtis, in Oleson).

While the mortar and pestle became standard equipment of the kitchen, changing very little in form throughout antiquity, grinding methods changed considerably. As early as the third century BCE a key innovation was the rotary hand-mill, which was cheaper and easier to operate than earlier mills and more versatile in being able to produce flours of different grades. This passage from the *Moretum*, a poem attributed to Vergil, provides a description of a rotary hand-mill. It consisted of a lower stone (*meta*), slightly convex in shape, upon which sat an upper stone (*catillus*), slightly concave at the bottom. The miller fed the grain through a receptacle above, the hopper, and ground the kernels as they fell between the two stones by turning a handle vertically inserted into the *catillus*.

3.16. "Vergil," *Moretum* 16–29

> A poor heap of grain was poured out on the ground: he helps himself to as much of this as the measure, which runs up to sixteen pounds in weight, allowed. From there, he goes forth and takes his place at the mill, and sets his trusty lamp on a small shelf, firmly secured to the wall for such purposes. Then from his garment he frees both of his arms and, dressed in the hide of a shaggy goat, he thoroughly sweeps the stones and the hollow of the mill with the tail. Next, he calls his two hands to work, dividing them up for each task: the left is directed to serve the grain, the right to grinding it. The right hand turns and drives the wheel in continuous circles (the grain, crushed by the swift blows of the stones, runs down); the left hand, meanwhile, relieves her wearied sister, and changes places.

The rotary mill allowed for continuous action, an improvement over the recip-rocal motion of earlier mills. Ultimately, this allowed for the development of animal driven devices from the second century BCE onwards, the best evidence for which are the donkey mills and ovens preserved in bakeries such as those at Pompeii. This mill was driven by two donkeys harnessed to a wooden frame attached to the mill. As the animals rotated the mill, the grain was ground between the stones. Significantly, animals could endure the drudgery of this work instead of humans, who had only to feed the grain into the hopper and then collect and sieve the meal to produce the flour. This innovation also meant increased production, since bakeries could now operate for longer periods of time. This in turn, led to the growth of commercial bakeries, especially in urban settings where large market demand existed. We know of dozens of bakeries in Pompeii by the later first century CE (Pirson, in Foss and Dobbins); larger cities like Rome had many more. Furthermore, archaeological remains at Ostia and Rome point to increasing specialization in labor within the purpose-built bakery. At the same time, specialization and mechanization led to very harsh conditions, as the bakery became a center of animal and slave labor. This passage, from the *Golden Ass* of Apuleius, records the deprivations of the bakery as endured by Lucius, the main character of the novel, who has been trans-formed into an ass through magic.

3.17. Apuleius, *Golden Ass* 9.11–12

There (sc. in the bakery) the multiple rotations of the many beasts kept the millstones of varying circumference turning, and not merely by day but all night long they would sleeplessly produce flour by the continuous turning of the mills … When the day was nearly over and I was completely exhausted, they removed my rope collar, disconnected me from the millstone, and tied me up at the manger. But, although extremely tired, badly in need of some refreshment and almost dying of hunger, nevertheless, spellbound by my habitual curiosity and quite anxious, I postponed the food in front of me, which was quite plentiful, and observed with a sort of fascination the routine of this detestable mill. Good gods, what scrawny little slaves were there! All of their skin was painted with purple welts from their many floggings, their striped backs shaded more than covered by their torn, patchwork garments; some were clothed only in a flimsy loincloth, yet all of them dressed in such a way that their bodies were visible through their rags. Their foreheads were branded, their hair was half shaven and their feet were chained. Their complexions were an ugly yellow; their eyes were so worn away by the smoky darkness of the steamy murk that they could barely see …

Given these features, it is not surprising that the ancients took a dim view of bakers. The Roman poet Martial, author of several books of witty epigrams

Figure 3. Ruins of a bakery, featuring grinding mills and oven. Pompeii, Italy, first century CE. Photograph, c. 1875. Photo Credit: Adoc-photos/Art Resource, NY.

during the first and second centuries CE, provides confirmation in the case of a certain Cyperus, who escaped the profession only to develop an equally dubious reputation as a spendthrift.

3.18. Martial 8.16

You, Cyperus, a baker for a long time, now plead cases, and you seek two hundred thousand sesterces.[10] But you spend it all and continue to borrow. You have not stopped being a baker, Cyperus: you make bread and you make flour.[11]

Over time, however, the baking profession became essential to the life of cities, especially Rome. These two excepts, legal enactments from the fourth and fifth centuries CE, point to difficulties during the Late Empire, when it became increasingly important to support the trade and discourage evasion from it (3.19) while ensuring that important sectors like the military continued to be supplied adequately (3.20).

3.19. *Theodosian Code* 14.3, *Concerning Breadmakers and Packanimal Drivers*

Emperor Constantius Augustus to Orfitus, Prefect of the City.

If any man should suppose that a daughter of a breadmaker should be united to him in marriage, he shall be held obligated to the guild of breadmakers; and since he is bound to the guild of a breadmaker, he shall be forced also to be subject to its burdens. Because this necessary guild must be fostered, I prohibit those persons established as patrons of breadmakers to be summoned to the duties of any other compulsory service. Henceforth, they shall not be attached to the guild of raftsmen, in order that they may be freed from other compulsory public services and with the exertions of undisturbed minds they may perform only this service.

Given on the day before the nones of July at Milan in the year of the consulship of Arbitio and Lollianus—July 6, 355.

3.20. *Theodosian Code* 7.5, *Concerning the Baking and Transportation of Food Supplies*

Emperors Arcadius and Honorius and Theodosius Augustuses to Hadrianus, Praetorian Prefect.

No person shall be exempted from the baking of hardtack,[12] which must be prepared for our loyal soldiers, and from the transportation of supplies. Indeed, not even the estates of the imperial household shall be considered immune from these duties. If any person should neglect to fulfill these commands, a thing that We do not expect, his procurator shall be severely punished. If it should be established that the master was an accomplice in such contumacy, he shall pay without delay fourfold the amount demanded of him for his tax.

Given on the ninth day before the kalends of April at Rome in the year of the sixth consulship of Honorius Augustus and the consulship of Aristaenetus— March 24, 404.

The grape: Viticulture, vintages and pleasure

As one of the primary foodstuffs of the ancient economy, wine competed successfully in the marketplace with grain and olives throughout the Graeco-Roman period (Garnsey 1999). Moreover, wine overwhelmingly remained the

Figure 4. Calendar mosaic for the month of September depicting wine pressing during the grape harvest. Detail from The Seasons and the Months, the House of the Months at El Djem, Tunisia (ancient Thysdrus), third century CE. Museum, Sousse, Tunisia. Photo Credit: © Gilles Mermet/Art Resource, NY.

alcoholic beverage of choice in Mediterranean culture. Distilled spirits were unknown in antiquity, while beer, although popular in northern Europe, Egypt, and the Near East (Homan), remained synonymous in the ancient mind with a lack of culture and civilization.

In this section we shall trace the development of viticulture in Greece and Italy and its emergence as an economic force, while noting the importance and prestige that the ancients attached to various vintages. The latter feature is especially important, since the preference for certain vintages contributed to the formation of identity through drinking practices. This section will conclude with a brief survey of the pleasures of drinking, a prominent theme among both Greeks and Romans. The broad scope of the sources at our disposal—including technical treatises, geographical works, and inscriptions—is such that it is only possible to provide a careful but necessarily limited overview of this sprawling topic. Even so, the hope is to provide a useful context for understanding the ubiquity and importance of viticulture and the wine industry in the ancient Mediterranean world.

Greece

The spread of viticulture

The Greek literary sources for viticulture in the time of Hesiod and beyond remain thin, yet there is no question that over time wine production increased dramatically across the Greek world. The movement of Greek colonists from the eighth century BCE to Sicily and southern Italy ensured the spread of the vine, although the exact process by which viticulture was established in these areas remains difficult to know (McGovern 2007; Unwin). Nevertheless, by the fifth century BCE Herodotus could refer to southern Italy as Oenatria, a name that recalls *oinos* (wine) and points to a region rich in vineyards. By 600 BCE Massalia (Marseilles) in southern France was also a thriving center for wine. Here, Justin, in his *Epitome* (a summary or abstract of a written work) of the historian Pompeius Trogus (first century CE), represents the Greek colonists as teaching the Gauls not only about urban life and government but also about viticulture.

3.21. Justin, *Epitome* 43.4.1

> The Gauls learned from these peoples, therefore, a more civilized way of life, their barbarian ways being laid aside and also softened; and they learned to cultivate their lands and to enclose their towns with walls. At that time they also grew accustomed to live by laws, not by weapons; then they learned to prune the vine and to plant the olive; and such a brightness was laid upon both men and their affairs that it was not the Greeks who seemed to have immigrated into Gaul, but Gaul into Greece.

Furthermore, new markets for wine emerged over time in regions such as the Black Sea, Egypt, and the Danube, while in Greece itself demand for wine increased. This was especially the case in larger cities like Athens, where specialization in viticulture would have benefitted from increased supply opportunities. Solon's legislation at Athens favoring vines and olives over cereals in the sixth century perhaps points to evidence of this kind of increasing specialization (Unwin).

Elsewhere, finer vintages came to be associated with certain locations. Indeed, wine from the Aegean remained especially prestigious, evident in the recognition of Cos, Lesbos, and Rhodes, for example, as especially notable wine producing areas. Surpassing all of these, however, was Chios, according to Athenaeus. Note in his careful description, the medicinal properties of Chian wine. This is a prominent aspect in the wines described both by Athenaues and Pliny the Elder and should remind us that both of these authors are not presenting in their descriptive lists of wines the judgment of wine experts but derivations from the accounts of medical writers, who rated wines on their effectiveness as remedies (see Chapter 7).

3.22. Athenaeus, *Sophists at Dinner* 1.32f–33a

The most pleasant is the Chian, especially the vintage known as Ariusian. There are three kinds of it: one is dry; a second is rather sweet; the third is a mean between the two in taste and is called "self-tempered." Now the dry has a pleasant taste, is nourishing and is more diuretic; the sweet is nourishing, pleasing, and laxative; the "self-tempered' is midway between these two in its useful effects. Speaking in general, Chian wine encourages digestion, is nourishing, produces good blood, is very mild, and is pleasing in its rich quality.

By the fourth century BCE the interest of Hellenistic writers in various aspects of the natural world helped to ensure that viticulture received at least some literary attention. Theophrastus, an associate and successor of Aristotle, makes this clear in his *Enquiry into Plants*, a work that has provided the foundation for botanical studies in the West. This excerpt is important for its recognition of different vines and their need for the right kind of soil. The passage is typical in that it does not treat viticulture exclusively but as part of a broader study of plant life. Still, the insights of Theophrastus confirm the vitality of wine growing while providing a handbook type of approach that strongly influenced later Roman agricultural writers.

3.23. Theophrastus, *Enquiry into Plants* 2.5.7

Most important to all, one may say, is to render suitable soil to each; for then is the tree most vigorous. To put it simply, they say that low ground is most suitable for the olive, fig, and vine, and for fruit trees the lower slopes of hills. Nor must one overlook what soil suits each variety, even in those closely related. There is the greatest difference, one may say, between the different kinds of vine. For they say that there are as many kinds of soil as there are of vines. When planted as their nature requires, they produce good fruit; when not, they are unfruitful. And these remarks apply just as equally to all trees.

The farmer and his tasks

In the Greek world wine was already present in Mycenaean culture of the second millennium BCE (McGovern 2007; McGovern et al. 1996; Unwin). It was not until around 700 BCE, however, that some of the first written evidence in Greek for viticulture emerged. The source is the *Works and Days*, a didactic poem by Hesiod that adds much to our knowledge of life in early Archaic Greece through the advice it offers on practical living and occupations such as farming. The *Works and Days* also serves as a reminder that much of Greek agriculture remained centered on the household, which practiced mixed farming on a subsistence level. The use of slaves too played an essential role, especially since vines required much attention.

The following excerpt is significant for three reasons. First, Hesiod's description of the winemaking process confirms that viticulture was well established in Greece in the eighth century BCE. Second, the method he describes of exposing grapes to sunlight over an extended period would have dried the clusters to produce sugars for a sweet wine high in alcohol content. Indeed, the strength of ancient wine would result in the common practice of mixing it with water to reduce its power. Lastly, the mention of vats offers an early indication of a drinking implement, the growth and diversity of which over time is preserved through the likes of mixing bowls (kraters), pouring vessels of various sizes and quality, and vessels for storage and transportation (amphorae). These items are well preserved in the archaeological remains. As we shall see in this chapter and elsewhere, they were not only an essential feature of the drinking experience but also helped to mark it out as a discrete sphere of consumption with its own set of rules and equipment (Murray 1990; Lissarrague).

3.24. Hesiod, *Works and Days* 609–14

> When Orion and Sirius come into the middle of the heavens, and rosy-fingered Dawn looks upon Arcturus,[13] then, oh Perses, pluck off all the grape clusters and bring them home. For ten days and nights set them out in the sun, then cover them up in the shade for five, and on the sixth day draw off into vats the gift of much-cheering Dionysius.

The task of tending vines was one of the most labor-intensive activities of ancient agriculture. The Greek historian Xenophon described the vine planting process in detail in the nineteenth chapter of his *Oeconomicus*, a series of dialogues on estate management. Latin technical treatises, such as those of Columella and Varro, also offer much detail on these matters, as we shall see below. In the meantime, the pastoral love story of Daphnis and Chloe, written in Greek by Longus in the second or third century CE, provides a useful, if not idyllic, summary of many of the tasks associated with wine making in Lesbos, an island in the Aegean well known for its wine in antiquity. This particular passage preserves an ecphrasis (verbal painting)[14] of a rustic scene that was typical of love novels of this kind.

3.25. Longus, *Daphnis and Chloe* 2.1

With the fruit season already at its prime, and harvest time pressing forward, everyone was working in the fields. Some fixed the wine presses; others cleaned out wine jars; others wove wicker baskets. Someone attended to a small reaphook for cutting the bunches of grapes, another a stone that could squeeze the juice out of the grapes, and another a dry willow twig that had been pounded into shreds so that, by its light, the must could be drawn off at night. And so Daphnis and Chloe stopped looking after their goats and flocks and gave the others a helping hand. He lifted up the clusters in baskets, threw them in the winepresses, trod upon them, and drew off the wine into the jars; she prepared food for the grape pickers, poured out drinks of older wine for them, and harvested the vines that were nearer to the ground.

Italy

The spread of viticulture

In turning to Italy, viticulture seems to have developed rapidly in Sicily and southern Italy as a result of the westward migration of Greek colonists in the eighth century BCE mentioned earlier. Farther north in Etruria, modern Tuscany, there is evidence of viticulture from at least the seventh century BCE, although later on these vineyards were of lesser renown that those to the south. It seems that by the third century BCE Italy was exporting wine into Gaul, while the development of vineyards in Italy had the effect of reducing imports of wine from the Greek mainland and islands (Unwin).

By the late first century BCE viticulture had spread extensively throughout the Mediterranean world. Of particular importance is Strabo, whose 17-book *Geographica* in Greek is our most important source for ancient geography. As a native of the Black Sea area, Strabo was especially familiar with the wines of modern Turkey. Yet he also provides information on vintages from Greece, Syria, Egypt, and North Africa, as well as from Italy and areas to its north. In all of this, Strabo gives no indication that vineyards were cultivated in areas other than those close to rivers and coastal plains, where transportation was most cost effective. More inland locations for vineyards would come only later. The passages below provide information from three distinct areas of the Mediterranean world (Hyrcania, south-east of the area of the Caspian Sea; North Africa; and Aquilea near the head of the Adriatic); and while we cannot always be certain of Strabo's sources, these excerpts are typical of his belief that wine production was important enough to merit inclusion in his excurses on various places, even if it is difficult for us to verify all of the details (Unwin).

3.26. Strabo, *Geography* 11.7.2

But Hyrcania is very fertile, extensive, and generally flat; it is distinguished by remarkable cities ... And because of its special kind of prosperity, writers narrate in full such evidence: the vine produces one *metretes*[15] of wine, and the fig tree sixty *medimni*;[16] grain grows up from the seed that drops from the stock; bees make their hives in trees, and honey drips from the leaves.

3.27. Strabo, *Geography* 17.1.14

The entire country itself is without good wine, since the wine jars receive more seawater than wine; and this they call "Libyan" wine, which, as beer too, is used by most of the tribe of Alexandrians; but Antiphrae is ridiculed most.[17]

3.28. Strabo, *Geography* 5.1.8; 5.1.12

Aquilea has been given over as a mercantile center for those tribes of the Illyrians that live near the Ister; the latter load the products of the sea on wagons and carry them inland, and wine stored in wooden jars, and also olive oil ... The jars indicate the quantity of wine, for the wooden ones are larger than houses; and the good supply of pitch contributes much towards the thorough smearing that the jars receive.

The "how-to" of handbooks

The first account of Italian viticulture to emerge belonged to Marcus Porcius Cato, who produced *On Agriculture* (*de Agri Cultura*), a 162-chapter handbook that treated all aspects of viticulture, including the nature of a vineyard, necessary equipment and slave labor, the calendar of work, and information on selling wine. Most importantly, he believed that vineyards were potentially the most profitable form of farming. The next passage makes this clear, while providing evidence that a more commercially based model was emerging along side traditional, subsistence-based farming in the second century BCE.

3.29. Cato, *On Agriculture* 1.1.7

If you ask me what is the best kind of farm, I should say: a hundred iugera[18] of land, of all sorts of soils, and in the best location; first is a vineyard, if it produces good and plentiful wine; second, a well-watered garden; third, a thicket of willows; fourth, an olive yard; fifth, a meadow; sixth, grain land; seventh, a forest fit for timber; eighth, an orchard;[19] ninth, an acorn grove.[20]

Recipes and vintages

Cato also provided recipes for wine, as in this Coan vintage, a popular Greek brand of the day that featured seawater as an additive. As mentioned earlier, diluting wine with water was a common practice among the Greeks and Romans as a means of altering the taste and reducing the alcohol content. The second passage reveals that when wine went bad, the ancients were anxious to preserve it, sometimes through unorthodox but creative techniques. The excerpt also attests to Cato's frugality, a trait that appears throughout his text.

3.30. Cato, *On Agriculture* 112

If you wish to make Coan wine, take seawater at a distance from the shore, when there is no wind, 70 days before vintage, where fresh water does not reach. When you have drawn it from the sea, pour it into a jar, not filling it up to the top but to within five *quadrantals*[21] full. Place a lid on top; leave space for air. After 30 days transfer it slowly and carefully into another jar, leaving the sediment at the bottom. Twenty days later transfer it in the same way into a third jar; leave it as is until vintage. Leave on the vine the grapes from which you wish to make the Coan wine, allow them to ripen thoroughly and when it has rained and dried out, then pick them and place them in the sun for two days, or in the open for three days, if it has not rained. If it does rain, put them under cover in baskets and, if any berries have rotted, clear them out. Then, take the seawater mentioned above and pour ten *quadrantals* into a 50-*quadrantal* jar. Then pick the berries of ordinary grapes from the stem into the same jar until you have filled it. Press the berries by hand so that they may soak in the seawater. When you have filled up the jar, cover it with a lid; leave space for air. After three days remove the grapes from the jar, tread out in the pressing room, and store the wine in jars that have been washed, cleaned, and dried.

3.31. Cato, *On Agriculture* 110

> To remove a bad odor from wine: thoroughly heat a thick, clean piece of roofing
> tile in a fire. When it is hot, coat it with pitch, attach a cord, gently lower the
> piece to the bottom of the jar, and allow the jar to be sealed for two days. If the
> bad odor is removed the first time, it will be best; if not, repeat until you have
> removed the bad odor.

A second noteworthy voice on viticulture was Marcus Terentius Varro. His *On
Farming*, written more than a century after Cato's work, includes a treatment of
viticulture that is less comprehensive than Cato's but still valuable. Like Cato,
Varro let nothing go to waste, sometimes pressing the grapes a second time to
produce *lora*, an inferior liquid that he provided for his slaves instead of wine.
The practice of offering a less desirable beverage to those of a lower social class
is important for our understanding of ancient social relations. The topic receives
further attention in Chapter 5.

3.32. Varro, *On Farming* 1.54

> When the flow ceases beneath the press, some people cut around the edges
> of the mass and press it again; and when it has been pressed again they call
> it *circumsicium*[22] and they keep separately the juice that has been squeezed
> because it has the flavor of the knife. The pressed grape skins are thrown
> together into jars and water is added; this is called *lora*, because the skins
> have been washed (*lota*), and it is given to the laborers during winter instead
> of wine.

Furthermore, some grapes produced wine that quickly turned acidic and thus
had to be drunk within a year. Other vintages, however, matured with age
and so were stored until thought to be ready for consumption. This practice
of storing wines, though an uncommon modern practice, was not unusual
in antiquity. The fictional freedman Trimalchio, whom Petronius satirized in
his *Satyricon*, a picaresque but incomplete novel that reveals much about life
in municipal Italy during the first century CE, once offered guests wine that
was more than a century old. This is not possible, of course, yet the gesture is
consistent with the host's inflated sense of self and it underscores the prestige
associated with certain vintages, especially among the aspiring elite of the first
century CE.

3.33. Petronius, *Satyricon* 15.34

Carefully sealed wine bottles were immediately brought forth, on the necks of which labels had been attached with this title:

FALERNIAN

CONSULSHIP OF OPIMIUS

ONE HUNDRED YEARS OLD

While we were examining the labels, Trimalchio clapped his hands and said, "Ah, and so wine has a life longer than us poor folks. So, let's soak it up. Wine is life. I'm giving you real Opimian. I didn't put out such good stuff yesterday, and a much classier crowd was eating dinner."

Beyond Falernian, we are well informed about other vintages. Pliny the Elder, so named to distinguish him from his nephew, the famous letter writer and senator under the emperor Trajan, was an encyclopediast of the first century whose *Natural History* includes a valuable account of wines produced in different parts of the empire. Although Pliny often relied on earlier authors, his fourteenth book, devoted entirely to wine, seems largely to be the result of independent research and thus is especially valuable. In all, the *Natural History* cites 50 kinds of quality wines, nearly twice as many varieties of vines, and some 40 varieties of foreign wines. Furthermore, Pliny was intensely interested in ranking wines and categorized them into main classes by quality. In addition to Falernian, Setine was also a vintage of first rank during Pliny's day, while the next best wines were Alban, Surrentine, and Massic. Of third rank was Mamertine, of Messana in Sicily (Robinson; Tchernia and Brun). This insistence on ranking and categorizing what one drank was consistent with Roman social values that placed great emphasis on an individual's status. As we shall see in Chapter 5, the result was a system where the quality of food and drink was typically tied to the social class of the recipient. Finally, Pliny was an early advocate of the role of topography and soil in determining the quality of wine, beliefs later embraced by the French in their concept of terroir.

Profit and productivity

The Roman agricultural handbook reached its peak in the mid-first century CE with the publication of *On Agriculture* by Lucius Junius Columella. A Spaniard by birth, Columella owned several farms in the region near Rome and therefore was well positioned to write on contemporary agricultural practices. Like Cato, Columella wrote from personal experience on all aspects of viticulture. He too was bullish on the financial rewards of a wine enterprise based on the large, complex villa, yet his calculation of the profits of viticulture, as captured below, is now largely viewed as an overly optimistic defense of an industry in stiff competition with wines from southern Spain and Gaul during his own lifetime. Even so, while Columella's figures may be incomplete due to a lack of data from earlier times, he confirms that viticulture on his own estates was indeed a profitable enterprise (Unwin). The second passage is notable for its deep knowledge of vines, their properties, and the conditions under which they were most productive. Here, Columella relates that the character of a particular wine depended on the proper combination of soil, vine and climate, a belief forged through much practice and innovation over a long period.

3.34. Columella, *On Agriculture* 3.3.2–3

Meanwhile, learned students of agriculture must be taught one thing first of all—that the return from vineyards is a very rich one. And to pass over that old-time fertility of the land, concerning which both Marcus Cato long ago, and Terentius Varro more recently, reported that each *iugerum*[23] of vineyard yielded 600 *urnae*[24] of wine—for Varro asserts this most emphatically in the first book of his *Res Rusticae*—nor that this was the customary yield in one district but also in the country around Faventia[25] and in the Ager Gallicus,[26] which is now annexed to Picenum; certainly in our own times the district of Nomentum is illustrious by a most renowned reputation, and especially that part which Seneca[27] owns, a man of outstanding talent and erudition, on whose estates it is learned that every *iugerum* of vineyard has yielded for the most part eight *cullei*.[28] For those things that happened in our Ceretanum[29] seem to have been in the nature of a prodigy, in that a certain vine on your place exceeded the number of 2,000 clusters, and at my place, that 800 grafted stocks of less than two years yielded seven *cullei*; that first-class vineyards produced a hundred *amphorae*[30] to the *iugerum*, when meadows, pastures, and woodland seem to take care of the owner very well if they bring in 100 sesterces[31] for every *iugerum*. For we can hardly recall a time when grain crops, in at least the greater part of Italy, returned a yield of four to one.[32]

3.35. Columella, *On Agriculture* 3.2.14–15

The Nomentan[33] vines follow after the Amineans[34] in excellence, but in productivity they are even superior; to be sure, since they are typically loaded full and preserve very well what they have produced. But of these, too, the smaller is the more fruitful and its leaf is more moderately cleft, and its wood is not so

red as that of the larger variety—from which color the vines are named *rubel-
lanae*. These same vines are also called f*aeciniae* because they make more dregs
(*faeces*) than other varieties. Even so, they compensate for this deficiency by
their large number of grapes, which they produce both on a trellis and better
on a tree. They endure winds and rains valiantly, drop their flowers quickly, and
therefore ripen sooner, bearing up under every adversity except that of heat; for,
having clusters that are small berried and tough-skinned, they shrivel in the hot
weather. They are especially happy in rich soil, which can provide some richness
to clusters that are scanty and small by nature.

Another way to ensure profit, of course was to limit expenditure, especially
among farm personnel. Once again, Cato is instructive in this regard, as seen
here in the rations of wine he provided for his slaves. The allowance, not at all
generous, was nonetheless consistent with Cato's frugal provision of food and
clothing for his slave workers.

3.36. Cato, *On Agriculture* 57

Wine rations for the slaves: When the vintage is over, for three months let them
drink *lora*.[35] In the fourth month, issue one-half sextarius[36] of wine a day, that
is, two and one-half congii[37] a month. In the fifth, sixth, seventh, and eighth
months allow a sextarius a day, that is, five congii a month. In the ninth, tenth,
eleventh, and twelfth months allow one and one-half sextarii a day, that is, an
amphora a month. In addition, issue three and one-half congii per person for
the Saturnalia and the Compitalia.[38] The total of wine for each person per year
is seven amphorae. Add an additional amount for the chain gang proportional
to their work. Ten amphorae of wine per person is not an excessive allowance
for the year.

Pliny the Elder is equally useful for his insights into the changing wine industry
of his day. He notes the productivity of vineyards beyond Rome, especially in
Spain and Gaul. Indeed, in the case of Gaul vine growing continued to advance
northward from the time of Caesar's conquest of that country in the first
century BCE. Likewise, Pliny believed that the wines of Italy had supplanted
those of Greece as the most renowned (*HN* 14.13.87).

The wine trade, personnel, and changing tastes

On the basis of authors like Pliny and Strabo, as well as the distribution of
amphorae across coastal and riverine areas of the Mediterranean region, it is
possible to appreciate the spread of viticulture under Roman influence by the

first century BCE. While we wish we were better informed, we do know of associations of merchants (*mercatores*) at this time, who purchased wine from estates in Italy and then transported it by land before exporting it overseas. Moreover, within a century we find mention of wine warehouses (*cellae vinariae*) along the banks of the Tiber River (*Corpus of Latin Inscriptions* [*CIL*] 6.8826=*ILS* 7276) and a port for handling wine in Rome (*Portus Vinarius*) (Purcell). This inscription records a funerary dedication made to a *lagonarius*, a dealer in wine bottles, who would have worked at the *Portus*.

3.37. *Corpus of Latin Inscriptions* (*CIL*) 6.37807=*Select Latin Inscriptions* (*ILS*) 9429

> To the spirits of the dead. Comisia Fecunda set up this monument for her well-deserving husband and fellow freedman, Caius Comisius Successus, a dealer in wine bottles at the wine port, and for herself and her descendants.

Ostia, too, the official port of Rome some 12 miles down river toward the Mediterranean Sea, supported a flourishing wine trade as witnessed by two associations of wine merchants, the "traders of wine at the forum" (*negotiatores fori vinarii*) and the elaborately named "most outstanding guild of wine importers and dealers (*corpus splendidissimum inportantium et negotiantium vinariorum*)." Furthermore, it is clear that the wine industry needed to be flexible in response to changing tastes and populations. Pliny seems to have had this reality in mind when he claimed that his beloved Falernian vintage was degenerating during his own day because producers began favoring quantity over quality (Pliny, *HN* 14.8.62).

Perhaps the most dramatic example of a changing wine trade from the first century CE was to be found in Rome, where a population of perhaps 1,000,000 inhabitants provided a steady market for the inferior wine necessary for various public distributions and ceremonies. The popularity of wine bars (*thermopolia*) in towns like Pompeii and Herculaneum continued this trend of diffusing cheap wine among the masses, with the result that a vigorous drinking place culture developed in urban communities of the Roman Empire (Purcell). In the following excerpts Dio, who wrote a history of Rome in Greek, indicates that these taverns were well stocked for a thirsty populace in the year 79 CE. The Roman poet Catullus reprises the common depiction of the tavern as a pick-up joint, filled with disreputable characters who, in this case, could take advantage of Lesbia, the poet's promiscuous lover. Lastly, a poem ascribed to the emperor

Hadrian is his clever retort (*Ego nolo Florus esse*, "I do not wish to be Florus") to the poet Florus' criticism of the emperor's love of travel (*Ego nolo Hadrianus esse*, "I do not wish to be Hadrian"); it too depicts the tavern and sausage shop in less than flattering terms.

3.38. Cassius Dio, 65.16

At this same time these incidents occurred: in some tavern such a large quantity of wine overflowed its cask that it ran out into the street …

3.39. Catullus, 37

Slimy tavern and you, barflies, nine posts from the skull-capped brothers,[39] do you think that you alone have penises, that you alone can screw as many girls as there are and label the others as he-goats? Or since you are sitting in silly bliss 100 in a row (or 200?) do you think that I wouldn't dare to screw two hundred loungers at one time? But think again: for I'll write on the front of every tavern using you like dicks. My girl, who runs from my embrace, loved like no other, on whose behalf I have waged great wars, frequents this dump of yours. All of you, the fine and well-born, love her and indeed, all the small-time losers and alleyway sex fiends, a shameful thing; but, you beyond the rest, Egnatius, long-haired son of Spain, itself known for its long-haired rabbits,[40] whose bushy beard attracts the moneyed class, and teeth brushed white with Spanish piss.

3.40. Hadrian (*Minor Latin Poets*, 2), 1

I have no desire to be a Florus, walking about the bars, lurking about the cook shops, fodder for fat mosquitoes.

Finally, this kind of demand required intensive production, an increase in the number of vineyards close to major cities like Rome, and a focus on selling wines within Italy in order to meet local needs. The result was not so much the collapse of the overseas Italian wine trade, as was previously thought, but a shift by growers and sellers to maximize profits (Unwin).

The price of wine

Price data on various commodities in the Graeco-Roman world are generally not well preserved, and this is true of wine as well. As Unwin has argued, it is especially challenging to obtain accurate prices for wine because the product varied by quality, region, and fluctuations in harvests. Columella has provided a minimum figure of 15 sesterces per amphora of wine as a wholesale price in the first century, but this figure is far from certain. We do, however, have some evidence on retail prices from the graffiti preserved on the walls of Pompeii as seen in the first passage, dated to 79 CE. Here we have different grades of wine costing one, two, and four asses, with the most expensive being Falernian. By way of comparison, a loaf of bread at Pompeii was two asses, as was a prostitute.

3.41. *Corpus of Latin Inscriptions* (*CIL*) 4.1679

> Hedone[41] declares: Drinks cost one *as*. If you give two *asses*, you'll drink better.
> If you give four *asses*, you'll be drinking Falernian wine.

Equally interesting is an inscription from Samnium in central Italy that records an exchange between an innkeeper and a guest over the bill for a night's lodging. While we have no way of verifying the authenticity of this evidence, there would not be much sense in fabricating costs that were not reflective of current conditions. What we find is a modest charge of one *as* for a *sextarius* of wine (546 milliliters, about 18 fluid ounces) and bread. Inns had a notorious reputation, a feature that may help to explain the low cost of the fare provided.

3.42. *Corpus of Latin Inscriptions* (*CIL*) 9.2689=*Select Latin Inscriptions* (*ILS*) 7478

> L. Calidius Eroticus set up this monument while alive for himself and for Fannia Voluptas. "Innkeeper, let's add up the bill. You have one sextarius of wine and bread costing one *as*, food costing two *asses*. So agreed. A girl costing eight *asses*. Also agreed. Feed for my mule costing two *asses*. That mule will put me in the poorhouse!"

As we might expect, inflation played a role in pricing over time. The *Edict on Maximum Prices*, an inscription that records the massive but unsuccessful empire-wide attempt by the Romans to put a maximum cost on all goods and services in the early fourth century under the emperor Diocletian, records that a *sextarius* of ordinary wine was eight *denarii*, equivalent to 128 *asses* in the fourth century, while a similar amount of wine of the best quality was 480 *asses*. These figures reveal an increase of more than 100 times in the price of wine since the first century CE. On the other hand, beer ranged from 32 to 64 *asses* per *sextarius*, two to four times cheaper than wine. Finally, in terms of comparing these costs to income, the most common daily wage in the *Edict* tended to be about 800 *asses*, which would have been roughly six times the value of a single *sextarius* of ordinary wine.

The pleasures of drinking

The pure pleasure of drinking (*delectatio bibendi*) was a significant aspect of ancient practice and rightfully takes its place among those works that attempt to record a history of pleasure (Murray 1995). Among the evidence, it will be useful to explore several selections. The first excerpt comes from the *Anacreontea*, a collection of poems in imitation of Anacreon, a poet of the sixth century BCE, who composed poetry of various meters in which love and wine figured prominently (West, in Murray 1990). The fact that Anacreon was frivolously imitated from the Hellenistic period into the modern era confirms that the themes of drinking and "the art of feeling very, very good" continued to strike a popular chord (Roth). Noteworthy here is the emphasis on Dionysius, the god of wine (Seaford; Carpentier and Faraone). Known as early as the fifteenth century BCE among the Mycenaeans, Dionysius took on additional attributes over the centuries as he spread across the ancient world. Eventually, he was incorporated into the Olympian pantheon as the twice-born son of Zeus and Semele. He does not appear until the sixth century BCE in depictions from Attica but later on he became the focus of religious ritual, especially in Athens and Italy, where, as the god Bacchus, he was known from much before the second century BCE. The violence associated with many of these rites posed a challenge to the accepted social order. Nevertheless, his popularity continued unabated. Associated with wine and drinking and with nature and the Underworld, no god was depicted more often in ancient art than Dionysius; and while we may be tempted to look upon him as a construct of the literary imagination, to the ancients he was a real god, worthy of worship and ever to be associated with drinking and pleasure.

In the following selections, note several motifs common to poetry of this kind, including, dancing, handsome male wine attendants, Aphrodite as the goddess of love and symbol of sexual intercourse, and the sheer pleasure of the drinking banquet.

3.43. *Anacreontea* 38

Let us be joyful and drink wine and sing of Bacchus, the inventor of the choral dance, the lover of all songs, leading the same life as the Loves, the darling of

Cythere;[42] thanks to him, drunkenness was brought forth, thanks to him, the Grace was born, thanks to him Pain takes a rest and Trouble goes to sleep. So the drink is mixed and tender boys are bringing it, and distress has fled, mingling with the wind-fed storm: and so, let us take our drink and let our worries go. What is the use of hurting yourself with cares? How can we know the future? The life of mortal man is unclear. I wish to be drunk and dance, to perfume myself and have fun […] and with beautiful women too.

3.44. Athenaeus, *Sophists at Dinner* 11.463a

And the delightful Anacreon says:

I do not like the man who, while drinking his wine beside the full mixing bowl, speaks of quarrels and tearful war, but I like him who, mixing together the splendid gifts of the Muses and Aphrodite, remembers the lovely good cheer of the banquet.

Scholia were drinking songs, especially popular in Attica, where the singer would hold a myrtle branch and, when finished, pass it to another, who was asked to sing a song before sending it along to the next celebrant. The poets Pindar and Alcaeus composed such songs. The first passage is perhaps the most frequently quoted of all *scholia* because of its strong gnomic appeal; the second expresses sentiments common to the drinking experience.

3.45. Athenaeus, *Sophists at Dinner* 15.694.7; 695.19

To have health is the best thing for mortal man; second is to be born handsome; third, to have honest wealth, and fourth, to enjoy youth with our friends.

Drink with me, be young with me, love with me, wear wreaths with me, rage with me when I am raging, be sober when I am sober.

While celebratory drinking was common, the association of drinking with elegance and refinement is also to be found in the sources. Observe in the next excerpt the drinking cup utilized by Nestor to provide restorative drink to the war-weary Greek soldiers. Its refinement is consistent with Nestor's stature as a man of wise counsel in Homer's epics, as are the fine furniture and Pramnian wine, a vintage of uncertain origin but highly regarded in ancient Greece as a dark wine of excellent quality and aging potential. The addition of substances such as cheese and barley to produce a mulled wine was a common practice in antiquity, as was a wide range of diluting or flavoring agents, including honey, resin, spices and seawater.

The second passage, closely connected to the first, is the so-called "Nestor's Cup Inscription," preserved on a drinking cup found in a cremation grave on the island of Pithecusae at the northern end of the Bay of Naples. Dated to the late eighth century BCE, the inscription either represents a clever joke that plays on a humorous comparison between Nestor's grand drinking vessel and the modest clay cup that carries the inscription, or a magical spell that works as an aphrodisiac (Faraone).

3.46. Homer, *Iliad* 11.628–41

> First, she pushed a table up toward them, elegant, with blue inlaid feet and highly polished; moreover she set on it a bronze basket with an onion in it, a relish for the drink, and pale gold honey along with ground meal of holy barley; and beside them a very beautiful cup, which the old man had brought from home, studded with golden nails. It had four handles, and two doves set on each, made of gold, and below were twin supports. Another man could hardly move it from the table when it was full, but old Nestor would easily hoist it up. In this cup the woman, skilled as a goddess, mixed a drink for them with Pramnian wine, and over it with a bronze grater she grated cheese of goat's milk, and scattered white barley meal over it; and she bid them to drink when she had made ready the mixture.

3.47. Hansen, P. A. *Carmina Epigraphica Graeca Saeculorum VIII–V A. Chr. N.*, Text und Kommentare 12 (Berlin, 1983) no. 454

> I am the cup of Nestor, good for drinking.

> Whoever drinks from this cup, instantly will a desire for lovely crowned Aphrodite seize him.

In a Roman context, the theme of *delectatio bibendi* also found expression in poetry, most notably that of Horace and Catullus. Horace, the most accomplished lyric poet of Latin literature, was keen to depict the pleasure of drinking, especially among friends (Davis, in Harrison). Recall *Odes* 1.20 (see 2.7) where his friend happens to be Maecenas, a trusted member of the inner circle of the emperor Augustus and an enlightened literary patron not only of Horace but also of Vergil and Propertius. The ode is a tribute to simple pleasures (Sabine in plain tankards) while also recognizing the importance of the aristocratic drinking experience through its deliberate mention of superior vintages (Falernian and

Formian) that would have been well known to Maecenas. Catullus 27 is the only one of its kind in the poet's collection. It is reminiscent of the drinking and singing mood of the Greek symposium; it is also interesting for its twist—the person in charge of overseeing the drinking, the *magister bibendi*, is a woman instead of a man.

3.48. Catullus, 27

Young cup bearer of old Falernian wine, bring in my cups of more pungent[43] wine as the law of Postumia[44] decrees, she an overseer drunker than the drunken grape. But you, waters,[45] the bane of wine, go off where you will, and depart to the more sober drinkers. This[46] is pure Thyonean.[47]

Two final testimonia cast the pleasures associated with drinking in a more colorful context. Lucian, a second-century rhetorician and satirist, wrote *True Histories* as a parody of the fanciful tales of adventure that ancient writers often presented as true (for more on Lucian, see Chapter 2, "Satire"). This account is notable for its themes of danger and sexuality. At the same time, the focus on the vine itself as the subject of the adventure underscores the connection of drinking with fantasy and pleasure, a theme that would have resonated strongly with Lucian's audience. Athenaeus' description is of the Sybarites of southern Italy, whose wealth and luxury became a *topos* (literary commonplace) in ancient literature. The ability to ensure the steady flow of wine from vineyard to wine cellar is typical of what the Sybarites were imagined to be, although there is no archaeological evidence to support this claim. In English, the words "sybarite" and "sybaritic" denote opulent luxury and unrestrained pleasure seeking.

3.49. Lucian, *True Histories* 1.8

Next, after passing through the river at a place where it was crossable, we found a marvelous thing in grape vines. The part that came out of the ground, the trunk itself, was flourishing and thick, but the upper parts were women, completely perfect from the waist up. They were like our pictures of Daphne turning into a tree as Apollo is just catching her. Branches full of grapes grew out of their fingertips. And what is more, the hair of their heads was tendrils and leaves and clusters. As we approached, they welcomed and greeted us, some of them speaking Lydian, some Indian, but for the most part Greek. They even kissed us on the lips. And everyone who was kissed at once became drunk and tipsy. At any rate, they did not allow us to gather any of the fruit, but howled in pain when it was plucked. Some of them wanted us to embrace them. Two of my comrades who approached them could no longer get free, but they were bound at the genitals. They had grown in and struck root. Already, branches had grown from their fingers, tendrils wrapped around them, and they were on the verge of bearing fruit like the others. Abandoning them, we fled to the boat, and when we arrived, we told everything to the men left behind, including the intermingling of the vines with our comrades. Then, taking some jars, at once we provided ourselves not only water but also wine from the river, set up camp for the night on the nearby beach, and at dawn put to sea with a moderate breeze.

3.50. Athenaeus, *Sophists at Dinner* 12.519d–e

Most of them own wine cellars near the seashore, into which the wines are sent through pipes from their rustic estates; part of it is sold outside the country, part of it is carried over in boats to the city. They also frequently hold many public banquets, and with crowns of gold they award the men, who have striven brilliantly for honors, and they publish their names at the state sacrifice and games, proclaiming not so much their good will to the state but their service in providing dinners; they crown even the cooks who have prepared the best dishes served on these occasions … They too were the first to invent chamber pots, which they carried to their drinking parties.

Olives and olive oil

Olives joined grain and grapes to complete the triad of the Mediterranean diet. Consumed as a fruit (primarily as an appetizer), olives were especially important for their oil, which was utilized for many purposes, including medicine, perfume, lighting, athletics, and bathing. Olive oil was also essential for cooking; as one of the main sources of fat in the ancient diet, it was essential for providing nutritional balance and for making a grain-based diet more palatable. Furthermore, olive oil enjoyed a higher "smoking point" (the boiling point at which a liquid begins to smoke, typically resulting in flavor and nutritional degradation) than water, thereby increasing its appeal as a cooking medium. Additional refining would have produced even higher boiling points (Dalby 2003, s.v. "olive oil").

Columella considered the olive tree the "queen of all trees," and ancient myth further enhanced its reputation. Roman olive traders considered *Hercules Olivarius*, "Hercules the olive-farmer," as their patron, while the Greeks

Figure 5. Charred olives from the eruption of Mount Vesuvius. Pompeii, Italy, first century CE. Museo Archeologico Nazionale, Naples, Italy. Photo Credit: Erich Lessing/Art Resource, NY.

attributed the first olive tree to Athena on the acropolis in Athens. In this excerpt Herodotus conveys the mystique and cultural importance of the olive tree in his account of its survival at Athens during the Persian invasion of Greece in the early fifth century BCE.

3.51. Herodotus, 8.55

On the next day he (sc. Xerxes, commander of the Persian army) summoned to his presence the Athenian exiles, who were serving with the Persian forces, and commanded them to go up into the Acropolis and offer sacrifice there according to Athenian custom; either some vision or other while he slept had suggested this course to him, or possibly his mind was unsettled by the burning of the temple. The Athenian exiles did as they were commanded. I tell of these details for a particular reason: there is a place on the Acropolis that is sacred to Erechtheus—"the earth-born,"[48]—and an olive tree and a spring of salt water are within it. According to Athenian legend, Poseidon and Athena put them there, when they competed for possession of the land, as markers of their claims to it. Now this olive tree was destroyed by fire with the rest of the sanctuary by the barbarians; nevertheless, when the Athenians who were ordered to offer sacrifice went up to that sacred place on the very next day, they saw that a new growth eighteen inches long had sprung from the stump. This they told the king.

The olive did not grow everywhere, however. Success typically depended on a dry season for developing its oil content, a cool winter without frost, and an altitude below 800 meters (Garnsey 1999). Given the proper conditions, olive trees could produce fruit for many hundreds of years in the most favorable regions of Greece and Italy. In fact, Pliny in his *Natural History* cites 15 varieties known to him. Here, Columella confirms several of the advantages that the olive tree offered to the ancient farmer, qualities that have endured in modern times.

3.52. Columella, *On Agriculture* 5.8

The cultivation of every kind of tree, however, is easier than that of the vine, and the olive tree, which is the foremost of all trees, requires the least expense of all. For, although it does not bear fruit every year but generally in alternate years, nevertheless it is thought of most highly because it is maintained by very light tending and, when it is not covered with fruit, it requires hardly any expenditure; also, if anything is spent upon it, it promptly multiplies its fruit. If it is neglected for many years, it does not deteriorate like the vine, but even during this period it nevertheless offers something to the head of the household and, when it is cultivated again, it recovers in a single year.

Turning to its role in the ancient diet, olive oil (*elaion* in Greek, *oleum* in Latin) served as a marinade for meat and fish, a cooking medium, a dressing for cooked food and green vegetables, and as a conserving agent. Its appeal was further enhanced by its high boiling point and especially by its health benefits. We now know that olive oil is high in monounsaturated fats ("MUFs," commonly identified as "healthy" dietary fat) as well as antioxidants, vitamins, and nutrients. The ancients were not aware of these many advantages, of course, yet they benefitted from them nonetheless by relying on olive oil for the fat requirements in their diet.

The Greeks and the Romans believed that the best oil came from "white," i.e. "green" olives, picked early, although it was the ripe "black" olives that contained more oil. Oil extraction was accomplished by crushing mills, the most common of which was known as the *trapetum* invented around the fourth century BCE, and by oil presses, both of which crushed the flesh of the fruit and pressed the pulp to release the oil. Crushing the stone was thought to reduce the quality, so this was avoided if possible. In a final step, the mixed oil, water and olive juice (*amurca*) settled in vats until the oil rose to the top and could be skimmed and stored in amphorae.

Like wine, the quality of olive oil ultimately depended on a host of factors, including fruit variety, growing conditions, harvesting practices, and storage. Because quality was so closely tied to these factors, and because, once extracted, the oil had to be kept in a dark place with limited contact with air, monitoring was critical. Cato elaborates on some of the duties of the olive oil watchman.

3.53. Cato, *On Agriculture* 67

> Further duties of the watchmen: Those in the pressing room must keep their vessels clean and see to it that the olives are completely worked up and that they are well dried. They must not cut wood in the pressing room.[49] They must skim the oil frequently. To the workmen he must give a sextarius of oil[50] for each pressing and what they need for the lamp. He must throw away the lees every day. He must continually clean out the *amurca*[51] until the oil reaches the last vat in the cellar. He must rub the fruit baskets with a sponge. He must change the vessel every day until the oil reaches the jar. He must be careful to see that no oil is stolen from the pressing room or the cellar.

Finally, while most oil was likely consumed locally, the best quality product was traded over long distances. Furthermore, certain regions became well known in antiquity as producers of luxury olive oil. These regions included Attica and Samos in Greece, and Venefrum in Italy. Moreover, Roman expansion had the effect of bringing the olive to other areas as well, such as Baetica in Spain and Cyrenaica in North Africa, both of which came to be important regions for high-quality oil.

Beef and pork

Beef was closely linked to wealth and status in the Graeco-Roman world and therefore was more likely to be consumed by elites than by other classes. This reality can be traced as far back as the heroic warriors of Homer's epic poems. In this passage Vergil's depiction in the *Aeneid* of Aeneas and his men feasting on meat is typical of the connection between beef and elite status in Graeco-Roman literature. In this instance the festal host is Evander, an Arcadian king who helped Aeneas defeat Turnus, the fiery king of the Rutuli, with the result that the Trojans are able to found the Roman race in Italy.

3.54. Vergil, *Aeneid* 8.175–83

> After he had said this, he orders the dishes and wine cups, which had already been removed, to be brought back, and he himself sets up the guests on grassy seats, and chief in honor he welcomes Aeneas to a couch of shaggy lion's hide and he invites him to a maple throne. Then chosen youths and the priest of the altar eagerly bring the roasted flesh of bulls, they load in baskets the gifts of Ceres, milled and baked, and they serve the wine of Bacchus. Aeneas along with his youthful Trojans feast then on a long chine of beef and the sacrificial meat.

As a luxury item, meat was most commonly available at feasts accompanying religious sacrifices. Wealthy and powerful cities like Athens and Rome could slaughter hundreds of cattle at some of these festivals; the later Hellenistic monarchs and Roman emperors did likewise. Even so, the extent of meat eating is difficult to gauge. Meat seems to have been sold at small neighborhood bars such as those at Pompeii, and it seems to have been especially popular among specific groups such as Roman soldiers (see Chapter 6). Another group for whom meat eating was critical was athletes, who were advised to eat much more meat than non-athletes. Athenaeus' depiction of a certain Milo is consistent with this view, which also tended to stereotype athletes as physically fit but mentally deficient.

3.55. Athenaeus, *Sophists at Dinner*, 10.413a

> This is what Milo was like, when at Zeus' feast he lifted up the weight of a four-year old heifer from the earth and carried the huge animal lightly on his shoulders through the entire crowd, as if it were a newborn lamb. This was an astonishing feat; but, stranger, he did something more remarkable than this in front of the altar in Pisa;[52] for he cut up into pieces of meat this unyoked hiefer that he carried around and he ate the whole thing all by himself.

Nevertheless, the ancient Mediterranean emphasis on grain, which was cheaper to produce than meat, meant that the latter was not consumed in antiquity on a regular basis and certainly less so than it is today in Western Europe and the United States (Garnsey 1999). While consumption may have been limited, the evidence clearly suggests a hierarchy among meats. Beef remained at the top of the chain, but a broad range of additional options was equally, if not more, popular. Chief among these was pork, a result of the widespread practice of pig keeping in the Mediterranean world. Pigs were routinely sacrificed at religious festivals, especially those connected with fertility such as the Thesmophoria and the Eleusinian mysteries. In the private sphere pork enjoyed an appeal that often cut across class lines. Pliny reminds us of this in the following excerpt, where he depicts pork consumption not only in the eating houses of the poorer classes but also at the *cenae* of the wealthy.

3.56. Pliny, *Natural History* 8.77

> M. Apicius discovered that we may apply the same method of increasing the size of the liver of sows as of that of geese. It involves stuffing them with dried figs, and once they are sufficiently fattened, they are soaked with wine mixed with honey, and quickly killed. No creature offers a greater variety to the eating house (*ganeae*) of the poor man; the flesh of the hog has nearly 50 different flavors, all the other animals have but a single one. As a result, there are entire pages of regulations of the censors[53] that forbid that the belly, kernels, testicles, womb, and jowls (*sincipita*) be served up at dinners. However, when Publius, a poet of mimes,[54] was freed from being a slave, he is said to have given no dinner worth remembering without serving up the belly of a sow, to which he also gave the name of *sumen*.

Concerning pork, we must also not overlook the sausage seller. A character of low social standing in ancient comedy, he was nonetheless a very popular vendor within the ancient city. We must consider too the opulent but garish feast provided by the freedman Trimalchio in the *Satyricon* of Petronius (see Chapter 2, no. 32). As Wilkins observes, Trimalchio does not provide his guests the higher status items of beef or fish but a pig that has been inventively prepared by stuffing it with all manner of foods, including live birds that fly forth when it is cut open. The episode reminds us of the appeal of pork while also perhaps suggesting undertones of vulgarity attributable to the host's servile origins (Wilkins 2006).

At the same time, the range of possibilities extended far beyond beef and pork. The sources mention mutton and goat, and the game typically obtained through the popular aristocratic pastime of hunting in antiquity, boar and deer. Poultry, and all sorts of other birds, must also be included in the mix. Varro provides detailed advice on the rearing of captive birds, while the following recipe for flamingo as preserved by Apicius confirms that there was always room for the conspicuous consumption of the exotic, a reality made possible by the vast sweep of the Roman Empire. As mentioned previously, also prominent here is the heavy reliance on spices and wine in Roman cookery, essential ingredients for masking difficult flavors.

3.57. Apicius, *On Cookery* 6.2.21=Grocock and Grainger 228–9

Flamingo. Pluck the flamingo, wash, dress, tie the legs together, place in a saucepan, add water, salt, dill and a little vinegar. When cooked halfway, make a little bundle of leek and coriander and let it cook (with the bird). When it is nearly cooked, add wine that has been boiled down to give it color. Combine in a mortar pepper, caraway, coriander, asafoetida,[55] root, mint, rue: grind; moisten with vinegar, add dates, pour over some of the cooking wine. Pour it into the same saucepan, thicken with corn flour, pour the sauce over the bird and serve. The same recipe can also be used for parrot.

Finally, the ancients made sure to utilize the entire animal for culinary purposes. Hence, we have evidence of dishes that included the head, ears and various internal organs, such as the intestines and the udder of a sow. As Wilkins has noted, this had to do with an ancient interest in anatomy in general but also with texture among the foods to be consumed. In this latter respect the Greeks and Romans are much closer to modern French, Spanish, and Chinese tastes than to those of Britain and America. Protein may have been important but so too was textural variety (Wilkins 2006).

Fish

Fish eating differed from meat eating and grain consumption in fundamental ways in antiquity. Raising cattle and pigs or planting and harvesting wheat involved expense but, with the exception of catastrophic drought or disease, they were relatively safe investments. On the other hand, fishing was a far riskier proposition. The sea, after all, was mysterious, its creatures hidden from view. Furthermore, there was always the possibility that the fish might eat the fisherman, an inversion of the natural order that induced fear and contributed to the perception of the fisherman as an isolated opportunist who lived at the margins of the civilized world (Purcell, in Wilkins et al. 1995). Indeed, according to one Greek epigram, the only thing that a fisherman was good at catching was lice (Homer, *Epigram* 17). Alciphron, who wrote fictional letters in elegant Greek about the occupations of the lower orders (see 2.28), captures the hard-luck nature of fishing in this amusing epistle.

3.58. Alciphron, *Letter* 20 [1.17]

"Trawlwell" to the "Harbor master."

The hell with the lookout place at Lesbos! Seeing the sea darkened with ripples here and there, he shouted as if it were a whole school of tunny-fish, young or old, which was coming. We believed him and cast our nets around nearly the whole bay. Then we started to haul it in, and the weight was too great for a regular load of fish. So we had hopes, and we called out to some of those nearby, promising them a share if they would grab on with us and give us a lift. At last, with great labor, late in the day, we reeled in a fine, big camel, already rotten and bursting forth with worms. This is the kind of catch I made; and I have told you about it not to make you laugh, but so that you may know how many are the snares that fortune uses to keep me—a luckless man—down.

Ancient pisciculture was unique in other respects as well. The nature itself of the Mediterranean ecosystem was one challenge. We now know that this environment, though apparently uniform, was in fact as fragmented as the land and that it supported less abundant populations of fish than the oceans (Horden and Purcell). Another obstacle was the technological limitations of catching fish by line or with nets, methods that changed little over time. Even so, many desirable species were obtainable through migratory patterns, which often brought fish of all kinds in contact with islands and coastlands. This, in turn, allowed the ancients to develop more productive strategies like the fishpond mentioned below.

Perhaps most important of all is how the ancients perceived fish as fitting into their diet. On the one hand, fish was considered a non-food, most notably among Christians, a belief that allowed it to be eaten during times of fasting. Fish operated on a metaphorical level too in Christianity, evident in Jesus' exhortation that his disciples become "fishers of men" (Matt. 4.19). On the practical level, despite the claims of some scholars (Gallant), fish could never compete with grain and meat for calorific value. To be sure, the ancients thought of fish as a supplement to a cereal diet, as do we. We never think, for example, "should I fill up on bread or sardines?" Why? Because we know, as did the ancients, that it is the bread that will fill us up while the sardines will provide minerals, proteins, and essential oils. It is perhaps due to this realization that fish easily took on the status of a cash crop in antiquity. The fisherman realized that he was able to acquire more protein by selling fish than by simply eating it, while the purchase of fish allowed the consumer to diversify and expand the typical grain and vegetable based diet. Converting fish into *opson*, a relish popular among the Greeks, or into *garum*, a fermented fish sauce that became a lucrative and widely traded product in the Roman world, created additional economic opportunities. This kind of processing also increased nutritional usefulness by making the resource sustainable in times of shortage. Not to be overlooked too in the economics of fishing was the fish market. It remained a fixture of the ancient town and provided a venue for fresh fish, especially for the connoisseur willing to pay top dollar for the most sought after species.

At the same time, it is important to understand this evidence in a wider context. Fish was certainly available to those who lived on the coast and near rivers but it would have been less available to those living at a distance from these areas. Availability would have been further restricted by the inability of fish to stay fresh for very long. Given these realities, it has been difficult to reach a scholarly consensus on the proportion of fish in the ancient diet and especially its availability to poorer people. Still, there is general agreement that, when compared to cereals or legumes, fish cannot have contributed significantly to the protein requirements of the ancient population.

All of these factors help to explain the prominence of fish in Greek and Roman literature. Indeed, we find nearly 40 entries on different species of fish in Dalby's encyclopedia (2003, s.v. "fish"), as well as much information on varieties and methods of cooking, especially in the works of Athenaeus and Archestratus. Oppian, a Greek poet from Galatia (modern Turkey), even dedicated a poem, *On Fishing*, to the Roman emperor Marcus Aurelius in the second century CE. Note here the attributes that he describes as necessary for a successful fisherman. To be sure, it is difficult to imagine any angler possessing all of these qualities; instead, what the passage suggests are the very real difficulties and challenges that were inherent in this occupation.

3.59. Oppian, *On Fishing* 3.29–49

First of all the fisherman should have body and limbs that are swift and strong, neither too fat nor too thin. For many times he must fight powerful fish in order to land them—fish that are very strong as long as they circle and wheel in the arms of their mother sea. And he must be able to leap easily from a rock; and when the toil of the sea is at its peak, he must quickly travel a great distance and dive into the deepest depths and remain among the waves and continue to labor at such works as fisherman toil at with stout hearts. The fisherman should be cunning of wit and wise, since fish devise many and various devices when they come upon unforeseen snares. He should also be bold and brave and temperate and not be fond of too much sleep; but he must be keen of sight, ready of heart, and open-eyed. He must endure well wintery weather and the parching season of Sirius.[56] He must have a strong desire for hard work and a love of the sea. In this way will he be successful in his pursuits and dear to Hermes.[57]

Comedy was a genre particularly interested in the piscine world. In Athenian comedy, fish, fisherman, and fish recipes were common; so too was the colorful haggling between buyer and seller at the market, a practice akin to the economy of the modern bazaar (Paulas). Here, Archippus, a contemporary of Aristophanes, offers a typical portrait of the scheming fishmonger in this fragment from his lost comedy, *The Fishes*, which also featured a chorus that even imitated fishes.

3.60. Athenaeus, *Sophists At Dinner*, 6.227A

The most despicable fish-seller, Hermaeus, the Egyptian, who violently peels the skin of monkfish and dogfish, and guts sea bass, and sells them, so they tell us.

Elsewhere, the impulse for competitive consumption among the wealthy helps to explain stories about spectacular singletons, those specimens whose extraordinary size dictated that they be brought as soon as possible to the most important figure in the ancient community. The social and political meanings behind the quest for fine fish have been carefully analyzed in recent years (Davidson, in Wilkins et al. 1995; Davidson 1997). Such tales were also tied to the recognition that the fish supply was unpredictable and often fleeting, and so an unusual catch had to be recognized in a significant manner. Juvenal's satire about the big fish brought to the emperor Domitian's court at Rome by a poor fisherman who traveled all the way from the Adriatic coast incorporates much of this thinking while viciously satirizing the emperor and his court.

3.61. Juvenal, *Satire* 4.59–72

… nevertheless, our fisherman is in a hurry, as if the South Wind were urging him on. And when the lakes were below him, where Alba, although in ruins, preserves the flame of Troy and the lesser Vesta,[58] a mob, gawking in wonder, delayed his advance for a little while. As it fell away, the folding doors swung open on easy hinges. The senators, shut out, look on as the big catch is admitted.

It is brought in to King Atrides.[59] Then, the man from Picenum said, "Accept this gift too large for a private kitchen. Let this be a holiday. Hurry up, stretch your belly by cramming it full and eat up this turbot preserved for your glorious times. The fish itself wished to be caught." What could be more blatant? And nonetheless, the emperor's coxcomb rose up. There is nothing that god-like power cannot believe about itself when it is praised. But there was no platter that measured up to the fish.

Finally, because fishing on the open sea was hazardous, the ancients skillfully utilized coastal wetland lagoons, which were much easier to develop and control. It was on the basis of such practices that ancient expertise in pisciculture developed, especially among the Romans, who created elaborate fishponds for both fresh and saltwater species. There is much archaeological evidence for these *piscinae*, as they were called, but ample literary testimony as well. In this passage Columella provides specific instructions on how to construct a fishpond near the coast. It is interesting to note that Columella's treatise is consistent with conventional Roman thinking on the importance of agriculture, yet he still recognizes the value of fish farming for the successful estate and treats it at some length in his eighth book.

3.62. Columella, *On Agriculture*, 8.17.1–2

We consider that pond to be the best by far, which is so situated that the incoming ocean tide drives out the water of the earlier tide and does not allow any old water to remain within the enclosure. For a pond is most like the open sea if the winds stir it up and its waters are constantly renewed; nor is it able to grow warm, since it rolls up a wave of cold water from the depths to the uppermost part. Moreover, the pond is either cut out of rock, an instance which is very uncommon, or constructed of plaster on the shore. But, no matter how it may be built, if the swirl of water that is constantly flowing in keeps it cold, it ought to have recesses near the bottom, some of these simple and straight where the scaly flocks may withdraw, others twisted into a spiral, and not too wide, where the lampreys may take refuge.

Figs, honey, and the bean

In addition to grains, olives, meat, and fish, the regular diet featured a wide range of vegetables and fruits that were well suited to the Mediterranean climate. In general, the sources do not have much to say about these foodstuffs unless a special point is being made or they are included as part of a comprehensive overview (Wilkins 2006). Common vegetables included lettuce, cabbage, leek, celery, and cucumber, as well as onion, radish, garlic, and turnip. Among fruits, the most popular were apples, grapes, and pears, while cheese and eggs enjoyed widespread appeal as dairy products.

Figs

Especially valued was the fig. As a standard foodstuff of the ancient Mediterranean diet, figs produced more calories per unit area than any other crop in antiquity. Dried figs, which receive the most attention in the sources, were more flavorful than fresh figs and served as an important source of dietary sugar, most commonly as a dessert or as a sweetener in cakes (Dalby 2003, s.v. "fig"). Furthermore, because of their high sugar content, dried figs could keep for several years if properly packaged. Elsewhere, Athenaeus and Columella portray dried figs as the food of slaves and the rural poor (Ath. 2.54f–55a, 2.60b–c; Columella, *Rust.* 12.14), while Aristophanes reveals that they provided emergency rations in times of food shortage (*Acharnians* 799–810). The fig leaf too had several culinary uses, while both fresh and dried figs were effective as laxatives.

The following excerpt, recorded by the geographer Strabo, preserves a divination contest between two of antiquity's most fabled seers. While the story underscores how this type of insight enabled one to see things that others could not through a form of knowledge similar to that of the gods, the tale is also important for underscoring the popularity and, more importantly, the fertility of the fig tree—and hence, its centrality to the ancient diet. Much as we saw earlier in Herodotus' description of the olive tree that survived the Persian Wars in Athens (no. 51), this tale underscores the cultural significance of the fig and the prominence attached to certain varieties in the ancient texts, especially those figs connected with major cities like Athens and Rome.

3.63. Strabo, *Geography* 14.1.27

> Next, one arrives at the mountain Gallesius, and Colophon, a city of Ionia, and the sacred grove of Apollo Clarius, where there was once an ancient oracle. The story is told that Calchas, the prophet, went there on foot with Amphilochus, the son of Amphiaräus, on his way back from Troy, and that, after meeting a prophet more skilled than himself near Clarus, Mopsus, the son of Manto, the daughter of Teiresias, he died of grief. Now Hesiod recasts the myth as follows, making Calchas

put forward this question to Mopsus: "I am amazed in my heart at all these figs on this wild fig tree, even though the tree is small: can you tell me the number?" And he has Mopsus reply: "There are 10,000 of them, and their measure is a *medimnus*;[60] but there is one fig over and above that number, which you cannot put in the measure."[61] "Thus he spoke," Hesiod adds, "and the number that the measure could hold proved to be true. Then the sleep of death closed Calchas' eyes.

Honey

The ubiquity of the fig notwithstanding, the chief sweetener among the ancients was honey, which was used in cooking, confectionery, and as a preservative. It was also used widely in medicine. Beekeeping was already well established in antiquity by the time of the Greeks and Romans, and the literary sources provide much incidental information on methods, regulations, and taxes on bee-keeping and honey production. The ancients also paid close attention to the honey-producing qualities of certain flowers and regions. Most favored was honey from Hymettus in Attica, which produced a honey that was pale in color and sweet in flavor.

In this famous passage from the *Aeneid*, Vergil compares the workers who built Carthage to bees constructing their hive. Here the bees work together as social animals to create an ordered community, an image that reflects a Stoic view of the body politic. The simile is equally important for its insight into the ancient fascination with bees and honey, a theme that extends from the scientific writings of Aristotle to the Roman farming treatises of Varro and Columella. Vergil himself had earlier treated this topic in greater detail in the fourth book of his *Georgics*, a poem on the various forms of rural industry.

3.64. Vergil, *Aeneid*, 1.418–36

Meanwhile, the two men pressed on where the pathway led. Soon they were climbing a long ridge, which, overlooking most of the city, gave a view down over the facing towers. Aeneas held in wonder the massive buildings, once simple huts, he marveled at the gates, the noise of the city, and the paved streets. There the Tyrians were zealously pressing on: some were laying courses for walls, and rolling up stones by hand to build the citadel, others picked out a building site and plowed a boundary furrow. Laws and magistrates and a sacred senate were being chosen. Here some men were dredging harbors, there others set the deep foundation of a theater, and quarried huge pillars to adorn the future stage. Just as bees in early summer amid the flowering fields are busy at their work in the sun light, and bring along the young to mature bee-hood; or when they stuff their combs with honey, and expand all the cells with nectar, or accept the plunder of newcomers, or, like soldiers on the alert, drive away the drones, an idle tribe, from the hives; labor thrives, and the honey, fragrant with thyme, smells sweet.

Beyond the literary sphere, honey played an important role in religion and myth. Homer records its use as a libation for the dead (*Iliad* 23.170), and it was also utilized in the rites of various cults. In everyday cooking honey found wide use as an ingredient in recipes that required a sweetening agent, including wine. In this excerpt Apicius provides a recipe for *conditum*, a spiced wine that was made with honey and allowed to mature before drinking. This version was made for travelers, who added the concentrate to whatever wine they had available. As Dalby has noted, such evidence points to the ancient interest in the health benefits thought to derive from adding spices and herbs to wine in the correct measure (Dalby 2003, s.v. "conditum").

3.65. Apicius, *On Cookery* 1.2=Grocock and Grainger 134–5

Spiced honey wine for travelers. Spiced honey wine that keeps forever, which is given to travelers on the road: put pounded pepper with skimmed honey in a small vat just as for spiced wine and, when it comes time for drinking, mix part of the honey with some wine. But it is recommended to add some wine to the honey mixture in order to make the honey flow more freely.

Beans

We know of some 20 different species of legumes that have been utilized in various parts of the world over their long history (Brothwell). In ancient Greece and Italy the most common varieties included black-eyed peas, chickpeas, lentils, lupins, and especially the broad bean (fava bean). It is the bean that will be our focus here.

Peter Garnsey has eloquently described the complex legacy of the bean as symbol, food, and social marker. As a symbol the bean carried both positive and negative connotations. The Pythagoreans held it in especially low regard, believing it to consist of flesh and blood—its consumption equivalent to cannibalism. The Athenians took a more optimistic view, utilizing the bean for the appointment by lot of numerous office holders, thereby confirming it as a symbol of democracy (Garnsey 1998; Beer).

As a food, beans were an important component of the ancient diet. Indeed, no less an authority than Galen, the most influential physician in the Graeco-Roman world, recognized the fava bean as a nutritious part of the diet. In his *On the Property of Foodstuffs*, Galen was especially struck by the versatility of the bean, which could be boiled, roasted, or made into flour for cleaning and cosmetic purposes (Powell). Furthermore, beans contained considerably more protein than grain while also supplying other nutrients in which grains were deficient. In this respect beans truly were the "poor man's meat," as they were sometimes characterized.

At the same time, beans were a food widely connected with physical disorders for those who consumed them. Some of these maladies, such as favism, which caused weakness, pallor, jaundice, haemoglobinuria, and even death, were quite serious (Garnsey 1998). Others were less severe, as in the case of flatulence, which, as we might expect, was especially well suited to comedy and satire. As an example from the latter genre, we find this portrayal of the Roman emperor Claudius in the *Apocolocyntosis* or *The Pumpkinification of Claudius*, a work attributed to Seneca in the first century CE.

3.66. Seneca, *The Pumpkinification of Claudius (Apocolocyntosis)* 4

At once he gave up the ghost, and that shadow of a life came to an end. He died, moreover, while he was listening to comedic actors, so you know that it is not without reason that I fear them. This final utterance of his was heard in this world, when he had made a great noise with that end of him which talked easiest: "Oh my, I think I've shit myself." Whether he did or not, I do not know: but he certainly made a shitty mess of everything else.

Beans were perhaps most interesting as a marker of social status. Compared to grain, they were generally of lower status in antiquity. As we saw earlier, the rich would have monopolized the best bread wheat in order to obtain the most refined flour for the highest-quality bread. Heavier wheat, barley, and legumes would have comprised a lesser category, with fodder crops occupying the lowest rung in this value system. That beans appear where they do in this scheme is not so surprising. It is clear from the agricultural sources that they were widely grown in the ancient Mediterranean and that they served as a significant substitute for or supplement to beef and grain. But the wealthy did not embrace beans, at least not in bulk, largely because they did not have to. That they did not eat them at all would not seem to be entirely accurate either, however. They surely would have consumed beans from time to time, whether as a dessert or in sauces. The cookbook of Apicius suggests as much, as we find a recipes for boiled beans with spices and honey named after Vitellius, a Roman emperor and well-known gourmand of the first century CE (Garnsey 1998). There was also a recipe for beans named after Baiae, a retreat on the Bay of Naples popular among the rich and famous in Roman times. We might even suppose that this dish occasionally found its way to the tables of these wealthy resort-goers.

3.67. Apicius, *On Cookery* 5.6.4=Grocock and Grainger 218–19

> Beans from Baiae.[62] Boil, chop finely. Serve with rue, green celery, leaks, oil, vinegar, *liquamen*, a little *caroenum* or *passum*.[63]

The association of beans with social status raises the larger and more complex issue of the relationship of food and identity and of food as a substance to bring people together but to set them apart at the same time. This topic will be explored more fully in Chapter 5.

Food supply, shortage, and famine

The food supply of the ancient Mediterranean rested largely on the principle of self-sufficiency. This was especially true for the Greek city-states of the Archaic and Hellenistic periods and for Roman farmers of the Republican era. The peasant farmer sought to produce enough food to meet the needs of his family and, in a good year, to achieve a modest surplus, which could then be preserved for times of shortage or sold at the local market. The permanent market itself, which coincided with urbanization in the Graeco-Roman world and gradually replaced archaic methods of exchange, was a key component in the food supply chain (Frayn; de Ligt). Here, peasants could sell their goods, typically under the supervision of the Greek city-state or the Roman imperial government. Local markets and fairs provided additional purchasing opportunities for rural inhabitants, and landlords of large estates in Italy would sometimes open their own markets to compete with these traditional fairs. Some markets were also connected to religious festivals, especially in Greece. Underlying this system was the strong attachment to the land itself and the virtue that was thought to derive from the steady application of one's labors and talents to farming. This notion was embraced by Roman elites, including emperors like Augustus, who promoted agricultural renewal as part of a broader program of state reform and restoration in the first century CE. It found additional expression in the robust technical literature of Roman writers like Cato and Columella, who, as we have seen already, wrote eloquently about all aspects of estate management.

When the ancient sources speak of food supply they are talking mainly about grain. As we saw earlier in this chapter, grain, most notably wheat and barley, was the most favored foodstuff of the ancient diet and as such the ancient city went to great lengths to ensure its availability and safety. This goal was not always achievable, however, as instability resulting from political turmoil, corruption, crop failure, or adverse weather conditions could lead to food shortages, food crises, and sometimes to famine. The next excerpt, perhaps more amusing than true, is interesting in that it suggests, however much exaggerated, the precautions surrounding food storage and security on the household level and the anxiety that accompanied this essential task. The story concerns Lacydes, who was head of the Academy founded by Plato in the third century BCE, as told by Diogenes Laertius, a Greek author who wrote about the lives of famous philosophers. The second excerpt, preserved in the Roman history of Ammianus Marcellinus, moves the issue of food security to a public setting, revealing that even the rumor of a threat to Rome's grain supply could provoke a revolt. In this instance, however, the weather improves and the grain ships arrive unharmed.

3.68. Diogenes Laertius, *Lives of Eminent Philosophers* 4.8.59

A very funny story is told of his housekeeping. Whenever he brought anything out from the storeroom, he would close the door up again and toss his signet ring inside through the opening to ensure that nothing stored up there should be stolen or carried away. So, as soon as his rascally servants figured this out, they broke the seal and carried off what they desired, afterwards throwing the ring in the same way through the opening into the storeroom. Nor were they ever detected in this.

3.69. Ammianus Marcellinus 19.10.1, 4

1. While in the extreme East these storms were swiftly passing one upon the other, the eternal city (*sc.* Rome) was fearing the disaster of a coming shortage of grain, and Tertullus, who was prefect[64] at the time, was frequently assailed by the violence of the common people who were very threatening, as they anticipated famine, the worst of all ills; and this was clearly unreasonable, since it was not his fault that food was not brought at the proper time in the ships, which

unusually rough weather at sea and adverse gales of wind drove to the nearest harbors, and by the greatness of the danger thoroughly terrified them from entering the Port of Augustus... .

4. And soon by the will of the divine power that gave increase to Rome from its cradle and pledged that it should last forever, while Tertullus was sacrificing in the temple of Castor and Pollux at Ostia, tranquility soothed the sea, the wind changed to a peaceful southern breeze, and the ships entered the harbor under full sail and crammed the storehouses full with grain.

This excerpt from Ammianus raises two important aspects of the food supply system: the presence of long-distance, large-scale grain operations and of an elite class to oversee this trade. Concerning the former, we are best informed about Athens and Rome. Athens was the largest Greek polis of the classical period; its population, including that of Attica, perhaps reached 250,000 in the fifth century CE. During this period Athens exploited the agricultural lands of Attica but also imported large amounts of grain from elsewhere. In this passage Demosthenes, the most famous of the Athenian orators, delivers a speech against a certain Leptines in the early fourth century BCE in which he provides some figures on the amounts of grain imported to Athens from the Black Sea area. His aim is to make a case for the important role of Leucon, the ruler of the Bosporan kingdom on the Crimea. Most interestingly, Attic oratory served as the primary source of textual evidence for the history of the Athenian grain supply, an indication that bread and politics could never be easily separated in Athenian public discourse (Moreno).

3.70. Demosthenes, *Against Leptines* 31–3=Meijer and van Nijf, no. 118

You perhaps know this—that we consume the greatest amount of imported grain of all peoples. Now the grain that reaches our harbors from the Black Sea is equal to the entire amount from all other trading places. And this makes sense; for not only is that region very rich in grain, but also Leucon, who oversees the trade, has granted exemption from dues to merchants transporting grain to Athens, and he proclaims that those sailing to your port will have priority of lading. For Leucon, holding an exemption for himself and his children,[65] has granted this to all of you. Observe what this amounts to. He collects a toll of one-thirtieth from the grain exporters from his country. Now about 400,000 bushels arrive at Athens from the Bosporus; one could check the figures by the accounts of the grain commissioners.[66] So for every 300,000 bushels, he grants 10,000 bushels to us, and for the remaining 100,000, he gives about 3,000. Now, so minimal is the threat of his depriving our state of this gift, that he has set up a depot at Theudosia, which our merchants claim is in no way whatsoever inferior to the Bosporus, and there also he has granted the same exemption to us. I pass over in silence many things that could be told about the other benefits that this man and also his ancestors have bestowed upon you; but the year before last, when there was a widespread grain shortage, he not only sent an amount sufficient for your requirements, but so much of an additional quantity that Callisthenes had a surplus of fifteen talents of silver to disperse.[67]

As a city of perhaps one million inhabitants in the first century CE, Rome required a level of supply that far exceeded the productive capacity of the city's surrounding territories. As at Athens, this situation called for exploiting grain from other sources, although in far greater amounts than were required by any city in the Greek world. While supplying the city was typically left to private enterprise, threats to the supply, whether perceived (as recorded by Ammianus above) or actual, prompted various forms of intervention. One such form was by individual magistrates, who, from the fourth to second centuries BCE, sought to win public favor by securing additional supplies of grain from areas under Roman control or from regions in which they had some personal influence. By the time of the Principate in the first century CE, the supervision of the food supply was ultimately overseen by the emperor, who took this task very seriously, both in his capacity as chief benefactor of the city and as a means to prevent social uprisings. While ancient biographies routinely mention the emperor's care for or neglect of his food supply responsibilities, a particularly illustrative example comes from the *Res Gestae Divi Augustus*, the inscriptional record of the achievements of the emperor Augustus, which was to be set up on bronze pillars at the entrance of his mausoleum in the Campus Martius in Rome. Among the document's emphases are the expenditures he made as the city's greatest benefactor. While the account is highly selective and many of its claims are difficult to confirm, it contains much information not found elsewhere and it attests to the strong tradition of self-advertisement and self-glorification that was embraced by Roman elites at this time (Cooley).

3.71. *The Deeds of Divine Augustus (Res Gestae) 5.2* (22 BCE)

During a very great shortage of grain I did not decline to undertake the charge of the grain supply, which I administered in such a way that within a few days

I freed the entire city from fear and immediate danger at my own cost and by my own efforts.

3.72. *The Deeds of Divine Augustus (Res Gestae)* 18 (18 BCE)

From the year when Gnaeus and Publius Lentulus were consuls, whenever the taxes were not sufficient, I made payments of grain and money from my own granary and inheritance, sometimes to 100,000 persons, sometimes to many more.

Continuing with the Roman evidence, we know that by the later second century CE adult male citizens in Rome were receiving a set monthly ration of grain (*frumentatio*) at a set price; by the mid-first century BCE this distribution was free. Known as the *plebs frumentaria*, these recipients had grown to such large numbers by the first century that Augustus reduced the roster to about 200,000. Equally important, he appointed an overseer of the public supply of grain (*praefectus annonae*), who supervised storage and distribution while watching over the food supply in general. Recipients could now secure their monthly ration by presenting a ticket (*tessera*), which could be sold or bequeathed. The *frumentatio* was never substantial enough to make ends meet for the recipient and his family, however, and so public markets and, where possible, produce from the family farm, served as additional sources of food.

The *annona* system was complex, requiring harbors and warehouses, guilds operating as commercial organizers, merchants, shippers, and various administrators (Aldrete and Mattingly, in Potter and Matttingly). We are well informed about several of the trades involved in this system. The first excerpt records legislation passed by the emperor Claudius in the first century CE to encourage private ship owners (*navicularii*) to import grain to Rome by offering benefits of status for those who contracted to provide a certain minimum tonnage in service to the *annona*. The second passage, a funerary inscription of an actual ship owner, reveals that most of these individuals appear to have been freedmen, foreigners and others of low status, and that many of them were located in important port cities of Spain, Gaul, Italy, and Africa, which exported goods to Rome. Furthermore, it is possible that senators and provincial elites served as invisible partners who provided financial backing for these shippers. This arrangement would have allowed such elites to make a profit while still adhering to the social ethos that saw trade as a sordid pursuit for gentlemen, who were expected instead to embrace land ownership and agriculture as the proper source of wealth.

3.73. Suetonius, *Claudius* 18–19

Once, after a series of droughts had caused a scarcity of grain, a mob stopped
Claudius in the Forum and pelted him so hard with curses and stale crusts that
he had difficulty in regaining the Palace by a side-door; as a result, he took
all possible steps to import grain, even during the winter months—insuring
merchants against the loss of their ships in stormy weather (which guaranteed
them a good return on their ventures), and offering a large bounty for every
new grain-transport built, proportionate to its tonnage. The ship owner, if he
happened to be a Roman citizen, was exempted from the Papian-Poppaean
Law; if only a possessor of Latin rights, he acquired full Roman citizenship; if a
woman, she enjoyed the privileges granted to mothers of four children.[68] These
regulations have never since been modified.

3.74. *Corpus of Latin Inscriptions (CIL)* 13.1942 = *Select Latin Inscriptions (ILS)* 7029

To the departed soul of Quintus Capito Probatus the Elder, a resident of Rome,
a sevir Augustalis[69] at Lugdunum[70] and at Puteoli,[71] Nereus and Palaemon,[72] his
freedmen, dedicated this monument for their patron, which he established for
himself and his descendants while he was alive and he dedicated it beneath the
depiction of a cutting tool.[73]

Finally, the state did not limit its interests to the supply of grain alone but
the *prefectus annonae* and his subordinates took charge of more specialized
commodities like olive oil and wine as well. One estimate has placed an absolute
minimum figure for the number of shiploads necessary to carry a year's supply
of wheat, oil, and wine for the city of Rome at 1,702, or about 17 ships per
day during the prime sailing season, which typically extended from March to
October. These figures may well be too low but they nevertheless indicate the
size and scope of Rome's supply needs and help to account for the large and
diverse pool of personnel attested in the sources for several centuries (Aldrete
and Mattingly, in Potter and Mattingly).

Shortages were an endemic feature of the Graeco-Roman food supply system.
Any number of causes could lead to shortages of varying duration and intensity,
including crop failure, problems with transportation, storage or distribution,
and manipulation of supplies for profiteering. Most rural farmers employed a
strategy aimed at minimizing risk. When shortages did threaten, local residents
would pressure political leaders to act before the shortage became worse. In
reality, the powers of such authorities to mitigate the effects of such crises were

limited (Garnsey 1988; 1998; 1999). One alternative was for local elites or grain traders to provide assistance in return for recognition and honors. This form of private philanthropy (euergetism) for the public good, an essential feature of ancient social relations, will receive more attention in Chapter 5. In this excerpt a merchant from Rhodes provides grain to the city of Ephesus at less than market prices. In return, he receives an honorary inscription and citizenship. The inscription, found in the theater of Ephesus, dates to about 300 BCE.

3.75. *Sylloge Inscriptionum Graecarum (SIG³)* 354 = Meijer and van Nijf, no. 121

> Resolved by the council and the people; Dion, son of Diopithes moved: since Agathocles, son of Hegemon of Rhodes, when he was importing grain to the city amounting to 14,000 *hekteis* and found that the grain in the agora was being sold at more than six drachmas, he was persuaded by the *agoranomos*[74] and wished to do a favor for the people, and sold all his grain more cheaply than it was being sold in the agora, be it resolved by the people, to grant citizenship to Agathocles of Rhodes on a basis of full equality, to himself and his descendants; the priests shall allot him a tribe and *chiliastys*[75] and the temple administrators shall record these honors in the sanctuary of Artemis, where the other grants of citizenship are recorded, so that all may know that the people knows how to return thanks to its benefactors. He was allotted the tribe Bembine and the *chiliastys* Aegoteus.

It seems equally clear that rural peasants suffered just as much, if not more, as urban inhabitants in times of shortage. Galen, the medical expert of the second century CE, reveals in this passage how food shortages compelled the peasantry to consume foods at the very bottom of the food chain simply to survive.

3.76. Galen, *Wholesome and Unwholesome Juices in Food* 1

> Among many of those under the subjugation of the Romans, the food shortages that have occurred over many years in succession have shown clearly to those not entirely lacking in intelligence that the consumption of bad foods plays a primary role in the formation of disease. For those who dwell in the cities, as it was their custom to gather and store grain sufficient for the entire next year immediately after the harvest, took from the fields all the grain as well as the barley, beans, and lentils, and they left the other fruits of the fields to the peasants, that which they call pulses—and they took to the city even a good number of these. Now the peasants ate what had been left for them during the winter and then they had to rely on unhealthy foods during the entire spring, eating branches and twigs

of trees and shrubs, and bulbs and roots of indigestible plants; they filled their stomachs with what are known as wild herbs, as much as they could get their hands on, stuffing themselves until they were sated; they even boiled up and ate fresh grass—a thing they had never tasted before, not even as a test.

Famine may be defined as an interruption of essential foodstuffs with the catastrophic result of unusually high death rates from epidemic disease that typically accompanied the incident. While shortages were common, famine was not frequent in antiquity (Garnsey 1988). As seen earlier, such tragedies were averted by a combination of subsistence strategies and public and private intervention. When famine did occur, it was often man-made, usually the result of military sieges or of political and strategic manipulation of the food supply network to gain some kind of advantage. Such incidences were typically localized and temporary. Of the handful of famine accounts preserved in the ancient sources, none is more dramatic than the Jewish historian Josephus' narrative of the starvation inflicted upon the residents of Jerusalem by the Romans under Titus during the siege of 70 CE.

3.77. Josephus, *Jewish War* 6.193–200

Meanwhile, those perishing of famine were falling in countless numbers and enduring indescribable hardships throughout the city. In every house, if even a shadow of food would appear anywhere, it meant war, and the closest of relatives fell to blows, snatching the pitiful ways and means of life from each other. For the dying there was no credit for poverty, but the robbers even searched them, lest someone who was holding food beneath a fold of his garment might be pretending to die. These criminals, gaping with hunger like mad dogs, staggered and reeled along, hurling themselves at the doors like drunkards; in their confusion they burst into the same houses twice or three times within a single hour. Necessity drove them to gnaw on everything, and they persisted to collect and eat offerings that even the most foul of animals would reject: thus in the end they did not abstain from belts and shoes, and they stripped off and chewed the leather of their shields. For others, shreds of withered grass provided sustenance; indeed, some collected stalks and sold a trifling number for four Attic drachmas. But why is it necessary to tell of the shameless reliance on inanimate articles of food provoked by the famine? For I am here about to make known a deed, which neither the Greeks nor barbarians have learned through inquiry, and as horrible to speak of as it is unbelievable to hear. As far as it concerns me, out of fear that posterity might suspect me of monstrous fabrication, I would gladly have omitted this tragedy, had I not countless witnesses among my

contemporaries. Furthermore, it would be a horrible compliment that I should
pay my country in suppressing the account of the woes she actually suffered.

Suggestions for Further Reading

Alston, R. and Nijf, O. van. eds. 2008. *Feeding the Ancient City*. Leuven.

Beer, M. 2009. *Taste or Taboo. Dietary Choices in Antiquity*. Exeter.

Braund, D. and Wilkins, J. eds. 2000. *Athenaeus and His World: Reading Greek Culture in the Roman Empire*. Exeter.

Brothwell, D. R. and Brothwell, P. 1969. *Food in Antiquity: A Survey of the Diet of Early Peoples*. New York.

Burkert, W. 1979. *Structure and History in Greek Mythology and Ritual*. Berkeley.

Camporesi, P. 1993. *The Magic Harvest: Food, Folklore and Society*.

Carpentier, T. H. and Faraone, C. A. eds. 1993. *Masks of Dionysus*. Ithaca, NY.

Cooley, A. 2009. *Res Gestae divi Augusti: Text, Translation and Commentary*. Cambridge.

Dalby, A. 1996. *Siren Feasts: A History of Food and Gastronomy in Greece*. London.

—2003. *Food in the Ancient World A to Z*. London.

Davidson, J. N. 1997. *Courtesans and Fishcakes: The Consuming Passions of Classical Athens*. London.

Dietler, M. 2006. "Alcohol: anthropological/archaeological perspectives." *Annual Review of Anthropology* 35: 229–49.

Dunbabin, K. M. D. 1993. "Wine and water at the Roman *convivium*." *Journal of Roman Archaeology* 6: 116–41.

Erdkamp, P., ed. 2012. *A Cultural History of Food in Antiquity*. London.

Faraone, C. A. 1996. "Taking the "Nestor's Cup Inscription" seriously: erotic magic and conditional curses in the earliest inscribed hexameters." *Classical Antiquity* 5: 77–112.

Flower, B. and Rosenbaum, E. eds. 1958. *The Roman Cookery Book: A Critical Translation of the Art of Cooking by Apicius*. London.

Foss, P. and Dobbins, J. eds. 2007. *The World of Pompeii*. London.

Foxhall, L. 1995. *Olive Cultivation in Greek Farming: The Ancient Economy Revisited*.

—2007. *Olive Cultivation in Ancient Greece: Seeking the Ancient Economy*. Oxford.

Frayn, J. 1993. *Markets and Fairs in Roman Italy*. Oxford.

Gallant, T. 1985. *A Fisherman's Tale: An Analysis of the Potential Productivity of Fishing in the Ancient Greek World*. Ghent.

Garnsey, P. 1988. *Famine and Food Supply in the Graeco-Roman World*. Cambridge.

—1998. *Cities, Peasants and Food in Classical Antiquity. Essays in Social and Economic History*. Cambridge.

—1999. *Food and Society in Classical Antiquity*. Cambridge.

Grant, M., trans. 2000. *Galen on Food and Diet*. London.

Grocock, C. and Grainger, S. text, comm. and trans. 2006. *Apicius: A Critical Edition with an Introduction and an English Translation*. Devon.

Harrison, S., ed. 2005. *A Companion to Latin Literature*. Oxford.

Homan, M. M. 2004. "Beer and its drinkers: an ancient near eastern love story." *Near Eastern Archaeology* 67: 84–95.

Horden, P. and Purcell, N. 2000. *The Corrupting Sea: A Study of Mediterranean History*. Oxford.

Humphrey, J., Oleson, J., and Sherwood, A. 1998. *Greek and Roman Technology: A Sourcebook*. London.

Hyams, E. 1987. *Dionysius: A Social History of the Wine Vine*. Reprint. London.

Ligt, L. de. 1993. *Fairs and Markets in the Roman Empire: Economic and Social Aspects of Periodic Trade in a Pre-Industrial Society*. Amsterdam.

Lissarrague, F. N. 1990. *The Aesthetics of the Greek Banquet: Images of Wine and Ritual*. Princeton.

McGovern, P. E. 2007. *Ancient Wine: The Search for the Origins of Viticulture*. Princeton.

—2010. *Uncorking the Past: The Quest for Wine, Beer and Other Alcoholic Beverages*. Berkeley.

McGovern, P. E., Fleming, S. J., and Katz, S. H., eds. 1996. *The Origins and Ancient History of Wine*. Luxembourg.

Meijer, F. and Nijf, O. van. 1992. *Trade, Transport and Society in the Ancient World. A Sourcebook*. London.

Moreno, A. 2007. *Feeding the Democracy: The Athenian Grain Supply in the Fifth and Fourth Centuries B.C*. Oxford.

Murray, O., ed. 1990. *Sympotica: A Symposium on the Symposion*. Oxford.

Murray, O. and Tecusan, M., eds. 1995. *In Vino Veritas*. Rome.

Oleson, J., ed. 2008. *The Oxford Handbook of Engineering and Technology in the Classical World*. Oxford.

Paulas, J. 2010. "The bazaar fish market in fourth-century Greek comedy." *Arethusa 43*: 403–28.

Potter, D. S. and Mattingly D.J., eds. 2010. *Life, Death, and Entertainment in the Roman Empire*. Michigan.

Powell, O., ed., trans., comm. 2003. *Galen, On the Property of Foodstuffs*. Cambridge.

Purcell, N. 1985. "Wine and wealth in ancient Italy." *Journal of Roman Studies* 75: 1–19.

Robinson, J., ed. 2006. *Oxford Companion to Wine*. Oxford.

Roth, M. 2000. "'Anacreon' and drink poetry; or, the art of feeling very, very good." *Texas Studies in Literature and Language* 42: 314–45.

Sallares, R. 1991. *The Ecology of the Greek World*. London.

Seaford, R. 2006. *Dionysos*. London.

Sherrat, E. S. 2004. "Feasting in Homeric epic." *Hesperia* 73: 301–37.

Sirks, B. 1991. *Food for Rome: The Legal Structure of the Transportation and Processing of Supplies for the Imperial Distributions in Rome and Constantinople*. Amsterdam.

Slater, W. J., ed. 1991. *Dining in a Classical Context*. Ann Arbor.

Standage, T. 2005. *A History of the World in Six Glasses*. New York.

Tchernia, A. 1986. *Le vin de l'Italie romaine: essai d'histoire economique d'après les amphores*. Rome.

Tchernia, A. and Brun, J. P. 1999. *Le vin romain antique*. Grenoble (France).

Thurmond, D. 2006. *A Handbook of Food Processing in Classical Rome: For Her Bounty No Winter*. Leiden.

Unwin, T. 1996. *Wine and the Vine: An Historical Geography of Viticulture and the Wine Trade*. London.

Wilkins, J., Harvey, D., and Dobson, M. 1995. *Food in Antiquity*. Exeter.

Wilkins, J. and Hill, S. 2000. *The Boastful Chef: The Discourse of Food in Ancient Greek Comedy*. Oxford.

Wilkins, J. and Hill, S. 2006. *Food in the Ancient World*. Oxford.

Eating, Drinking, and Believing:
Food, Drink, and Religion

All sorrows are less with bread.

Miguel de Cervantes

The relationship between the human and the divine is an essential feature of any people. This is no less true of the Greeks and Romans, whose religious practices and beliefs continue to attract intense scholarly interest. Food and drink figured prominently in ancient religion, whether in public or private sacrifices, in ceremonies of the life cycle such as birth, marriage and death, and in the numerous religious celebrations of specific groups, both large and small, within the ancient community.

Before we examine more closely the ways in which the ancients utilized food and drink in a religious context, however, we must first understand what we mean when we say "Graeco-Roman religion." To begin, as James Rives has reminded us, when many people think of "a religion" today, they tend to do so in terms of a coherent and distinct set of beliefs and principles as they relate to human interaction with some superhuman force. This system might also include features such as: a set of sacred scriptures; some sort of professional or full-time authorities; specific places and times for worship; a moral code; and a number of associated practices and customs (Rives).

Yet when we turn to the Greeks and Romans, we find a system in which many, if not all, of these features are entirely missing. Instead, we find a way of thinking about and interacting with the divine that was much more fluid and open, with the result that the ancients could simultaneously maintain beliefs and practices that we might characterize as inconsistent with one another or even as mutually exclusive. At the same time, there were certainly many widely held assumptions about typical religious belief and practice, such as the importance of cult practice and belief in a polytheistic system. We shall have more to say about these features as the chapter progresses. In the meantime, an obvious response to this reality is to treat the topic as inclusively as possible. With this approach in mind, it will make sense to include magic and superstition in this chapter, for example, even though their characterization as "religion" might be considered to be contestable.

A second issue has to do with the ancient sources themselves. As mentioned earlier, sacred scriptures did not play a central role in ancient Graeco-Roman religion. To be sure, there were no sacred texts that served a function similar to that of the Bible for Christians, the Torah for Jews, or the Koran for Muslims. This is not to say that we are lacking evidence. On the contrary, the testimony is plentifully preserved in a wide range of sources, including literary and philosophical texts, inscriptions, and papyri. It is simply that this evidence is far from complete. Nevertheless, it is from these sources that we must stitch together our knowledge of ancient religion, despite the fact that many of the pieces simply no longer exist or that they often come from sources that are much later than the rites or practices they describe.

It is important to recognize one more feature as well. Many of the sources for Graeco-Roman religion reflect an aristocratic bias, that is, they are the works of literate elites produced for an elite audience. For example, we have calendars that preserve religious festivals in large cities such as Athens or Rome because these events often involved the support and participation of the wealthy. On the other hand, we are typically less well informed about religion in rural areas of the Mediterranean world. The evidence, therefore, is inevitably one-sided and so we must remember that our view of ancient religion will never be as full as we would like.

Mindful of these general features, this chapter will focus for practical and thematic reasons on specific instances in which food and drink intersected with belief in a Graeco-Roman setting and the meaning we can ascribe to such evidence. The testimony itself is varied and colorful. It includes the festivals and ceremonies of the ancient community, which routinely involved the sacrifice of animals and other foods to the gods in order to fulfill any number of vows— honoring a patron divinity, praying for a plentiful harvest, or protecting the city or the herdsman's flocks. Equally important, these rites often provided participants with a meal at the same time as they preserved the social order of the community. As mentioned earlier, food and drink was also a prominent feature at celebrations within certain cults and at key events in the life cycle, such as birth and death. Furthermore, we must not overlook various foreign cults as well as early Judaism and Christianity, all of which competed for the religious attention of both the Greeks and Romans with belief systems that placed great emphasis on ritual eating and drinking. In all of this evidence we will notice a common thread—the need among the ancients for establishing right relations with the gods and the significance of food and drink in maintaining this relationship.

Finally, while such evidence may not always match up with our own conceptions of religion, one conclusion is clear: that for the ancients, the divine remained ever difficult to know. At the same time, this challenge did not prevent the believers from repeated attempts to discern the will of the gods and to gain their favor. To be sure, the ubiquity and diversity of practices such as animal sacrifice and magic attest to this persistence.

The food of the gods

In Graeco-Roman religion there were numerous divinities of varying stature and importance. The ancient pantheon included not only the 12 major gods, who were immortal, but also a host of lesser gods. This latter category included, for example, mortal heroes, who received worship on the basis of their putative ability to affect the ancient community for better or for worse, and nymphs, female spirits of nature who represented the divine powers of mountains, forests, waters, and trees as well as places, regions, and cities. We must add to this mix as well the personification of concepts such as Fame, Persuasion, Health, and many others, all of whom might enjoy cultic worship (Stafford). If we were to tally up such evidence, in the case of Greek religion alone, the number would come to several thousand divinities (Mikalson).

In addition to their sheer number and diversity, the gods typically took on human form and displayed human emotions, as conceived by their mortal worshippers; in other words, they not only looked like but also acted like humans. Furthermore, this anthropomorphic view encouraged the concept of a divine society. We see evidence for this in the sanctuaries or favorite places for these deities on earth and also on Olympus, where the gods lived together in colorful and eccentric family relationships (hence, the term "Olympian" gods for the major pantheon), as typically portrayed in mythology.

Turning to food and drink, the major difference of course between gods and mortals was that the gods remained immortal. Given this critical advantage over humans, it follows that the gods did not have to be concerned with finding and preparing food. Instead, they subsisted on ambrosia and nectar, the food and drink of immortality. That these products often enhanced or preserved human life when provided by the gods to their mortal favorites is most commonly confirmed in epic poetry, where divine-human interaction is an important narrative strand. In the first passage, taken from Homer's *Iliad*, Zeus implores Athena to utilize these substances to strengthen the fasting Achilles during the Trojan War. The second passage, also from Homer's *Iliad*, underscores an additional feature: that the gods did not have blood in their veins since they consumed neither bread nor wine, but a special fluid known as *ichor*. The episode of Diomedes' wounding of Aphrodite, who was assisting her son Aeneas in battle against the Greeks, makes this clear.

4.1. Homer, *Iliad* 19.344–54

"There he sits in front of his ships with their raised sterns grieving for his dear friend. The others have settled down to their meal, but he fasts and tastes no food. But go, instill deep within his chest some nectar and sweet ambrosia so that hunger does not come upon him." So saying, he urged on Athena already eager for action. She, like a falcon, wide winged and shrilly crying, leapt down from the heavens through the air. The other Achaeans were speedily arming themselves for battle. She distilled nectar and sweet ambrosia into Achilles' chest so that grievous hunger would not come upon his limbs.

4.2. Homer, *Iliad* 5.334–42

But once he caught up with her, pressing hard upon her through the great throng of battle, then the son of great spirited Tydeus, reaching forward to strike, overtook her and cut the surface of her defenseless hand with a sharp spear. Immediately the spear bore right through her flesh on the wrist above the palm, through the ambrosial robe, which the Graces themselves had made for her with their labor. Immortal blood flowed from the goddess, ichor, such as flows through the veins of the blessed gods; for they do not eat bread, nor do they drink sparkling wine, and so they are bloodless, and we call them immortal.

The centrality of sacrifice

While the gods themselves had no dietary concerns, the human act of sacrificing animals or other foods to them nevertheless remained a central feature of Greek and Roman religion. This primitive way of communicating with the gods has led to various interpretations, most notably Burkert's psychological and ethological approach and the sociological and cultural approach of Vernant and Detienne. These interpretations have argued that sacrifice assuages feelings of guilt at the slaughter of the sacrificial animal while promoting solidarity at the same time. More recently, emphasis has shifted to the priests and gods by arguing that animal sacrifice attempts to establish contact with a divine being, and that the act itself is so important and fraught with uncertainty that it becomes subject to complex and extensive regulations (Naiden). To be sure, sacrifice was encoded with economic, political, social, and cultural meanings consistent with its nature as a ritual act located at the very center of the ancient community. At the same time, however, the external form of a religious act is all that we possess in this case. As a consequence, we know very little about the worshipper's state of mind, that is, the levels of intellectual commitment or emotional involvement that he or she brought to this act on any given occasion (Rives).

Given its importance in the divine-human relationship, sacrifice occurred in many different contexts, from the marriage of a son or daughter in the private realm to public rites held at a sanctuary or as part of a city-wide celebration. Those who offered sacrifice might vary too, from the head of the household to professional priests trained in sacrificing and cooking the animal. From the perspective of food studies, the sacrificial act is especially important, as it demonstrates the human belief in offering up one of life's most essential necessities—food itself—in an effort to communicate with and display reverence for the gods. In the instance of animal sacrifice, there was the additional and welcome possibility of a distribution of meat for the human participants. Consequently, the sacrifice was significant both in a symbolic and a practical sense. The excerpts below highlight the nature and diversity of the sacrificial act—Greek and Roman, bloody and bloodless, noble and not so noble, while also including the use of wine in a ceremonial context.

Animal sacrifice

The most popular form of sacrifice in the ancient city was blood sacrifice, the ritual slaughter of an animal, typically a domesticated animal like a sheep, pig, or cow. Part of the victim was offered to the gods by being burned on an altar; the participants consumed the rest according to fixed rules. Cattle were especially favored as victims in this ritual, since, as the most costly of sacrificial animals, they were thought to be quite pleasing to the gods. A second form of animal sacrifice involved no meal for the participants because the animal was

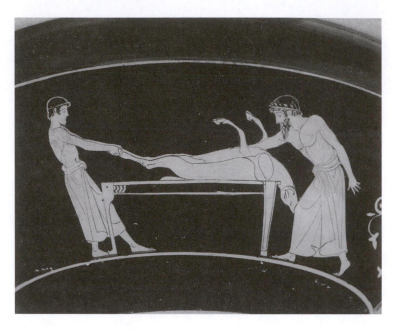

Figure 6. Slaughter of a sacrificial animal. Workshop of red-figured skyphos. Douris Painter, fifth century BCE. National Museum, Warsaw, Poland. Photo Credit: Erich Lessing/Art Resource, NY.

burnt completely (holocaust) as an offering to the gods. This type was associated primarily with certain cults of the dead and hero-cults.

The alimentary type, as it involves food for the celebrants, will be the focus here. In the following passage the myth of Prometheus' deception of Zeus provides Hesiod with the opportunity to explain why human diners at a sacrifice received better fare than the gods. The excerpt is important as an instance of aetiology, an attempt to explain a practice that seemed odd or counterintuitive by providing an *aition*, or cause, for the distinctive feature in question. Notable, too, is the emphasis on the sacrifice as a shared, although unequal, meal.

4.3. Hesiod, *Theogony* 535–57

For when the gods and mortals were at variance in Mecone, with eager spirit he (sc. Prometheus) divided up a large ox and set it before Zeus, trying to trick the god's mind. For on the hide he set down before him the flesh and the intestines, rich with fat, hiding them in the stomach of the ox; and then in turn he placed before him the ox's white bones, arranging them with cunning artifice, hiding them with glistening fat. Then the father of men and gods addressed him: "Son of Iapetus, renowned among all the princes, my dear man, how unfairly you have allotted the servings!" Thus Zeus, who knows eternal counsels, spoke sneeringly; but crookedly scheming Prometheus addressed him in turn with a faint smile, and he did not forget his deceptive craft: "Zeus, most renowned, supreme among the immortal gods, choose whichever from these the heart in your breast bids you." Thus he spoke, plotting deception. But Zeus, who knows eternal counsels, recognized the trick and was quick to see through it; and he saw in his spirit evils for mankind that would come to pass. He took up the white fat with both hands, and when he saw the white bones of the ox, the result of the trickery, his heart became enraged and anger overtook his thoughts. And ever since that time the tribes of mortals who live upon the earth burn white bones upon smoking altars for the immortal gods.

Epic poetry frequently portrayed the sacrificial act. The passage below depicts an idealized sacrifice by Nestor, king of Pylos, to Poseidon upon the return home of Telemachus, the son of Odysseus. While this ritual may strike us as bloody and violent, the ancient sources tended to emphasize other aspects, such as the importance of following a set procedure as we see below; additionally, in this particular instance it is Nestor's wealth, generosity, and leadership role as king that are especially significant. The sacrifice also provided the poet with an opportunity to fill out his narrative by treating in a highly formulaic way a scene that represented a routine activity of daily life.

4.4. Homer, *Odyssey* 3.430–63; 470–2

Thus he (sc. Nestor) spoke and all of them bustled to work. The cow came from the plain, from the swift, well-balanced ship came the companions of great-hearted Telemachus, and the smith came, holding in his hands his bronze tools, the finishers of his trade—the anvil, the hammer, and the sturdy tongs, which he used to make gold. And Athena came to partake in the holy rites. Old Nestor, the driver of chariots, provided gold. Next, the smith fashioned the gold and put it around the cow's horns so that the goddess might rejoice in beholding the pleasing gift. Stratius and noble Echephron led the cow by the horns, and Aretus came from a chamber bringing water in a cauldron embossed with flowers for them to wash their hands; in the other hand he held barley-meal in a basket. Thrasymedes, the steadfast warrior, holding a sharp axe in his hands, stood by to strike the cow dead. Perseus held the bowl for the blood. Old Nestor, the driver of chariots, began the sacred rites of hand washing and the sprinkling of barley-meal, and he prayed to Athena at length, casting some hairs from the victim's head into the fire. Then, when they had prayed and scattered forth the barley grain, Thrasymedes, the high-spirited son of Nestor, came near and struck the blow. The axe cut the tendons of the neck and loosed the strength of the cow, and the daughters and the wives of the sons and the revered wife of Nestor, Eurydice, the eldest of the daughters of Clymenus, raised a shrill cry. Then the men raised the cow from the wide-wayed earth and held it, and Peisistratus, leader of men, cut its throat. And when the dark blood flowed out and its life left its bones, quickly they cut up the body, and cut out the thigh pieces according to the proper procedure, and covered them with a double layer of fat, and upon them they placed pieces of uncooked meat. The old man burned them on splints of wood, and poured sparkling wine on them, and beside him the young men held five-pronged spits in their hands. But when the thighs had burned up and they had tasted the intestines, they cut up the rest into smaller pieces, placed it on spits and held the pointed spits in their hands and roasted them …

When they had roasted the outer flesh and had taken it off from the spits, they sat down and feasted. Worthy men waited on them, pouring wine into cups made of gold.

Among the Romans, an especially important form of sacrifice was the *suovetau-rilia*, the sacrifice of a pig (*sus*), sheep (*ovis*), and bull (*taurus*) at the conclusion of a lustration (*lustratio*), a ceremony of purification and of averting evil. In its public aspect, the ceremony denoted a new beginning and thus was commonly enacted at the time of a census of the Roman people; in a military context, upon the arrival of a new commander; or when two armies were joined together. In this passage the Arval Brothers (*fratres arvales*), a priestly college in Rome whose main ritual obligation was the festival of the goddess Dea Dia, offer such a sacrifice, when work to repair lightning damage in the grove sacred to the goddess required that several trees be uprooted and destroyed. Consisting of 12 members chosen from senatorial families, the Arval Brothers were known for their lavish feasting in support of this goddess and the imperial family.

4.5. *Corpus Inscriptionum Latinarum (CIL) 6.2107.2 = Inscriptiones Latinae Selectae (ILS) 5048*

Seven days before the Ides of November (November 7), the Arval Brothers gathered in the grove of Dea Dia on the Campanian Way (*via Campana*) at the fifth milestone at the direction of the master, Caius Porcius Priscus. And they performed there a sacrifice because some trees in a grove sacred to Dea Dia were struck by lightning and burned in a powerful storm; and in expiation for removing those trees, striking them with iron and burning them up in a fire, for grinding up their remains and also for replacing them with other trees, and for initiating the task and rebuilding altars sacred to Dea Dia for the occasion— in expiation for these things a purificatory sacrifice was performed with the offering of a full-grown pig, ram and bull …

In the next passage Pausanias provides a vivid account of a rare sacrifice involving domesticated and wild animals along with game birds in the annual rites at Patrai, a chief port of western Greece, in honor of Artemis, goddess of the hunt. The final excerpt, more genial in tone, is an ode written by Horace, who has pledged a sacrificial goat to celebrate the anniversary of his narrow escape from a falling tree.

4.6. Pausanias, 7.18.12–13

In this case the sacrifice is offered on the following day, and the festival is no less a state function than quite a popular holiday. For the people throw upon the altar living birds and provisions and all kinds of slaughtered animals as well, and there are wild boars, deer and gazelles; some bring wolf cubs and bear cubs, others the full-grown beasts. They also place the fruit of cultivated trees upon the altar. After this, they set fire to the wood. At that time I have seen a bear and some of the beasts forcing their way outside at the first raging of the fire, some of them actually escaping by their strength. But those who threw them in drag them back to the pyre once again. There is no recollection that the beasts ever wounded anyone.

4.7. Horace, *Odes* 3.8.1–16

What am I, an unmarried man, doing on the first day of March, what do the flowers mean, the casket full of incense, and the ashes laid on newly-cut turf— at this you marvel, you learned in the lore of either language? I had vowed to Liber[1] a delightful feast and a pure white goat when I was nearly done to death by a falling tree. This festal day, each time the year revolves, will draw forth a well-pitched cork from a jar set to drink the smoke in Tullus' consulship.[2] Maecaenas, drink up 100 cyathi[3] for your uninjured friend, and keep the lamps lit until dawn: keep at a distance every loud shout and cause for anger.

Of course, not everybody in the Graeco-Roman world agreed with animal sacrifice. Such opposition was part a much larger debate on the proper attitude towards animals, an argument that extended from the Pre-Socratic philosophers of the sixth century BCE to Aristotle (who famously did not attribute reason and belief to animals) and beyond. The most well known opponent was Pythagoras, who founded a sect or society that bore his name during the sixth century BCE in southern Italy. One of the most influential but mysterious intellectual figures of antiquity, Pythagoras argued against animal sacrifice, based in part on his belief in the transmigration of the soul (metempsychosis). This doctrine, which made mankind literally akin to animals, helped to advance his argument for vegetarianism as the best way to live one's life. This belief was among those preserved by later writers, especially the prominent Neoplatonist philosopher Porphyry, a scholar and student of religions who lived in the third century CE. In fact, Porphyry is the author of the most important work in defense of animals, *On Abstinence from Animal Food*, in four books. The work forbids meat on ascetic grounds, rejects animal sacrifice, and makes a claim for rationality and justice for animals. A final book offers an anthropology of vegetarian nations. This excerpt, taken from his second book, argues that simple offerings of fruits of the earth are just as pleasing to the gods as costly animal sacrifices.

4.8. Porphyry, *On Abstinence from Animal Food* 2.13–15 (trans. Taylor)

13. Someone, however, perhaps may say, that we also take away something from plants [when we eat, and sacrifice them to the gods]. But the ablation is not similar, since we do not take this away from those who are unwilling that we should. For, if we omitted to gather them, they would spontaneously drop their fruits. The gathering of the fruits, also, is not attended with the destruction of the plants, as it is when animals lose their animating principle. And, with respect to the fruit which we receive from bees, since this is obtained by our labour, it is fit that we should derive a common benefit from it. For bees collect their honey from plants; but we carefully attend to them. On which account is it requisite that such a division should be made [of our attention and their labour] that they may suffer no injury. But that which is useless to them, and beneficial to us, will be the reward we receive from them [of our attention to their concerns]. In sacrifices, therefore, we should abstain from animals. For, although all things are in reality the property of the gods, yet plants appear to be our property, since we sow and cultivate them, and nourish them by other attentions which we pay to them. We ought to sacrifice, therefore, from our own property, and not from the property of others, since that which may be procured at a small expense, and which may easily be obtained, is more holy, more acceptable to the gods, and better adapted to the purposes of sacrifice, and to the exercise of continual piety. Hence, that which is neither holy, nor to be obtained at a small expense, is not to be offered in sacrifice, even though it should be present.

14. But that animals do not rank among things that may be procured easily, and at a small expense, may be seen by directing our view to the greater part of our race: for we are not now to consider that some men abound in sheep, and others in oxen. In the first place, therefore, there are many nations that do not possess any of those animals which are offered in sacrifice, some ignoble animals, perhaps, excepted. And, in the second place, most of those that dwell in cities themselves, possess these but rarely. But if someone should say that the inhabitants of cities have not mild fruits in abundance; yet, though this should be admitted, they are not in want of the other vegetable productions of the earth; nor is it so difficult to procure fruits as it is to procure animals. Hence an abundance of fruits, and other vegetables, is more easily obtained than that of animals. But that which is obtained with facility, and at a small expense, contributes to incessant and universal deity.

15. Experience also testifies that the gods rejoice in this more than in sumptuous offerings. For when that Thessalian sacrificed to the Pythian deity oxen with gilt horns, and hecatombs, Apollo said that the offering of Hermioneus was more gratifying to him, though he had only sacrificed as much meal as he could take with his three fingers out of a sack. But when the Thessalian, on hearing this, placed all the rest of his offerings on the altar, the god again said that by doing so, his present was doubly more unacceptable to him than his former offering. Hence the sacrifice which is attended with a small expense is pleasing to the gods, and divinity looks more to the disposition and manners of those who sacrifice than to the multitude of things which are sacrificed.

Bloodless sacrifice

Not every offering involved slaughtered animals. The ancients sacrificed a wide range of additional items, including breads, fruits, vegetables, cakes, and various spices. Not surprisingly, much sacrifice of this kind occurred in the home, as in the following excerpt, where an ancient commentator (scholiast) on a passage from the *Wealth*, a comedy written by Aristophanes, notes the simple ceremony that marked the acceptance of a new person into the Greek household. In addition to what it tells us about food offerings, the passage reminds us that ritual religion and slavery could co-exist quite easily in antiquity.

4.9. Scholiast on Aristophanes, *Wealth* 768 = Rice and Stambaugh, 144

> In the instance of newly purchased slaves, when they enter the house for the first time, or in general any persons concerning whom they wish to have favorable omens—a newlywed, for example—it was customary to scatter sweetmeats at the hearth as a symbol of good seasons. These "showers" consisted of dates, sweet cakes, candied fruits, figs, and nuts, which the other slaves would scoop up.

Bloodless sacrifice displayed a public dimension as well, evident in the autumn festival of the Pyanopsia, whose central rite was an offering to Apollo, of a potpourri of boiled pulses. The Greeks connected this feast to Theseus, who, when driven ashore at Delos while on his Cretan expedition, vowed a thank offering to Apollo if he slew the Minotaur. The potpourri nature of the offering may be connected to Theseus' comrades, who, upon landing in Attica, gathered up the leftovers from their provisions and made them into a meal. Plutarch's biography of Theseus provides the account.

4.10. Plutarch, *Theseus* 22.4–5

> After he buried his father, Theseus made his vows to Apollo on the seventh day of the month Panepsion, for on that day they had safely returned to the city. The boiling of different kinds of pulses is said to have come about because the young men whom Theseus had rescued mixed together their leftover provisions, boiled them in a single pot, and ate the whole mixture among themselves. They also carry the "eiresione," the branch of an olive tree wreathed with wool, just as Theseus had carried at one time as a suppliant when he was weighed down with first fruits of every kind to signify the end of the time of scarcity, and they sing as they go:
>
> > "Eiresione brings figs and the finest bread for us, brings us honey in a pot, and oil to rub off from our bodies and a beaker of unmixed wine so that one may sleep sweetly."
>
> Some say, however, that these ceremonies are enacted in memory of the sons of Heracles,[4] who were continuously supported in this way by the Athenians, but most report the matter as I have done.

Certain sects also embraced bloodless sacrifice as a way to distinguish themselves from the meat-eaters of animal sacrifice. As mentioned earlier, one such group were Pythagoreans, some of whom were committed vegetarians, while others embraced a compromise position by consuming offerings such as goats and pigs but not cattle. Another group, the followers of Orpheus, maintained a strict diet of honey and cereals, the same foods they sacrificed to the gods. We must also include in this category the followers of Isis, an Egyptian goddess who was very popular in the Roman world and whose favor could only be secured through participation in an elaborate set of rituals by those who wished to worship her (Beard et al.). We witness this in the following excerpt from the *Metamorphoses* by Apuleius, where Lucius, the main character of the novel, has been turned into an ass and must abstain from meat and wine for a prescribed period of time as part of an initiation process, through which he hopes that the goddess will restore him to human form. The excerpt is equally interesting for the light it sheds on the fervency of belief that linked devotee to deity in some cults.

4.11. Apuleius, *Metamorphoses* 11.23

… Then, as the priest said, since the occasion demanded it, he escorted me, surrounded by a cohort of devotees, to the adjacent baths. After I had bathed in the usual manner, he invoked the gods for forgiveness and cleansed me with a sprinkling of very pure water. With two-thirds of the day already having passed, he led me back to the temple again and set me before the very feet of the goddess, gave me in secret certain instructions not be spoken aloud, and amid all the witnesses openly ordered this: that I abstain for the next ten days from dietary pleasures, that I not eat any meat or drink wine. Once I had duly observed these restrictions with venerable self-control, the day designated for my divine appointment now arrived, as the Sun on its downward curve led on the evening. Then, behold, crowds of initiates flowed together in accordance with the ancient practice of the mysteries, each person honoring me with different gifts. Next, after all the uninitiated had been sent away, the priest clad me in a primitive linen robe, took me by the hand and led me to the heart of the sanctuary itself.

Offerings of wine

Wine, too, commemorated any number of events or activities, including meals, arrivals and departures, the beginning and ending of the day, and truces and treaties. The first passage records the days of violets and roses, named after the flowers presumably left at the gravesite as part of the Roman ceremony to commemorate the dead. Here, wine was typically poured at the grave in order to provide sustenance for the deceased and to maintain the relationship between the living and the dead. On other occasions, water or milk and honey were used instead. In this instance wine is actually distributed as a gift to members of the college of Aesculapius and Hygia, a funerary club in Rome, whose calendar confirms this activity as an annual rite (see 5.57).

4.12. *Corpus Inscriptionum Latinarum (CIL)* 6.10234

> And also on March 22, the day of violets, let a handout be distributed with wine and bread in the same location for the attendees, as written for the days above. Also on May 11, the day of roses, let a handout be distributed with wine and bread in the same location for the attendees as written for the days above on this condition, decreed by all in assembly, that on the days written above, the distribution of bread and wine for those not in attendance be delivered and divided among the attendees.

In this excerpt, Thucydides records the libation made at the start of a military campaign, in this case the ill-fated Athenian expedition to Sicily in 415 BCE during the Peloponnesian War.

4.13. Thucydides, 6.32.1–2

> When the ships were manned and everything that they planned to take with them on the voyage had been put aboard, the sound of the trumpet signaled silence, and they offered up the customary prayers made before putting out to sea, not by each ship separately, but by all of them together, following the words of a herald. The whole army had wine mixed in bowls, and officers and sailors made their libations from gold and silver cups. And the rest of the crowd on the shore, the citizens and others who wished the expedition well, joined together in the prayers. Then, when the hymn had been sung and the libations finished, they put out to sea, first sailing out in a single column and then competing with each other as far as Aegina.

Questionable motives

To be sure, the celebration of a particular ritual or ceremony was not by itself a guarantee that the participants would always display religious scruples. In fact, the greedy celebrant was a stock character type in ancient comedy. Menander confirms this in his *Dyskolos*, as in the character of Knemon, who, while clearly exaggerating in the next passage, nevertheless provides enough truth to make his audience think more critically about the nature of religious observance. Epicharmus of Cos, a fifth-century BCE comic dramatist who is preserved only in fragments as cited by Athenaeus, provides a similar view in the second excerpt. No less did such character types escape the notice of philosophical authors such as Theophrastus, who were concerned at this time with assessing human character and the problem of extravagance in Greek society, as confirmed in the final passage. At the same time, these accounts underscore a simple but important truth—that a sacrifice meant a meal, no matter how one acquired it or what one's view might be concerning religion and belief.

4.14. Menander, *Dyskolos* 447–53

Knemon: How these thieves perform! They bring their picnic baskets, their wine jars, not for the gods but for themselves. The incense and sacrificial cake is sufficiently holy. The god takes all of that, placed upon the fire; and they lay on the tailbone and the bile, since they are inedible for the gods—then they gulp down all the rest.

4.15. Athenaeus, *Sophists at Dinner* 2.36d

(A.) A sacrifice leads to a banquet, and a banquet leads to drinking. (B.) That sounds fine to me, at least! (A.) But drinking leads to drunken carousing, and drunken carousing leads to piggish behavior, and piggish behavior leads to a lawsuit, <and a lawsuit leads to being found guilty,>* and being found guilty leads to shackles, stocks, and a fine.

4.16. Theophrastus, *Characters* 9

The sponger is the sort of person who, in the first place, goes back to a man whom he has defrauded and asks for a loan; then, after performing a sacrifice to the gods, once he salts the meat and stores it away, he goes to dinner at another man's house; he invites his slave along as well, and gives him meat and bread taken from the table and says to everyone as they listen, "Enjoy yourself, Tibeios."[5]

Festal calendars and festivals of Greece

In many cities of the Graeco-Roman world, major religious festivals at which food and drink played a prominent role were listed on official calendars, which

---

* Addition to text made by a commentator.

were either inscribed in stone or painted on walls in a public place for all to see. These calendars, combined with literary and other evidence, are important sources for religious feasts and festivals in the ancient city. Major festivals fell under the control of religious elites, such as the *pontifices*, one of the colleges of priests in Rome. At the same time, we also possess calendars of smaller groups, such as those associated with various demes in Attic Greece or of associations, known as *collegia*. In general, such evidence reveals the diversity and complexity of ancient civic and religious life and the centrality of food and drink in these settings.

Among the ancient Greeks there was no single calendar, but most communities developed their own, which might differ from others in the names of the months and the date of the New Year. Best known is the Athenian calendar, which dates to the time of Solon, the great lawgiver in Athens of the sixth-century BCE. Although modified over time and surviving only in fragmentary form, a full calendar can be reconstructed by combining these remains with information from other sources. The Athenians enjoyed as many as 120 festival days each year, the most of any city-state. The Athenian year began in mid-summer, in theory with the appearance of the first new moon after the summer solstice. The 12 lunar months were named after various festivals or divinities, with Athena, patroness of the city, and Demeter, goddess of the crops, receiving special attention (Bruit Zaidman and Schmitt Pantel).

Especially noteworthy is the Panathenaea, the greatest festival of Athenian religious life, which celebrated annually the birthday of Athena during the month of Hekatombaion (July/August). The actual source, in this case an inscription, provides information on regulating the distribution and purchase of sacrificial victims for the attendees. Note especially that portion size was determined by social rank and that the larger populace also received meat on this occasion.

4.17. *Inscriptiones Graecae (IG)* II.2.334 = *Sylloge Inscriptionum Graecarum (SIG)* 3.271 = **Rice and Stambaugh 119**

...when the *hieropoioi*[6] make the sacrifices, they are to distribute the portions of meat from two of them, that to Athena Hygieia[7] and that in the old temple, performed in the traditional way, in the following proportions: five shares to the *prytaneis*,[8] three to the nine *archons*, one to the treasurers of the goddess, one to the *hieropoioi*, three to the board of generals and division-commanders, and the usual shares to the Athenians who participate in the procession and the maidens who act as *kanephoroi*;[9] the meat from the other sacrifices they are to distribute to the Athenians. From the 41 minas which represents the rent on the sacred land, the *hieropoioi*, along with the cattle-buyers, are to buy the sacrificial cattle; when they have conducted the procession, they are to sacrifice all of these cattle to the goddess on the great altar of Athena, except for one which they are to choose ahead of time from the finest of the cattle and sacrifice on the altar of Nike; all the rest of the cattle bought with the 41 minas they are to sacrifice to Athena Polias[10] and Athena Nike[11] and distribute the meat to the Athenian people in the Kerameikos[12] in the same fashion as in the other distributions of meat. They are to assign the portions to each deme [residential district] in proportion to the number of participants in the procession from each deme...

While sacrifice was integral to the life of the ancient community, such festivals were by no means exclusive to Athens. Athenaeus' description of the Hyacinthia, a three-day feast celebrated by the Spartans each summer in honor of Hyacinthus, a mythological figure beloved by Apollo but killed by the jealous suitor Zephyrus, captures much of the joy and pageantry of the public sacrifice as well as the welcome distribution of meat to all the people, even slaves.

4.18. Athenaeus, *Sophists at Dinner* 4.139e–f

But on the middle of the third day there is an elaborate show and a large assembly for a festival that is worthy of mention ... numerous choruses of young men come in and sing some of their native poems ... some of the unmarried girls are carried in lavishly ornamented carriages fitted with wickerwork, while others process on two-horse racing chariots; and the whole city is in a state of movement and of pleasure for the festival. On this day they also sacrifice a large number of animals, and the citizens offer dinner to everyone they know, as well as to their own slaves. No one misses the sacrifice, and the city empties out to see the show.

Even more illuminating is part of a calendar from Kos, an island located in the southeastern Aegean Sea. Dated to the mid-fourth century BCE, the calendar preserves detailed instructions for performing a festival for Zeus Polieus (Zeus, Protector of the City) on the nineteenth and twentieth days of the month Batromius (perhaps equivalent to January). It is from the latter date that the excerpt reprised here is taken. In addition to the detailed instructions regarding the foods and how they are to be apportioned, note the large number of officials involved in a festival of this importance. The number includes *hieropoioi*, who helped to slaughter the animals; heralds, who likely held some sort of hereditary or semi-professional position that allowed them to make pronouncements on sacred matters; the shawm, or flute player, who was required at most sacrifices; incense-burners, who were a normal part of the sacrificial scheme; and the Nestoridai, presumably a hereditary group who played some special role. Less clear is the role of the physicians, bronze-smiths, and potters. This inscription is especially valuable for preserving the sense of pomp and ritual that characterized a city wide festival of this sort (Kearns).

4.19. *Lois sacrées des cités grecques (LSCG)* 151 = Rhodes-Osborne 62 = Kearns 5.3.2

> On the twentieth: the chosen ox is sacrificed to Zeus Polieus. The parts to be wrapped in the skin are wrapped. Half a *hekteus*[13] of barley is sacrificed at the hearth along with two loaves of half a *hekteus*, one in the shape of a cheese, and the parts in skin. Portions of the ox for the priest are the skin and a leg (the priest provides the offerings), half the breast and half the belly. The incense-bearer is given the hip end of the leg belonging to the *hieropoioi*.[14] For the heralds, a double portion of back meat, the parts under the shoulders, and a three-legged spit of blood parts. For the Nestoridai, a double portion of [back meat?], for the physicians, meat, for the shawm-player, meat, and to each of the bronze-smiths and the potters, (meat from) the head. The rest of the meat belongs to the city. None of these is taken outside the city.

Festal calendars and festivals of Italy

As with the Greeks, the Romans utilized public calendars to record the dates of religious festivals, market days and days when the law courts and public assemblies could meet. The calendar below, from Antium outside of Rome, is a fully restored version of the month of April. It dates to the first century BCE. The first column indicates the modern days of the month (note that there are only 29 days according to the Roman reckoning). In the second column the sequence of letters (A–H) mark eight-day periods with a market day on the ninth. This recurring cycle of letters continued to run throughout the year without a break at the end of a month. The letters in the third column indicate the (notional) lunar phases of the month: K (Kalends) on the first (new moon); NON (Nones) on the fifth or seventh (first quarter); EIDUS (Ides) on the thirteenth or fifteenth (full moon). The Romans calculated dates by counting backwards and inclusively from these three points: for example, April 10 = 4 days before the Ides of April. The remaining letters in the third column indicate whether or not public business could be conducted on a particular day: F (*fastus*) designates days when the law courts were open; C (*comitialis*) indicates days when public assemblies or law courts could meet; N (*nefastus*) indicates when no assembly or court could meet. NP (of uncertain meaning but possibly *nefastus publicus*) designated no court or assembly meetings, and usually indicated notable public festivals (Beard et al.). As the accompanying notes indicate, the month of April included several feasts, one of which, the Parilia, is considered in more detail below.

4.20. Calendar from Antium, Italy (Beard, North and Price [1998] II.3a, 63–64)

Aprilis

1.	A	[K<alends of> AP]R<IL>. F
2.	B	F
3.	C	C
4.	D	C
5.	E	NON. N. To Public Fortune[15]
6.	F	N
7.	[G]	N
8.	[H	N]
9.	A	[N]
10	B	N
11.	C	N. To Great Idaean Mother of the Gods[16]
12.	D	N
13.	E	EIDUS. NP. To Jupiter Victor
		to Jupiter Libertas[17]
14.	F	N
15.	G	FORDI<CIDIA>. NP[18]

16.	H	N
17.	A	N
18.	B	N
19.	C	CERIA<LIA>, N[P].To Ceres, Liber, Libera[19]
20.	D	N
21.	E	PARIL<IA>, N[P].[20] Rome founded
22.	F	N
23.	G	VINAL<IA>. To Venus Erucina[21]
24.	H	C
25.	A	ROBIG<ALIA>. NP[22]
26.	[B]	C
27.	[C	C]
28.	D	C
29.	E	C

The Parilia, the Roman festival of the god or goddess Pales, was celebrated on April 21 and originally seems to have been a rural festival associated with the flocks and herds of the Roman community. The Augustan poet Ovid distinguished between a rural and urban Parilia and connected the festival with the founding of Rome and the city's sacred boundary, the *pomerium* (Beard et al.). By the first century BCE, the Parilia was also identified as the birthday of the city of Rome, acquiring the alternative title "Romaia" by the second century CE. There is also testimony to suggest that the Parilia was a festive occasion in the community, as recorded by Propertius, another Augustan-era poet.

4.21. Propertius, 4.4.73–80

It was the festival of the Ploughtail (the Fathers called it the Parilia); this was the birthday of Rome's walls, the annual banquet of the shepherds, a time of revelry in the city, when village dishes flow rich with plenty and the drunken crowd kicks high its filthy feet over scattered heaps of burning hay. Romulus decreed that the guardsmen should relax at their ease and that the camp be silent, with the call of the trumpet suspended.

Beyond the calendar of Antium, three additional public festivals at Rome help us to appreciate the centrality of food and drink in widely divergent contexts. This passage records the Saturnalia, a festival that involved the exchange of gifts every December 17. In its public aspect the festival involved a sacrifice and banquet at the temple of Saturn; at the same time, private parties, which might last for several days, allowed additional opportunities for feasting and for exchanging gifts (Beard et al.). The Saturnalia was especially popular during the time of the later Roman Empire and eventually was incorporated into the Christian celebrations of Christmas and New Year. In the following passage Macrobius reveals that social inversion at the dining table was an important part of this festival, as slaves were served dinner before their masters. Some ancient sources even suggest that the masters themselves waited on their slaves at this dinner.

4.22. Macrobius, *Saturnalia* 1.24.22–3

Amid these remarks, the head slave, whose responsibility it was to burn incense before the Penates,[23] to maintain the provisions, and to oversee the activities of the domestic servants, informed his master that the slaves had feasted according to the annual ritual custom. For at this festival, religiously observant households first of all honor the slaves with a dinner prepared as if for the enjoyment of the master; and only after they have finished is the table reset for the heads of the household. So, then, the head slave entered to announce the time of dinner and to call the masters to table.

The *ludi Romani* (Roman Games) was originally a single-day celebration in honor of Jupiter Optimus Maximus (Jupiter, the Best, the Greatest), whose temple on the Capitol in Rome was dedicated in 509 BCE. By the time of the emperor Augustus, the *ludi Romani* extended for more than half the month of September and included horse and chariot racing, theatrical shows, and, as we see in this passage, animal sacrifice that would have produced meat for consumption. Such *ludi* became an important feature of Roman religious ritual—and increasingly popular, as attested by the more than 60 days devoted to such games on the Roman calendar by the first century CE. This account belongs to Dionysius of Halicarnassus, a Greek historian and literary critic during the time of Augustus, who was especially interested in the influence of Greece upon such Roman traditions.

4.23. Dionysius of Halicarnassus, *Roman Antiquities* 7.72.15–16

After the procession concluded, the consuls and the priests whose function it was immediately sacrificed oxen, and the mode of conducting the sacrifice was the same as ours (i.e., the Greeks). After washing their hands, they purified the victims with clear water and sprinkled grain on their heads; after this, they prayed and then bid their assistants to sacrifice them. Some of these assistants struck the still standing victim on the temple with a club, and others received it upon the sacrificial knives as it fell. And after this they skinned the ox and cut it up, taking off a piece from each of the viscera and also from every limb as a first-offering, which they sprinkled with grits of spelt and carried to the officiating priests in baskets. These placed them on the altars, made a fire beneath them, and poured wine over them as they burned. It is easy to see from the poetry of Homer that each of these ceremonies was performed according to the customs established by the Greeks with reference to sacrifices.

A final piece of testimony underscores the connection between food and political identity in a religious context. The Fornacalia, or Feast of the Ovens, was a winter celebration named after the bake houses (*fornaces*), where a sacrifice used to be made among the *curiae*, groups of families that provided the basis for the early political and military organization within Rome (Scullard). These *curiae*, originally 30 in number, had their own banqueting halls where the celebration took place. In an interesting twist, anyone who did not know his own *curia* or forgot to attend the meeting could make up the sacrifice on an alternate date at a general assembly of all 30 *curiae*. Dionysius witnessed this celebration and likens the Romans' *curia* to the Spartan mess hall and its simple meals.

4.24. Dionysius of Halicarnassus, *Roman Antiquities* 2.23.2–5

Together with their own priests the members of each *curia* performed their appointed sacrifices, and on holy days they feasted at their own table. For a banqueting hall had been built for each *curia*, and in it a common table for all members of the *curia* was consecrated, just as in the Greek *prytanea*.[24] These banqueting halls had the same name as the *curia* themselves, and are still called by the same name in our own times. It seems to me that Romulus took over this institution from the practice of the Spartans in the case of their *phiditia*,[25] which were in vogue at that time … At any rate, I myself have seen in the sacred buildings meals set before the gods upon ancient wooden tables, in baskets and modest earthen plates, consisting of barley bread, cakes and spelt, with the first offerings of some fruits, and other things of a similar kind, simple, inexpensive, and lacking all vulgar display.

Feasting and calendars among select groups

Festal calendars were also kept by *collegia*, associations in the Roman world that were most commonly comprised of citizens of the same occupation (see Chapter 5, nos. 57, 58). In ancient Greece, *orgeones*, here translated as "worshippers," were apparently hereditary groups of citizens devoted to the cult of a hero and/or heroine, and on whose behalf they feasted in a shrine, which they owned for that purpose. This decree is part of a third century BCE inscription found at the Areopagus, a hill where judicial proceedings took place in Athens. The surrounding text, however, describes this inscription as "ancient," and so it likely dates to the fifth century BCE. Note that the "worshippers" were adult males but family members, including women, were allowed to share in the sacrificial meats. The final line records a man receiving a woman's portion (presumably a smaller share than that typically enjoyed by a man), a practice that was not common—and perhaps the reason for its inclusion in the text.

4.25. *Lois sacrées: Supplément (LSS) 20.12–23*

Decreed by the worshippers. The host is to perform the sacrifice on the seventeenth and eighteenth of Hekatombaion.[26] He is to sacrifice on the first day to the heroines a young pig; and for the hero [he is to sacrifice] an adult victim and set a table. And on the next day [he is to sacrifice] to the hero an adult victim. And he is to record whatever he spends. And he is to spend no more than the income. And let him distribute the meats to the worshippers who are present, and to their sons up to one half [viz. a worshipper's share] and to the women of the worshippers, giving to the free ones the equivalent share and to their daughters up to one half and to one (female) attendant up to one half. And he is to hand over to the man the share of the woman.

Feasts at sanctuaries, shrines, and as thank-offerings

Not all eating and drinking events were connected with large urban festivals, major divinities, or specialized groups. Simple shrines and sanctuaries throughout the Mediterranean world attest to the ubiquity of celebration and sacrifice in any number of settings. In the following passage the Greek historian and Spartan sympathizer Xenophon describes in vivid detail the nature and operation of a rural Greek shrine located on his property. Especially interesting is the emphasis on the fertility of the site and the camaraderie shared by family members and locals on festal occasions.

4.26. Xenophon, *Anabasis* 5.3.8–13

It so happened that flowing through the grounds was a river named Selinus; and at Ephesus too a Selinus river flows past the temple of Artemis. In both streams were fish and mussels; in the plot of land at Scillus may be found many wild animals to be hunted. Here Xenophon built an altar and a temple from the sacred money, and afterwards he would take ten percent of the crops and offer sacrifice to the goddess with it. All the citizens and the men and women in the neighborhood shared in the festivities. The goddess provided barley meal, bread, wine, and dried fruit for the worshipper and a portion of the sacrificial victims from the sacred land and a portion of the animals seized in the hunt. For Xenophon's sons and the sons of other citizens used to hold a hunt during the festival time, and men who wished to do so would join in. They captured some animals in the sacred precinct and some on Mount Pholöe, wild boars and gazelles and deer.

The place is located on the road from Sparta to Olympia and is about 20 stades from the temple of Zeus in Olympia. Within the sacred precinct there is a meadow and hills covered with trees suitable for raising pigs, goats, cattle, and horses, so that even the beasts of burden belonging to those who attend the festival may be well fed. Around the temple itself is a grove of cultivated trees, which produce all kinds of dessert fruit in season …

The cult of Bacchus, the Greek god Dionysius, spread from southern Italy to Etruria and Rome in the second century BCE. This development provoked deep concern in the senate because of the orgiastic nature of the rituals, which might include shouting, singing, frenzied dancing, drinking, and sexual license. The passage below is a portion of the text of a senatorial decree against the cult as preserved on an inscribed bronze tablet discovered in south Italy. Addressed to towns of Italy that were still independent of Rome at this time, the decree did not ban the cult but it did strictly regulate its activities by ordering a search for Bacchic priests in both Rome and Italy, prohibiting initiates to gather for rites, and instructing investigators to seek out criminals and performers of immoral acts. Other provisions called for the destruction of shrines, forbade the mixing of men and women on ritual occasions, prohibited men from being priests, and banned secret rites and the swearing of oaths.

4.27. Final Decree of the Senate on the Cult of Bacchus, *Corpus Inscriptionum Latinarum (CIL)* 10.104=*Inscriptiones Latinae Selectae (ILS)* 18

(3–6) None of them shall seek to have a Bacchic shrine. But if there are some who say that it is necessary for them to have a Bacchic shrine, they should come before the urban praetor in Rome, and when it has heard their case, our senate should pass a decree on this matter …

(10–17) No one shall be a priest. No man or any woman shall be a master. None of them shall seek to have money in common. No one shall seek to appoint either a man or woman as master or acting master, or seek hereafter to exchange mutual oaths, vows, pledges, or promises. No one shall seek to perform rites in secret nor shall anyone seek to perform rites in public or private or outside the city, unless he has approached the urban praetor and is given permission by a senatorial decree …

(19–21) No one shall seek to perform rites when more than five men and women are gathered together, nor shall more than two men or more than three women seek to be present there, except by permission of the urban praetor and the senate as written above.

Rites of passage

In the Graeco-Roman world the transition from one life status to another, as found in birth, coming of age, marriage, and death, often combined a religious emphasis with eating and drinking. The reasons for marking these occasions with food and drink are not entirely clear, although they may have something to do with the fundamental change in economic and social relationships that each change provoked, since each involved a transition from one life status to another. Indeed, one need look no further than the modern wedding reception or the Irish wake among a host of other potential ceremonies and rites to observe the cultural persistence of this phenomenon in the present day (Donahue).

At the same time, we should not view these rites as simply the manifestations of "family" or "popular" religion. The former term does not fit with
ceremonies that often displayed a community as well as a family component,
while the latter designation is not only vague but also corresponds poorly
with Graeco-Roman notions of religion (Bruit Zaidman and Schmitt Pantel).
Instead, we are better served by thinking of these transitions in the anthro-
pological context of "rites of passage." As we shall see, this is perhaps the best
way to make sense of rituals and beliefs that sometimes seem quite alien to
modern sensibilities. Equally important, it also removes the temptation of
bringing modern religious beliefs to bear on the ancient evidence. Finally,
much work has been done on these aspects of the family in recent years.
For additional perspectives, readers are encouraged to consult the works of
Cohen and Rutter, Rawson (2003, 2011), Evans-Grubbs, and Hope, as listed
at the end of this chapter.

Birth rites and birthdays

The birth of a child had a profound impact on the ancient family and so it is not
surprising to find that both the Greeks and Romans relied upon specific rituals
and ceremonies in order to integrate the newborn into the household. While
these rites are well known, we are less well informed about the role of eating
and drinking to celebrate this occasion. We do know that in the Greek world a
sacrifice was held on the tenth day after the birth and that this was followed by a
banquet to which all members of the family were invited. On the other hand, the
evidence is more forthcoming for the birthdays of those who survived beyond
childhood. In the case of imperial birthdays, feasting was widespread. Augustus
is known to have provided banquets and entertainment on his birthday at Rome,
and members of the imperial family also enjoyed this honor, as in the case
of the emperor Caligula, who marked the birthday of his concubine Drusilla
with a banquet for senators and equites, the social class immediately below
that of senators. Among the literary sources, the first passage from the Latin
poet Propertius vows to celebrate the birthday of his beloved Cynthia. The text
captures the deep emotions typical of elegiac poetry but is also noteworthy for
its promise of a lavish birthday celebration. Alciphron (see 2.28) makes similar
promises of drinking and revelry in one of his letters to a fictitious farmer.
The *cordax* he mentions in this passage was a lascivious dance well known in
antiquity.

4.28. Propertius, 3.10.19–32

Then, when you have consecrated the garlanded altars with incense and an auspicious flame glows throughout the house, let us think about the table, and let the night hasten by amid our drinking, and the jar of perfume anoint our nostrils with the fragrance of saffron. Let the horse-throated pipe grow weary with all-night dancing, and the language of your naughtiness show no restraint, and let sweet celebrations remove unwelcome sleep; let the public air of the nearby street reverberate with noise; let us play at fortunes with a toss of the dice to reveal for whom the boyish Cupid beats harder with his wings.

When the hour has been spent in much drinking, and Venus will make ready the sacred ceremonies of the night, let us perform anniversary rites on our bed and thus complete the course of your birthday.

4.29. Alciphron, *Letters of Farmers* 2.15

Eustachys to Pithacnion

I am celebrating the birthday of my son, and I invite you to our big celebration, oh Pithacnion; and not you alone, but bring your wife and children and your hired man; yes, and if you like, your dog too, for she is a good watchdog and she frightens off those who have designs on the flocks by her loud barking. A dog like that would be a welcome participant in our feast. We are going to have a very pleasant party; we shall drink until we are drunk, and after our fill, we shall sing; and whoever is able to dance the *cordax* will step into the midst and entertain the crowd. So then, my dear friend, don't be late. For it is a good idea at parties to get the drinking bout started first thing in the morning.

For Christians, the sacrament of baptism, signifying a second birth through initiation in the faith, provided yet another occasion for celebration. In this passage the Christian poet, writer, and bishop Gaius Apollinaris Sidonius (see 5.52) requests that a friend prepare a lavish banquet to celebrate the consecration of a baptistery. This excerpt is also useful as an example of Sidonius' interest in pleasure and comfortable living, pursuits that were not incompatible with the conduct and lifestyle of a bishop in fifth-century Gaul.

4.30. Sidonius, *Letters* 4.15

Sidonius to his friend Elaphius, greetings

Prepare a feast of many courses and a very large spread of couches; the people are coming to you by multiple routes and in very large crowds (thus the brotherhood of your close friends has resolved), indeed now that the time of the coming dedication has been published for all. For you write that the baptistery, which you have been constructing for a long time, can now be consecrated. You are invited to this feast because of your vow, I because of my episcopal post, many because of the claims of duty, and everybody because of the faith that they hold.

Coming of age

At the Apatouria, a three-day festival held in October/November, an Athenian father would present his son, less than a year old, to the phratry to which he belonged. The phratry was a religious and political organization of several households, which served as an intermediary between the family and the state. At this time the father swore an oath that he and his wife were Athenians, thus ensuring the citizenship of the child. There were no collective rites of this sort for daughters of male citizens, since, unlike sons, they did not become full citizens. Instead, a select few might assume religious positions, such as attendants to a particular deity. This inscription, from the deme of Decelea in Attica in the early fourth century BCE, reveals how carefully the phratry sought to verify the admission of young boys into its ranks. Most interesting for our purposes is mention of the *koureion*, described in later sources as an occasion when the young man cut his hair and offered an animal sacrifice on the third day of the festival to mark his induction into his phratry. The sharing of meat on this occasion thus served the important function of integrating into the wider community a person who was no longer a child but one on the brink of adulthood.

4.31. Rhodes-Osborne 5, side B, lines 108–26

I bear witness that this candidate whom he is introducing is his own legitimate son by a wedded wife. This is the truth, by Zeus Phratrius:[27] if I keep my oaths, may much good befall me, but if I swear falsely, the opposite.

Menexenus proposed:

It should be resolved by the members of the phratry concerning the introduction of the boys on other respects in accordance with the previous decrees. But, in order that the members of the phratry may know those who are going to be introduced, they shall be recorded with the leader of the phratry in the first year after the *koureion* sacrifice, by name, the name of the father, his deme, and by the mother and her father's name and deme; and, when they have been recorded, the leader of the phratry shall display the record wherever the Deceleans congregate, and the priest shall inscribe the record on a white tablet and display it in the sanctuary of Leto.[28] The priest is to inscribe the phratry decree on a stone marker …

The Romans shared a similar interest in the coming of age ceremony. For example, Augustus, the first emperor of Rome, staged a magnificent entertainment and granted the citizens a festival at public expense upon shaving for the first time. On a more modest scale this inscription from the first century CE records a gift of sweet wine and pastries for the people of Surrentum in municipal Italy, as provided by a certain priest of the emperor Tiberius at a ceremony where boys assumed the *toga virilis*, the white toga of manhood at about the age of 15. The inscription, a summary of the donor's benefactions, accompanied a statue erected in his honor by the town council.

4.32. *Corpus Inscriptionum Latinarum (CIL)* 10.688

To Lucius Cornelius M[---], son of Lucius of the Menenia tribe,[29] a priest of Tiberius Caesar Augustus at Rome, an augur,[30] an aedile,[31] a duovir quinquennalis,[32] a two-time superintendent of the local craftsmen, who gave sweet wine and pastries to the people on the day of assuming the toga of manhood …

Marriage

Graeco-Roman marriage was essentially a family affair. The father of the bride or her guardian arranged the marriage with the parents of the groom or even the groom himself, if he was older and already the head of his own household. The transition to married status was significant for both the bride and the groom, although more so for the bride, who left her home and the control of her father for a new home and the control of her husband. Since the family, and not the state, was at the center of ancient marriage, the rituals themselves could be quite diverse in form and might be directed toward any number of deities connected with the families involved. Even so, the goal of marriage remained clear: the production and rearing of legitimate children for the continuation of the family and, by extension, the civic community (Rawson 2011).

While there was room for variation in the marriage ceremony itself, food and drink remained a constant feature and played highly symbolic role. In Athenian custom the father or guardian of the bride held a sacrifice and a banquet at his house on the day of the ceremony at which a young boy handed around bread to the guests in order to recall the Greeks' transition from a life of savagery to one of settled cultivation as symbolized by milled grain. Consistent with this symbolism, the bride was expected to bring a frying pan for cooking barley to the feast, while a child brought a sieve. In the evening, as the bride prepared to enter her new home, the bridegroom's parents offered her sesame and honey cake, and a quince or a date as symbols of fertility. Later, she was showered with nuts and figs as she was led around her new familial hearth, a further symbolic indication of the importance of fertility. On the following day further sacrificing and banqueting occurred and the newlyweds received more gifts. Food and drink thus played a practical role in ancient marriage rites by uniting the families in celebration but also a symbolic function through its emphasis on fertlity as a fundamental aspect of ancient marriage (Mikalson; Kearns).

Much of what we know about marriage, especially in Greece, is preserved on vases. Furthermore, given that the rites were located within the family, written evidence tends to be scanty. Even so, we do possess some revealing and colorful testimony. In the first passage, Menelaus, the ruler of Lacedaemon and husband of Helen, offers a feast to guests invited for the wedding of his son and daughter, as well as to Telemachus and a traveling companion, who are visiting Sparta in search of Telemachus' father, Odysseus. The food and drink offered to the travelers provides additional insight into the particulars of the menu as well as the aristocratic networking system known as *xenia* (2.14). The second excerpt, an anonymous fragment, perhaps part of a Greek comedy from the late third century BCE, portrays a speaker, who may be the father of the bride, mentioning certain gifts, including a piece of land that may have been part of the dowry. The foods mentioned at the end of the passage would seem to refer to the wedding feast; they are not extravagant but make their own entrance in an amusing manner. In the final excerpt Plutarch reveals that Pericles, the famous Athenian general and statesman of the fifth century BCE, was reluctant to drink at the wedding feast of a relative. The vignette not only reveals Pericles as a man of moderation but also the wedding as a celebration of great joy and revelry.

4.33. Homer, *Odyssey* 4.15–19; 52–8

So the neighbors and relatives of the renowned Menelaus were feasting in the high-roofed hall; among them a divine minstrel was playing the lyre and singing, and two tumblers leading the dance whirled up and down in their midst.

Then in a beautiful golden pitcher a handmaid brought water for their hands and poured it over a silver basin for them to wash, and then she set up a polished table beside them. And the revered housekeeper brought bread and placed it in front of them and served generous portions from the other dishes she had. And a carver raised up platters of all kinds of meats and set them before the guests, and he placed beside them golden drinking cups.

4.34. *Select Papyri III* (Loeb 236–9)

Since it seems that you wish to conclude this marriage quickly, right now I make an agreement with you for your good fortune …

(*Traces of 17 lines follow, including the phrases,* I give you the land too … towards you and Bion … rejoiced in modest manners)

… stewed a bitter little snail, tassel hyacinths came dancing … chopped small, an artichoke made an entrance, a beet held a certain rhythm, and there was bread (?) of flour. Since all of these fine foods made their appearance, …

(*Unintelligible remains of five more lines*)

4.35. Plutarch, *Pericles* 7.4–5

He refused invitations to dinner and all such friendship and familiarity, so that in the long period that elapsed while he was governing, he did not go to the house of a single friend in order to dine—except that when his cousin Euryptolemus gave a wedding feast, he attended until the celebratory drinking, then he immediately got up and left. For conviviality is prone to break down and prevail over all dignity, and decorum, which is assumed for appearance's sake, is very difficult to maintain in everyday dealings with people.

Death

Whether nourishing the spirit of the deceased at the gravesite or commemorating the dead in a public celebration, food and drink were essential elements of the life cycle's ultimate transition from the world of the living to that of the dead. In the private realm the family would make offerings each year at the gravesite. We know little of the nature of these offerings, but among the Greeks they likely included libations of milk and honey to nourish the spirit of the deceased and perhaps a meal at the grave plot to follow. The Romans provided similar offerings on the day of roses and the day of violets, both named after the flowers presumably laid at the tomb by family members each year (Hope). We get some idea of the importance with which the ancients viewed these annual rites through a courtroom excerpt on the disadvantages for those who died without an heir. The text belongs to Isaeus, one of the ten canonical Attic orators in Greece during the fourth century BCE.

4.36. Isaeus, *On the Estate of Menecles* 2.46

> He (sc. my opponent) now wants to deprive me of my father's estate, whether it be large or small, and to make the deceased childless and nameless, so that there may be no one to honor the family cults on his behalf or to offer the annual sacrifice to the dead for him, but that he may be robbed of all the honors he deserves.

Also popular were testamentary feasts to honor the memory of the dead, especially those enjoyed by various associations of workers found throughout the Roman Empire. Typical is this inscription from Cisalpine Gaul in which a certain M. Labikanus Memor honors his wife and his in-laws with a perpetual feast that is to be embellished with roses and perfume. The duty of safeguarding their memory is given to the local association of textile workers. It would seem that either M. Labikanus Memor or his father-in-law, C. Atilius Secundus, or both, were associated with the guild but the connection is not clear. The inscription likely dates to the late second or third century (Liu).

4.37. *Corpus Inscriptionum Latinarum (CIL)* 5.2176

> Marcus Labikanus Memor set up (this monument) for Atilia Secundina, daughter of Caius, his most faithful, modest and disciplined wife, who lived 17 years, seven months and seven days, and also for Caius Atilius Secundus and Serr(ia ?) Valeriana, freedwoman of M(arcus), his dearest parents-in-law, while they were alive, and in their memory roses, perfume and banquets in perpetuity were assigned to be carried out by the guild of textile workers of Placentia in the district of Clastidium.

When we turn to the celebration of death in a civic context, two events help to underscore the diversity and complexity of these rites. Among the Greeks was a three-day festival of Dionysius known as the Anthesteria, named after Anthesterion, the month (roughly February/March) in which it was celebrated. The first day, the *Pithoigia*, included the ceremonial opening of the vats containing the new wine that had been fermenting since the previous autumn. The next day, *Choës*, was concerned with communal drinking, and took its name from the three-quart jugs from which the wine was generously poured and imbibed. The final day, *Chytroi*, the day of "cooking pots," was named after the vessels in which mixed vegetables were prepared and then offered to Hermes Psychopompus ("Conveyer of Souls"). It was at this time that the souls of the dead were thought to wander among the living, only to be sent back to the Underworld at the end of the day by celebrants who raucously shouted that the Anthesteria was concluded. The meaning or function of this complex festival is difficult to know, and many interpretations have been offered, from fertility to the celebration of plant life. It is more likely that the festival fulfilled several functions at the same time—social, religious, and carnivalesque—with drinking and cooking taking center stage in this colorful tribute to the cult of the dead (Parke).

More spectacular perhaps, but equally difficult to interpret, were Roman gladiator games (Fagan), which began as part of the funerary tribute of prominent individuals. It is possible that these contests were conceived with the notion that the spilling of blood was a means of appeasing the gods below the earth. The next passage describes the funeral of a prominent Roman in 183 BCE. Note especially the distribution of meat, banqueting, and games, benefactions that served as a precursor to the bread and circuses routinely offered at Rome by the emperor centuries later.

4.38. Livy, 39.46.2–4

A public distribution of meat was provided for the funeral of Publius Licinius and 120 gladiators fought, and for three days funeral games were given, and after the games a feast. At this time, when the tables had been arranged throughout the whole Forum, a storm arose with great winds and forced most of the people to set up tents in the Forum; these were taken down a bit later, when the weather had cleared up all around.

Magic

As with ancient religion, the literature on magic and superstition is both vast and ever growing. Given the nature of this book, it will be most useful to provide a general definition of magic and then to choose passages that help

Figure 7. Mosaic from the "House of the Gladiators" of two gladiators facing each other and ready for fight. Their names, Hellenikos and Margareites, appear in Greek above their heads. The composition was probably commissioned after gladiatorial games, which took place in the Kourion theatre. Kourion, Cyprus, third century CE. Photo Credit: Edgar Knobloch/Art Resource, NY.

to illuminate this practice while underscoring the place of food and drink in this particular realm. For useful recent studies, see Collins (in Boys-Stones), Dickie, Faraone and Obbink, and Ogden (2002) in 'Further Readings' at the end of this chapter.

Broadly defined then, magic typically denoted the use of supernatural means ("occult") as a manipulative strategy to influence the course of nature. To put it another way, religion asked for something to happen, while magic deliberately attempted to make that thing happen. In this context we find food and drink used most often as a medium through which the practitioner sought to achieve his or her particular wish. Sometimes the food was consumed, at other times it was applied to the body as a mixture. Most popular were charms for foreknowledge or memory, love spells, and spells of attraction. Regardless of the motive, it will become clear that magic utilized food and drink in imaginative and sometimes highly unusual ways.

Love spells of attraction

The first extract, from a collection of papyri dating to the fifth century CE, is written in Egyptian letters and translated into Greek. Although this spell is Egyptian in origin, "apple spells," whereby one commonly threw soft fruit at his beloved in the hope of winning her over, were quite popular among the Greeks and Romans. The motif was reprised in the popular myth of Hippomenes and Atalanta and, by extension, in the myth of Hades and Persephone, where pomegranate seeds are employed.

4.39. *Supplementum Magicum (Suppl. Mag.)* 72.1–14

> Spell using an apple. Say it three times over. I will pelt with apples … [gap] I will give this spell, which is always suitable for eating for mortal men and immortal gods. Whichever woman I give the apple to, whichever woman I throw the apple at and hit with it, may she put everything else aside and fall crazily in love with me. Whether she takes it in her hand and eats it, or puts it away in her dress, may she not stop loving me. Cyprus-born Aphrodite, bring this spell to fruition.

This next selection, also a love spell of attraction, belongs to the *Greek Magical Papyri (PGM)*, a name given by scholars to a corpus of papyri from Graeco-Roman Egypt that contains a variety of magical texts dating from the second century BCE to fifth century CE. While these texts represent only a fraction of the spells that once existed, they nevertheless provide remarkable insight into the power and pervasiveness of magical belief in antiquity.

4.40. *Papyri Graecae Magicae (PGM)* 4.1390–8

> Love spell of attraction carried out with the assistance of heroes or gladiators or those who have died violently: Leave a bit of the bread, which you eat; break it up and shape it into seven bite-size pieces. And go to the place where heroes and gladiators and those who have died a violent death were slain. Say the spell to the pieces of bread and toss them. And pick up some polluted dirt from the place where you perform the rite and throw it inside the house of the woman whom you desire, go on home and go to sleep.

In this spell of attraction food was not to be ingested but smeared on the body part that the petitioner wished to utilize to fulfill his wish.

4.41. *Papyri Graecae Magicae (PGM)* 7.191–2

Eternal spell for binding a lover. Rub together some gall of a wild boar, some rock salt, some honey from Attica and smear the head of your penis.

Much like the preceding entry, this remarkable spell also uses a food product, in this case wine, to act as a medium for attracting the lover to the petitioner.

4.42. *Papyri Graecae Magicae (PGM)* 7.643–51

Cup spell, very remarkable: Say the spell that is spoken to the cup seven times: "You are wine; you are not wine but the head of Athena. / You are wine; you are not wine, but the guts of Osiris, the guts of IAO PAKERBETH SEMESILAM OOO E PATACHNA IAAA." (For the spell of compulsion: ABLANATHANALBA AKRAMMACHAMAREI EEE, who has been stationed over necessity, IAKOUB IA IAO SABAOTH ADONAI ABRASAX").

"At whatever hour / you descend into the guts of her, NN, let her love me, NN, [for] the rest of her life."

Spell to Acquire Foreknowledge and Memory

The final selection is noteworthy as an example of a spell to acquire foreknowledge and memory, which was also a popular in the magical sources.

4.43. *Papyri Graecae Magicae (PGM)* 3.424–30

A copy from a holy book. Charm that grants foreknowledge and memory: Take a kakouphon,[33] which in Egyptian is kakkou[phat, tear out] its heart, perforate it with a reed, [cut] the heart [into pieces], and put them into Attic honey when the goddess[34] advances. Then pulverize the heart on the first [day of the month] of the goddess, mix it with the honey, [and eat it] on an empty stomach while saying this formula seven times, once while tasting with the forefinger:

"Make me know ahead of time, once and for all, the things that are going to happen, the things that are about to happen, the things that have been done, and all [today's] activities." (*the charm continues for 37 lines*)

Eating, drinking and Judaism

Jewish attitudes toward food and drink come into sharp relief through the writings of the Jews themselves and of the non-Jews who wrote about them, especially the Romans. It is clear that, similar to the earlier periods of their history, the Jews of the Diaspora continued to attach great importance to food laws and fasting (Williams). To be sure, food and fasting played an important part in the definition and self-definition of the Jew (Grimm). Of particular interest is Philo, a wealthy Hellenized Jew of first-century Alexandria, who was deeply committed to uniting Jewish religion and morality with Hellenistic philosophy. One result of this approach was a relentless belief in controlling pleasure, especially through regulating food and drink. While it is difficult to know how closely Philo reflects the views of Diaspora Jews in general, he nevertheless provides valuable insight into contemporary attitudes toward food and fasting in the Alexandria of his own day. The first excerpt captures a fear of gluttony and corpulence that is typical of Philo's mindset. Moreover, it portrays a way of living that has much in common with Platonic thinking and later Christian beliefs in abstention and purity, a convergence that helps to account for Philo's strong influence on the Christians of Alexandria. The second passage, the conclusion to his treatise on drunkenness, implores man to embrace the true vine of virtue and not that of inebriation and license, while underscoring the metaphorical power of viticulture in ancient thought.

4.44. Philo, *Special Laws* 1.148–50

> The paunch is an outgrowth of the belly, and it happens that the role of the belly is to be the stable of that irrational animal desire, which, soaked by wine drinking and gluttony, is ever inundated with constant infusions of food and drink, and like a pig is happy to spend its life in the mud. And so, a very suitable place has been assigned to that adversarial and intemperate beast. But the opposite of desire is temperance, which one must practice and labor and take pains to acquire in every way possible as the greatest and most perfect good, both for the individual and for the state. Therefore, appetite, as profane, impure and unholy, has been expelled beyond the boundaries of virtue, and fittingly so. But let temperance, that pure and unblemished virtue that pays no attention to all concerns of food and drink and boasts to stand superior to the pleasures of the belly, approach the holy altars and bring with it the outgrowth of the belly as a reminder that it despises gluttony and greediness and all the things that inflame the tendencies to lust.

4.45. Philo, *On Drunkenness* 223–4

No plant of true joy sprouts in the soul of the wicked man, since it does not have healthy roots, but such as were burned and reduced to ashes, since in the place of water heaven has poured upon it the unquenchable fire of lightning, God having decided that as a well-deserved punishment for the wicked. In such a soul all that is planted is excessive desire, devoid of all good things, and blinded to all that is worthy of its contemplation, and he (sc. Moses) compares this lust to a vine; not that which is the mother of edible fruits, but a vine that produces bitterness and evil and villainy; a vine very rich in wrath and anger and the most savage moods, a vine that stings the soul like vipers and poisonous asps—a sting that is utterly incurable. Let us pray that these may be averted, and let us implore the all-merciful God to obliterate this wild vine and to declare perpetual banishment to the eunuchs and to all those who do not produce virtue, and that in their place he may plant worthy trees of right instruction in our souls ...

Roman views of the Jews varied, as some writers were sympathetic to the Jewish faith while others were more hostile. In this passage Tacitus provides the most detailed ethnographic account of the Jews. The Roman suppression of the Jewish revolt and eventual capture of Jerusalem under Titus in 66–70 CE provides the context. Note that Tacitus recognizes certain aspects of the Jewish diet, such as fasting, abstention from pork, and the use of unleavened bread, but that he also includes stereotypes such as worship of the ass and Jewish indolence.

4.46. Tacitus, *Histories* 5.4–5

To strengthen his position over this people forever, Moses introduced novel rites, quite opposed to those of the rest of the human race. In them everything we consider sacred is profane, and conversely they allow what for us is impure. In the heart of the temple they dedicated a statue of the animal,[35] which helped them to drive away their wandering and their thirst (sc. in the wilderness), sacrificing a ram apparently in mockery of Ammon;[36] a bull too is sacrificed, since the Egyptians worship the Apis bull. They abstain from pork in memory of an epidemic when the scabs to which this animal is susceptible once afflicted them. Even now they bear witness to their historic hunger by frequent fasts, and Jewish bread is still unleavened to recall the haste with which they seized the grain.[37] They say that rest was agreeable to them on the seventh day because that marked the end of their labors; then the allure of indolence led them to give over the seventh year to inactivity too.[38] Others say that this rest is in honor of Saturn, either because the Idaeans (who had been expelled with Saturn and whom we believe are the founders of their race) transmitted the principles of their religion; or because, of the seven planets that govern the human race, Saturn moves in the highest orbit and has the greatest power; in addition, many of the celestial bodies run on their own path and courses in multiples of seven.[39]

Just as Roman writers differed in their assessment of the Jews, so too did Roman leaders differ in their treatment of them. In this passage Josephus, a Jew who sought to portray Romano-Jewish interaction in a positive light, credits Julius Caesar with liberal treatment of the Jews. Caesar's favorable disposition toward the Jews may have been the result of assistance he had earlier received from two Jewish leaders in Egypt. Note the importance to the Jews of shared meals, which Caesar preserved for them while banning similar arrangements for non-Jews at Rome. The petition here comes from Parium in northwest Asia Minor, and the provincial governor shares Caesar's viewpoint.

4.47. Josephus, *Jewish Antiquities* 14. 213–16

Julius Gaius, consul of the Romans, to the magistrates, council, and people of Parium, greetings. The Jews from Delos, and some of the neighboring Jews, in the presence of some of your envoys, have petitioned me and declared that you are preventing them by decree from following their ancestral customs and holy rites. Now it is not pleasing to me that such enactments should be passed against our friends and allies, and that they should be prevented from living according to their customs and from contributing money to common meals and sacred rites, since they are not prevented from doing this even in Rome. For example, Gaius Caesar (sc. Julius Caesar), our consular praetor, prohibiting by edict religious associations from assembling in the city, did not prohibit these people alone from collecting contributions of money and holding common meals. In the same way, I too prohibit other religious associations, but allow these people alone to assemble and hold meals in accordance with their ancestral customs and conventions. And, if you have passed any decrees against our friends and allies, you will be well advised to set them aside, because of their virtue and favorable disposition towards us.

Food and drink among Christians

On the basis of a broad range of Christian texts from the first three centuries CE, including the New Testament, wisdom literature, gnomic sayings, and apologetic works, it is clear that the diet of Christians differed little from that of non-Christians across the Mediterranean world (for general studies, see Sivan, in Barchiesi and Scheidel; Grimm; Lieu; and Neufeld and DeMaris). It should perhaps come as no surprise therefore that bread and wine, the two most common foodstuffs of the daily dietary regimen, became the central components of the Eucharistic meal. Furthermore, by consistently emphasizing moderation and restraint in the eating and drinking habits of the faithful, Christian writers attempted to solidify Christian identity and to set Christians apart from their pagan contemporaries in a significant way. At the same time, the ubiquity of this call for moderation and the vehemence with which this message was delivered, suggest that a life of restraint was one that was not always so easy to live by.

A common diet

As Jews who were liberated from their own food restrictions, early Christians were free to eat the same items as non-Christians, with the exception of sacrificial meat. Thus do we find Paul urging the Corinthians to "eat whatever is sold in the meat market without raising any question on the ground of conscience, for the earth and its fullness are the Lord's" (1 Cor. 10.25) We find that the actual Christian diet of first-century Palestine seems to have diverged little from the triad of cereals, grapes, and olives, which had formed the core of the Mediterranean regimen for centuries by the time of emergent Christianity. The bread, wine, and olive oil produced from these foodstuffs, supplemented by fruits, vegetables and fish, where available, formed the dominant dietary regimen of the Graeco-Roman period (see Chapter 3), and the reliance of Christians on these items forms an important strand in the social the fabric of the New Testament. This is the case in the well-known account of the feeding of the 5,000 at Bethsaida:

4.48. Matthew, the Evangelist, 14.13–21 (*New Oxford Annotated Bible*)

Now when Jesus heard this, he withdrew from there in a boat to a deserted place by himself. But when the crowds heard it, they followed him on foot from the towns. When he went ashore, he saw a great crowd; and he had compassion for them, and cured their sick. When it was evening, the disciples came to him and said, "This is a deserted place, and the hour is now late; send the crowds away so that they may go into the villages and buy food for themselves." Jesus said to them, "They need not go away; you give them something to eat." They replied, "We have nothing here but five loaves and two fish." And he said, "Bring them here to me." Then he ordered the crowds to sit down on the grass. Taking the five loaves and the two fish, he looked up to heaven and blessed and broke the loaves, and gave them to the disciples, and the disciples gave them to the crowds. And all ate and were filled; and they took up what was left over of the broken pieces, twelve baskets full. And those who ate were about five thousand men, besides women and children.

As we saw in Chapter 3, wine was the primary beverage of the Mediterranean region and the focus of extensive Roman writings on viticulture, vintages, and medicine. It was no less important to the dietary regimen of early Christianity. In the passage below wine storage practices provide a metaphor for one of the best-known parables of the New Testament. Note especially how the parable underscores the vitality of the wine trade and helps us to conceptualize the reality that Jesus' listeners surely knew that wineskins expanded when new wine was poured in and continued to ferment. The wineskins would then harden and, if new wine was put into a hardened wineskin, continued fermentation could cause the skin to burst. Of course, wineskins were not the only metaphor that Jesus relied upon in his teachings, yet their appearance in this context provides a vivid reminder of the enduring cultural power of wine in everyday Mediterranean life and how readily and effectively it could be appropriated for conveying deeper truths.

4.49. *Matthew, the Evangelist,* 9.14–17 (*New Oxford Annotated Bible*)

Then the disciples of John came to him, saying, "Why do we and the Pharisees fast often, but your disciples do not fast?" And Jesus said to them, "The wedding guests cannot mourn as long as the bridegroom is with them, can they? The days will come when the bridegroom is taken away from them, and then they will fast. No one sews a piece of unshrunk cloth on an old cloak, for the patch pulls away from the cloak, and a worse tear is made. Neither is new wine put into old wineskins; otherwise, the skins burst, and the wine is spilled, and the skins are destroyed; but new wine is put into fresh wineskins, and so both are preserved."

The dangers of excess

An important theme in early Christian literature was the need for proper behavior among the faithful, especially in matters of eating and drinking. This is evident in the following passage taken from the *Shepherd of Hermas*, an apocalyptic compilation that portrays the central character and author, Hermas, as receiving prophetic visions from an angelic mediator in the guise of a shepherd. The teachings of the *Shepherd* reflect deep concerns over the

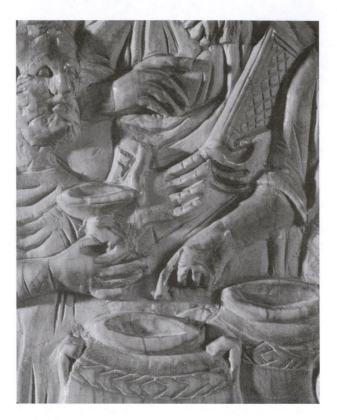

Figure 8. Detail of the Marriage at Cana, the blessing of water and changing it
into wine. From the back of the pulpit of Archbishop Maximian. Carved ivory
plaque, sixth century CE. Museo Arcivescovile, Ravenna, Italy. Photo Credit: Erich
Lessing/Art Resource, NY.

dangers of excessive food and drink, and it is not unreasonable to suggest that
such anxieties were based at least in part on a larger Mediterranean world where
a lack of moderation at table was not at all uncommon. Here, a "bad angel"
prompts gluttony and excess in those whom he possesses:

4.50. Shepherd of Hermas, *Mandate* 6.2.5

"Lord," I said, "I do not understand how to recognize him." "Listen," he
answered, "when any irascibility or wrath should come upon you, realize that
he is in you. Then there is desire for many activities and much extravagant
food and heavy drinking and many wild gatherings and various luxuries that

are completely unnecessary … and so, when these things arise in your heart, recognize that the angel of evil is in you."

Christian apologists

The Greek term *apologia* means a "defense." Some of the most important writings from early Christianity were apologies, or "defenses," of the faith written by Christian authors against the attacks of non-Christian critics. Chief among the early Christian apologists was Tertullian, who wrote for Christians in Carthage during the late second and early third centuries. Tertullian displayed a keen interest in matters of food and drink as we see in this excerpt, the fiery peroration to his treatise, *On Fasting*, in which he vigorously exhorts Christians to increase their abstinence as a means of attaining ritual purity. By equating the Pauline virtues of love, faith, and hope with common features of ancient dining—saucepans, kitchens, and waiters, respectively—Tertullian attempts to underscore the degeneracy of his audience, whom he sees as valuing temporal pleasures more than steadfast virtues. The contrast is made all the more vivid by the pairing of Paul's final virtue—love—with the most illicit form of that virtue, incest.

4.51. Tertullian, *On Fasting* 17

With you, love simmers in cooking pots; faith heats up in kitchens, hope lies upon serving dishes; but of greater account is love, because that is how your young men sleep with their sisters.

Minucius Felix, a North African contemporary of Tertullian, was the author of the *Octavian*, a dialogue in elegant Latin between the Christian Octavius and the pagan Caecilius Natalis of Cirta. In this excerpt Octavius recounts the common charges of cannibalism, excessive feasting, and incest leveled against early Christians. Such accusations were both graphic and provocative, and played upon the popular misconception that Christians were cannibals because they feasted on "the body and blood of Christ." Charges of incest grew out of the custom whereby Christians addressed one another as "brother" or "sister." In much the same way another common charge against Christians was that they refused to attend sacrifices as a way of abstaining from the blood of sacrificial animals. The apologists rigorously maintained that the sacrifice of animals was a profanation and that their own meat contained no blood.

4.52. Minucius Felix, *Octavian* 9.5–6

The story of the initiation of new recruits is as repulsive as it is notorious. A baby, covered in flour to deceive the unsuspecting, is put in front of the person to be admitted to the sacred rites. The recruit is compelled to inflict seemingly harmless blows to the flour, and kills the infant with wounds that remain secret and hidden. Greedily they lap up the infant's blood—how dreadful! The limbs they eagerly tear apart, and by complicity in the crime they take a pledge of mutual silence. These sacred rites are fouler than all sacrileges. And their style of feasting is well known. People talk about it everywhere, as witnessed by the speech of our compatriot from Cirta.[40] They assemble for banquets on the appointed day, with all their children, sisters, and mothers, people of either gender and of every age. There, after much feasting, when the party has warmed them and the drunken raging of libidinous incest has taken flame, a dog, which has been tied to the lamp, is goaded to rush forward by the toss of a scrap thrown beyond the reach of the leash tying him up. In so doing the telltale light is overturned and extinguished, and in the shameless darkness they copulate indiscriminately with unutterable desires; and all alike, even if not in practice at least in complicity, commit incest, since anything that happens through the action of individuals results from the intention of everybody.

Suggestions for Further Reading

Barchiesi, A. and Scheidel, W., eds. 2010. *The Oxford Handbook of Roman Studies.* Oxford.

Beard, M., North, J. and Price, S. 1998. *Religions of Rome.* 2 vols. Cambridge.

Betz, H. D., ed. 1992. *The Greek Magical Papyri in Translation. Including the Demotic Spells.* 10 vols. Chicago.

Boys-Stones, G., Graziosi, B. and Vasunia, P., eds. 2009. *The Oxford Handbook of Hellenic Studies.* Oxford.

Bruit Zaidman, L. and Schmitt Pantel, P. 1992. *Religion in the Ancient Greek City.* Cambridge.

Burkert, W. 1985. *Greek Religion.* Cambridge, MA.

Clark, G. 2000. *On Abstinence from Killing Animals.* London.

Cohen A. and Rutter, J., eds. 2007. *Constructions of Childhood in Ancient Greece and Italy.* Princeton.

Coogan, M. D., ed. 2010. *The New Oxford Annotated Bible. New Revised Standard Version with the Apocrypha.* 4th edn. Oxford.

Detienne, M. and Vernant. J-P. 1989. *The Cuisine of Sacrifice among the Greeks.* Chicago.

Dickie, M. W. 2001. *Magic and Magicians in the Greco-Roman World.* London.

Donahue, J. 2004. *The Roman Community at Table during the Principate*. Ann Arbor.

Evans-Grubbs, J. 2002. *Women and the Law in the Roman Empire: A Sourcebook on Marriage, Divorce and Widowhood*. London.

Fagan, G. 2011. *The Love of the Arena: Social Psychology and the Crowd at the Roman Games*. Cambridge.

Faraone, C. A. and Obbink, D., eds. 1991. *Magika Hiera: Ancient Greek Magic and Religion*. Oxford.

Grimm, V. E. 1996. *From Fasting to Feasting, the Evolution of a Sin: Attitudes to Food in Late Antiquity*. London.

Hart, G. D. 2000. *Asclepius: The God of Medicine*. London.

Hope, V. M. 2007. *Death in Ancient Rome: A Sourcebook*. London.

Huskinson, J., ed. 2000. *Experiencing Rome: Culture, Identity and Power in the Roman Empire*. London.

Kearns, E. 2010. *Ancient Greek Religion: A Sourcebook*. West Sussex.

Kinzl, K. H., ed. 2006. *A Companion to the Classical Greek World*. Malden, MA.

Lieu, J. M. 2004. *Christian Identity in the Jewish and Graeco-Roman World*. Oxford.

Liu, J. 2009. *Collegia Centonariorum: The Guild of Textile Workers in the Roman West*. Columbia Studies in Classical Tradition, v. 34. Leiden.

Luck, G. 1985. *Arcana Mundi: Magic and the Occult in the Greek and Roman Worlds*. Baltimore.

Mikalson, J. 2010. *Ancient Greek Religion*. Malden, MA.

Naiden, F. 2012. *Smoke Signals for the Gods: Ancient Greek Sacrifice from the Archaic Through the Roman Periods*. Oxford.

Neufeld, D. and DeMaris, R., eds 2009. *Understanding the Social World of the New Testament*. London.

Ogden, D. 2002. *Magic, Witchcraft, and Ghosts in the Greek and Roman Worlds: A Sourcebook*. Oxford.

—ed. 2007. *A Companion to Greek Religion*. Malden, MA.

Parke, H. W. 1986. *Festivals of the Athenians*. Ithaca.

Parker, R. 2011. *On Greek Religion*. Ithaca, NY.

Rawson, B. 2003. *Children and Childhood in Roman Italy*. Oxford.

—ed. 2011. *A Companion to Families in the Greek and Roman Worlds*. Oxford.

Rhodes, P. J. and Osborne, R., eds., w. intro., trans., and comm. 2003. *Greek Historical Inscriptions: 404–323 BC*. Oxford.

Rice, D. G. and Stambaugh, J. E. 2000. *Sources for the Study of Greek Religion*. Atlanta.

Rives, J. B. 2007. *Religion in the Roman Empire*. Malden, MA.

Rüpke, J., ed. 2007. *A Companion to Roman Religion*. Malden, MA.

Scheid, J. 2003. *An Introduction to Roman Religion*, trans. J. Lloyd. Bloomington, IN.

Scullard, H. H. 1981. *Festivals and Ceremonies of the Roman Republic*. London.

Stafford, E. J. and Herrin, J., eds. 2005. *Personification in the Greek World: From Antiquity to Byzantium*. Aldershot.

Taylor, T., trans. 1965. *Porphyry, On Abstinence from Animal Food*. London.

Van Andringa, W., ed. 2007. "Meat: sacrifice, trade and food preparation in the Roman empire." *A Special Edition of Food and History* 5:5–272.

Warrior, V. M. 2002. *Roman Religion: A Sourcebook*. Newburyport, MA.

—2009. *Greek Religion: A Sourcebook*. Newburyport, MA.

Williams, M. 1998. *The Jews among the Greeks and Romans: A Diasporan Sourcebook*. Baltimore.

Eating, Drinking, and Sharing:
The Social Context of Food and Drink

You must reflect carefully beforehand with whom you are to eat and drink,
rather than what you are to eat and drink. For a dinner of meats without a
friend is like the life of a lion or a wolf.

Seneca, *Letter* 1.19

On the most basic level, we eat out of necessity, that is, to ensure our survival. But there is another dimension, a more social aspect of eating, which finds expression in the act of dining. "To dine" means "to have dinner" but it can also mean "to give a dinner," and "to entertain at dinner," as in the phrase "to wine and dine" someone. It is this meaning of eating and drinking as a shared experience that Seneca understands as being most important when he recalls the phrase attributed to Epicurus, the famed Greek philosopher. Dining distinguishes us from the lion and the wolf. It helps to makes us human.

For the Greeks and Romans food was about consumption. But consumption was also about those who were doing the eating and with whom they were doing it (Nielsen and Nielsen; Dunbabin and Slater, in Peachin). It is this social dimension of eating and drinking that we shall explore in this chapter. We shall discover that food consumption was deeply embedded in the social system of the ancient world. More importantly, it will become clear that eating and drinking helped to confirm social status, or lack thereof, among the participants. This was especially true for the Romans, for whom the sources are generally more plentiful than for the Greeks.

We shall begin with the grand and extravagant banquets and symposia of the Greek world and their adaptation by various Roman dynasts and eventually by the Roman emperors. We shall then shift our focus to dining on a smaller scale, both among elites and the general populace. Among meals for elites, we shall focus especially on the Roman *convivium*, a dining arrangement that is essential if we are to understand the connection between eating, drinking, and status.

Among the lower orders of society, the food and drink received at public shows, purchased at the tavern, and procured through the patron–client relationship will be significant, as will be the emergence of cooks and flatterers as colorful components of this dining culture. We shall also explore eating and drinking within well-defined groups of non-elites, most notably the Roman *collegia*, associations that typically utilized food and drink to reinforce status differences within the group itself. Finally, we shall examine the social dynamic of food and drink as it intersected with sex and as it found expression in the unique setting of military life among the Spartans. Amid all of this evidence, two conclusions will be inescapable: the undeniable power of food and drink to unite the participants but also to separate them by reinforcing social distinctions.

The emergence of extravagant dining

The ancient sources do not date precisely the emergence of fine dining. Part of the reason surely has to do with the fact that eating and drinking were routine and ephemeral acts that did not always capture the attention of authors in the same way as warfare and politics. Livy records that luxurious dining practices had arrived in Italy by the second century BCE as part of the influx of wealth into Italy from the Greek East (see 5.12). But change was apparent well before this time. Texts and iconography from the third millennium BCE in Mesopotamia provide a good amount of testimony on the custom of reclining at formal and informal meals and at drinking parties, although much work remains to be done on these earlier practices and their connection to Greek, Hellenistic, and Roman dining and drinking customs. For our purposes, a useful place to start is Greece of the fourth century BCE, where tensions were apparent between the ideologies of the simple meal and the more lavish displays of elites, who sought to compete with those dining practices from elsewhere in the Mediterranean that were beginning to impinge on the Greek world (Wilkins 2006).

The first passage reflects something of this tension. Xenophon's imaginary dialogue between Hieron I, tyrant of Syracuse (478–467 BCE) in Sicily and Simonides compares the place of the tyrant and the private citizen in the realm of banqueting. Hiero argues that he has no more access to pleasure than a private person, even when it comes to the plentiful banquets he consumes as a despot. Important here is the emphasis on wealth, happiness and pleasure and the fact that food and drink now play a role in such debates. Curiously, the dialogue concludes without allowing the tyrant to respond to Simonides' advice on what makes for a happy ruler. Consequently, the *Hiero* has been variously interpreted from the Renaissance to modern times.

5.1. Xenophon, *Hiero* 1.17–25

"I know, Simonides," he said "that the reason most men judge that we have more enjoyment in eating and drinking than private citizens is this: they think that they themselves would find the dinner served at our table a better meal than what they receive. Anything, in fact, that surpasses what they are accustomed to gives them pleasure. For this reason all men welcome with pleasure the festivals, except the despots. For their tables are always plentifully laden, and have no need of an increase on feast days. As a result, they are first and foremost at a disadvantage compared to the private citizen in the joy of anticipation. But further, I am sure that your own experience tells you that the greater the number of excessive dishes set before a man, the sooner that a feeling of satiety from the food falls upon him; and so, in terms of the duration of his pleasure, the man who has many courses put in front of him is worse off than he who lives moderately."

"But surely by Zeus," said Simonides, "as long as the appetite endures, he who dines at the more expensive banquet has much more pleasure than he who is served with the less costly meal."

"Therefore, Simonides," said Hiero, "do you think that the greater a man's pleasure in any pursuit, the stronger is his devotion to it?"

"To be sure," he said.

"Then do you observe that tyrants approach their meal with any more zeal than private persons to theirs?"

"No, by Zeus, no, of course not," he said, "but with more disgust, according to the common opinion."

"Well now," said Hiero, "have you noticed all those culinary creations that are put before tyrants— pungent, bitter, sour, and alike?"

"Yes, certainly," said Simonides, "and these seem to me to be very much contrary to a man's constitution."

"And so don't you think," said Hiero, "that these dishes are the pursuits of a soft and delicate appetite? I well know, and you know too, that those who eat gladly have no need of these inventions."

"Well," said Simonides, "I certainly think that those costly perfumes with which you anoint your bodies provide more pleasure to those who are near you than to yourselves, just as the man who has consumed unpleasant food is less conscious of the disagreeable smell than those who come near him."

"Quite so," said Hiero, "and we may add that he who always has all sorts of food has no desire for any of these. Offer a man a dish that he rarely tastes, and he joyfully fills his belly."

Two additional forces in the fourth century BCE captured this growing interest in fine eating—the cookbook and the dining habits of the Eastern monarchs, who succeeded Alexander the Great upon his death in 323 BCE. The first Greek version of a cookbook belongs to Archestratus of Sicily, who produced the *Hedupatheia* (*The Life of Luxury*), an epic poem, of which some 340 lines survive. It provides a culinary tour of the Mediterranean for readers who sought the best foods (Olson and Sens; Wilkins and Hill). In general, cookbooks were important for advertising *truphe* (luxury)—what we would now term as haute cuisine—as well as for preserving regional specialties (Purcell, in Gold and Donahue 2004). They have also been invaluable for helping us to understand individual recipes (Dalby and Grainger), although less useful in providing insight into various cooking styles and systems. All of these features are evident in the next passage, where the focus on fish is typical of Archestratus and reflects the importance of maritime cuisine in Sicily. Note too, as we observed earlier, the absence of precise measurements in ancient recipes.

5.2. Athenaeus, *Sophists at Dinner* 7.321c–d=*Archestratos of Gela*, fragment 37 (Olson and Sens)

Whenever Orion is setting in the sky, and the mother of the wine-producing grape cluster sheds her hair,[1] then get a roasted sargue,[2] sprinkled with cheese, big, warm, and pierced with pungent vinegar; for it is hard by nature. And so I urge you to remember and treat every tough fish in this same fashion. But as for that which is good and naturally soft and rich-fleshed, sprinkle it with fine-ground salt only and baste it with olive oil; for it contains the epitome of pleasure within itself.

The Hellenistic monarchs of the later fourth century BCE were equally interested in culinary extravagance, especially to display their own generosity and royal status (Donahue 2004b). Especially notable was the sumptuous procession dedicated to Dionysius, god of wine, by Ptolemy Philadelphos of Alexandria in the first extract. A member of the same Ptolemaic line that would eventually include Cleopatra, the queen and consort of Julius Caesar and Marc Antony, Ptolemy erected in 275–274 BCE an elaborate pavilion for his guests while sparing no expense on the dinnerware and fare. The importance of festal setting as a qualitative distinction that helped to establish the social identity of benefactors and beneficiaries alike will receive additional attention later in this chapter. The second excerpt features a singularly engaged host, the Seleucid monarch Antiochus IV Epiphanes, who once presented a splendid festival in the royal park at Daphne near Antioch in order to match the impressive games put on by the Roman general Aemilius Paulus upon his conquest of Macedon in the second century BCE. In both of these passages the emphasis on opulence and generosity on a large scale is typical of the value system of the Hellenistic monarch. Such practices would later be adapted to great effect by various Roman dynasts and then by the emperors themselves.

5.3. Athenaeus, *Sophists at Dinner* 5.197a–c

Along the highest space in the ceiling were gold eagles that faced one another and were 15 cubits long. Set along the two sides of the pavilion were 100 gold couches with feet shaped like sphinxes; the apse facing the entrance was left open. Purple double-pile carpets of first-quality wool were spread on the couches, and quilts of many colors, splendid in workmanship, were on top of these. Smooth Persian carpets with beautiful designs of living creatures woven into them covered the space in the middle where people walked around. Gold tripods, 200 in number, were set beside the guests on silver stands, so that there would be two per couch; behind these were set 100 silver basins and an equal number of pitchers for them to wash with. Facing the symposium another couch had been set up to display the cups and drinking vessels and the rest of the items that were required; these were all made of gold, had inset jewels, and were marvelous in their workmanship. It seemed clear to me that offering a detailed account of the appearance and type of these vessels in turn would be a huge task; but the total weight of all the dinner vessels taken together was 10,000 silver talents.[3]

5.4. Athenaeus, *Sophists at Dinner* 5.195d–e

On one occasion 1,000 dining couches were spread for a feast, while on another there were 1,500 with the most extravagant trappings. The king himself managed the details; for he trotted along the procession on a cheap horse, bidding some groups to move forward and others to wait. At the drinking parties he himself stood at the entrance and led some people in, showed others to their couches, and escorted the servants carrying the dishes. And going around he would seat himself in one place and recline with others in another place. And sometimes he set down a morsel of food in the middle of eating it, sometimes a glass of wine, and sprung up, moved off somewhere else, and circulated through the party, receiving toasts, standing sometimes by one, sometimes by another, while at the same time laughing at the entertainments.

When we turn to the evidence of dining that involved non-royal elites during this period, among the possibilities is a singular account of a wedding breakfast provided by a certain Caranus about 300 BCE (Wilkins 2006; Dalby 1996). Caranus was Macedonian, and we must interpret this excerpt in the context of the spread of sumptuous eating in the successor kingdoms of Alexander the Great from the fourth century BCE onwards. Particularly striking is the amount and varieties of meats provided and the distribution of expensive gifts. Athenaeus characterized this meal as the most extravagant he had ever witnessed (3.126e). We have no way of confirming this statement, of course, but Caranus' feast does provide us with an opportunity to assess what "lavish" meant to the wealthy and how they may have adapted their eating and drinking practices in competition for prestige and status with other elites.

5.5. Athenaeus, *Sophists at Dinner* 4.128c–e

As I said, when Caranus had his wedding feast in Macedonia, the men who were invited numbered 20.[4] As soon as they reclined on the couches, they were given silver drinking cups, one for each, as a gift. Before entering the room, each was crowned also with a golden headband. The cost of each was five gold staters. When they had emptied their cups, on a bronze platter of Corinthian construction they were given a loaf of bread as big as the plate; also chickens, ducks, pigeons, a goose, and an abundance of such things all heaped up; and each guest took it and gave it over, platter and all, to his slaves behind him. Many other varied dishes were handed around, after which a second silver platter followed, on which again there was a large loaf, geese, hares, young goats, other elaborate breads, woodpigeons, doves, partridges, and many other fowls. "These too we gave to the slaves," he says, "and when we had had our fill of food, we washed our hands. Then many garlands made of all sorts of flowers were brought in and, in addition to all of them, golden tiaras of equal weight with the first garland."

The symposion

The symposium, the practice of "drinking together" (*symposion*) in Greece was a complex ritual of pleasure that must be considered alongside the emergence of elite dining. We are well informed about this practice through literary accounts of the event itself, especially by Plato and Xenophon, as well as through poetry produced for these occasions. The essential elements included: male participants wearing garlands and meeting in groups ranging in size from 14 to 30; a dining space (*andron*), which included couches upon which the diners reclined on the left elbow, with one or two diners to a couch; the practice of mixing water with wine according to established ratios (usually three or four parts water to one part wine) as determined by the leader (*symposiarch*) of the symposium; a repertoire of drinking implements; dining service provided by slave boys; entertainment in the form of music, dancing, or acrobatics; and a concluding procession in the streets to underscore the social cohesion of the group (Murray).

Male and most typically aristocratic, the symposium served as a venue for transmitting traditional values among men, including the homosexual bonding of young attendees. Citizen women were not allowed to attend (although female slave companions were). This excerpt is Xenophon's account of a private banquet on the occasion of the Great Panathenaea of 421 BCE. The setting, an *andron* belonging to the host Callias, reinforces the social identity of the drinkers as elite and separate from others. Xenophon himself would have been quite young at this time so the speeches of the participants are probably imaginary. The attendees are all historical figures however, including Socrates, who delivers a serious speech on the superiority of spiritual over physical love. In this passage he supports

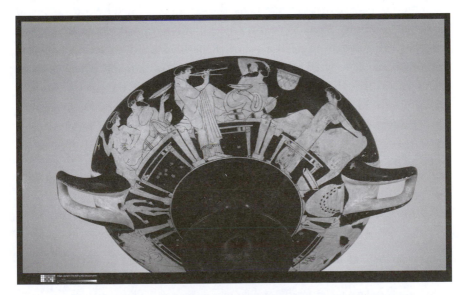

Figure 9. Terracotta kylix (drinking cup) of a Greek drinking party (symposium) featuring reclining male drinkers with musical and female accompaniment. Signed by Hieronas potter, attributed to Makron, c. 480 BCE. Metropolitan Museum of Art, Images for Academic Publishing.

moderate drinking as the best path to pleasure. Finally, this passage is typical of Xenophon's focus on conversation and not the foods served. The latter did receive attention in antiquity, however, through accounts of dinners (*deipna*) that preserve menu items and entertainments (see Dalby 2003, s.v. "symposion" [2]).

5.6. Xenophon, *Symposium* 2.24–7

> Here Socrates spoke again. "Well, gentlemen, he said, "as far as drinking goes, you very much have my approval; for wine does refresh our souls and puts our sufferings to sleep as the mandragora[5] does with men, while fostering a cheerful disposition, just as oil stirs up a flame. Yet it seems to me that men's bodies fare the same as those of plants that grow in the ground. For when a god gives a plant too much water to drink all at once, it is unable to stand up straight or let the breezes blow through it; but when it drinks only as much as it enjoys, it will grow up very straight and tall and, flourishing, come to full and abundant fruitage. And so it is with us; if we pour ourselves immense draughts, both our bodies and our minds reel quickly, and we shall not be able to draw breath, much less to say anything; but if the servants frequently besprinkle us—if I too may use a Gorgian saying[6]—with small cups, we shall thus not be driven on by the wine to become intoxicated, but, being persuaded, we shall be brought to a more playful mood."

Plato did not believe that the guardians, those most qualified by education and character to govern, should ever become intoxicated, as it would make little sense for the guardian to need a guard (*Rep.* 403d–e). Even so, he proposed drinking bouts supervised by those most qualified (presumably elites) as a safe test of a man's true character. We find this in his final work, the *Laws*, a dialogue on laws for the ideal state. Whether or not we believe this proposal to be serious, the scheme is rooted in the popular ancient belief that wine reduced one's inhibitions to reveal the true self. The interlocutors here are Cleinias, a Cretan, and an Athenian stranger, who dominates the dialogue.

5.7. Plato, *Laws* 1.649c–650b

> ATHENIAN. It seems then that we must be placed in those situations that naturally tend to make us especially confident and courageous when we are paying attention to how to be as free as possible from shamelessness and excessive audacity, and fearful at all times of daring to say, or allow, or do anything shameful.

> CLEINIAS. It seems fitting.

ATHENIAN. Accordingly, these are all the conditions in which we are of the character described—anger, lust, arrogance, ignorance, love of gain, and extravagance; and these also,—wealth, beauty, strength, and everything that intoxicates one with pleasure again, and makes him turn his thoughts. First, to provide a cheap and rather harmless test of these conditions, and, secondly, to gain practice in them, what more moderate device can we mention than wine, with its playful testing—as long as it is employed with caution? For consider: in the case of a man with a discontented and fierce disposition (from which springs countless iniquities), is it not more perilous to test him by entering into financial transactions with him, at one's own risk, than by associating with him with the insight of Dionysius? Or would you, if you wanted to apply a test to a man prone to sex, entrust to him one's own daughters and sons and wife, and thus place one's dearest family members in danger in order to discover the disposition of his soul? In fact, one might mention countless cases in a vain attempt to show the full superiority of this playful method of inspection, which is without either punishment or loss. Indeed, so far as that is concerned, I do not believe that either the Cretans or any other people will doubt that such a test is a fair test, and that it is superior to all others for cheapness, security, and speed.

CLEINIAS. That is true too.

ATHENIAN. This then, the knowledge of the natures and habits of men's souls—will be one of the most useful things to that art whose task it is to tend to them; and that art is (as I presume we say) politics. Is it not so?

CLEINIAS: Without a doubt.

A more dramatic example of a people's character is preserved in the next passage, a high-risk drinking game allegedly enjoyed at the symposia of the Thracians, whose territory centered on modern Bulgaria, Turkey, and Greece. While it is difficult to verify this practice, the account is consistent with the ancient perception of the Thracians as primitive, ferocious, and warlike.

5.8. Athenaeus, *Sophists at Dinner* 4.155d–e

Seleucus (*FGrH* 341 F4) says that there are some Thracians who play a symposium game that involves hanging, in which they attach a rope to something high and put a stone that moves easily when one stands on it directly below it. They draw lots; the man whose lot is drawn gets up on the stone, holding a small sickle, and places his neck in the noose. Someone else comes along and causes the stone to move. The stone slips out from under him, and if the man who is hanging does not cut the rope quickly enough with his sickle, he dies, and the others laugh and consider his death to be a great joke.

Not all symposia were so serious, however, as witnessed by the popularity of drinking games of various sorts in ancient Italy and Greece. Next we find a drinking game called *kottabos*, which involved tossing the drops of wine remaining in one's cup at a specific object, such as another person, a bronze target, or a cup floating in a bowl of water. Athenaeus provides some detail in a fragment from the *Birth of Aphrodite* by Antiphanes a fourth-century BCE writer of comedies, who often referred to food and drink. The second excerpt, by Alciphron (see 2.28), records a *symposion* among drunken farmers. Alhough fictional, the account helps us to imagine group drinking in a rural context, a depiction that is rare in the ancient sources.

5.9. Athenaeus, *Sophists at Dinner* 15.667b

(B.) Take the cup and show me how it's done.

(A.) You must curl your fingers like the claws of a crab, like you're playing the pipes; pour in a bit of wine, not too much, and then let it fly!

(B.) How?

(A.) Pay attention! Like this.

(B.) Poseidon! Look how high it went!

(A.) You can do it just like that.

(B.) I couldn't have gotten it that far if I were using a sling.

(A.) Alright—time to practice!

5.10. Alciphron, *Letters to Farmers* 2. 30

Scopiades to Cotion

Well, I'll be blest, Cotion, drunkenness is such an evil! I fell into a drinking party with some wretched guys (they were all heavy drinkers, and not one of them was content to drink moderately), the cup was going around continually (the penalty for those who declined was to give a party the next day, if anyone did decline the cup); as a result I know I drank more than I ever carried in my wineskin before, and here I am two days later, and I can tell you that I am still hung over and that I am vomiting stale wine.

From Greece to Rome: The feasts of Roman dynasts

The influence of Eastern luxury upon Roman dining practices was well underway by the second century BCE. In the next passage we find the Roman general Aemilius Paulus paying as much attention to detail in planning a banquet as in preparing for battle. Plutarch would have us believe that Roman militarism now had to compete with the dining table as part of a larger cultural shift in Roman thinking in the direction of all things Greek at this time. Even so, Rome's embrace of eastern luxury earned the disapproval of those who saw it as an unwelcome departure from the time-honored Roman virtues of frugality and simplicity. It is this traditional view of Roman public behavior that underlies Livy's sharp assessment in the second excerpt. In the final passage Sallust provides additional support for Livy's position in the person of Marius, the seven-time consul and a skillful general of humble origins, who vigorously eschews the trends of elegant dinners, highly paid cooks, and honors attained through material possessions rather than through warfare. The backlash we see here can be partly explained as xenophobia but also as anxiety in the face of change, and a Roman response that sought to counteract such change by evoking the time-honored values of the past that had helped to make Rome great. At the same time, the process of cultural exchange between Greece and Rome was as real as it was inevitable, and dining practices remain an important measure of gauging such interactions.

5.11. Plutarch, *Aemilius Paulus* 28.7–9

He also put on all kinds of games and contests and offered sacrifices to the gods, at which he gave feasts and banquets, utilizing the abundant wealth of the royal treasury, while in the arrangement and ordering of them, in seating and greeting his guests, and in paying to each one that degree of honor and kindliness that was properly his due, he displayed such precise and thoughtful perception that the Greeks were amazed, seeing that he neglected not even their pastimes, but that, although he was a man of such great affairs, he gave proper attention even to trifling things. And he was also pleased to find that, although preparations for entertainment were ever so many and magnificent, he himself was the most pleasant enjoyment and sight for his guests; and to those who wondered at his attention to details, he used to say that the same spirit was required both in arranging a battle line and in presiding at a banquet well, the object being, in the one case, to terrify the enemy as much as possible, in the other, to give the most pleasure to the guests.

5.12. Livy, 39.6.7–9

For the origin of foreign luxury was introduced into the City by the army from Asia. For the first time they imported bronze couches into Rome, valuable robes for coverlets, tapestries, and other fabrics, and what at the time was considered splendid furniture—tables with a single pedestal and sideboards. Then female lute and harp players and other festal delights of entertainments were added to banquets; moreover, the banquets themselves began to be planned with both greater care and expense. At that time, the cook, to the ancient Romans the most worthless of slaves, both in financial value and in utility, began to be worth something, and what had been an occupation came to be regarded as an art. Yet those things, which were then perceived as remarkable, were hardly even the seeds of the luxury to come.

5.13. Sallust, *War with Jugurtha* 85.38–40

"But those most arrogant men are greatly mistaken. Their ancestors have left them all that they were able—wealth, portrait busts, their own illustrious memory; they have not left virtue for them, nor could they have done so; that alone is neither granted nor received as a gift. They say that I am a common and inelegant man because I do not know how to put on a fancy dinner and because I do not pay any actor or cook higher wages than I do my overseer. This, fellow citizens, I freely admit; for I learned from my father and from other venerable men the following: that elegance is proper to women, hard work to men; that all virtuous men ought to have more fame than riches; and that warfare, not furniture, bestows honor."

The behavior of various Roman dynasts in the first century BCE confirmed Livy's fears. Much like the Hellenistic monarchs mentioned earlier, these men, backed by powerful armies, embraced the elegance and abundance of the banquet table with great enthusiasm. Note that all of these passages belong to Plutarch, a biographer who, as we have seen earlier, was always interested in revealing a man's character. Dining habits were particularly relevant to this task. The Roman dictator and general Cornelius Sulla provides a stunning display of festal excess in the first passage, as does Marc Antony in the second, where Plutarch recounts Antony's excesses by way of his own grandfather, who knew of these tales from a court physician on the scene.

5.14. Plutarch, *Sulla* 35.1–3

On consecrating a tenth of all his property to Hercules, Sulla feasted the people lavishly, and his provision for them was so much beyond what was necessary that great amounts of meat were cast into the river every day, and wine was drunk that was 40 years old and beyond. Amid the feasting, which lasted for many days, Metella lay sick and dying. And since the priests prohibited Sulla to go near her, or to have his house polluted by a funeral, he sent her divorce papers, and ordered her to be carried to another house while she was still alive. In doing this, he observed the law strictly, out of super-stition; but he broke the law limiting the cost of the funeral, a law he himself had introduced, and he spared no expense. He broke also his own ordinances limiting the cost of banquets, when he tried to soothe his sorrow by drinking parties and convivial banquets, where luxury and buffoonery held sway.

5.15. Plutarch, *Antony* 28.2–4

For they had an association called the "Inimitables." And every day they feasted each other, creating expenses that were incredible and beyond measure. Anyway, Philotas, the physician of Amphissa, used to tell my grandfather Lamprias, that he was in Alexandria at this time, studying his profession, and that having gotten to know well one of the royal cooks, he was easily persuaded by him (since he was a young man) to witness the great expense and preparation for a royal dinner. Accordingly, when he was led into the kitchen and saw all the other provisions in great abundance, and eight wild boars roasting, he expressed his wonder at the large number of diners. But the cook burst out in laughter and said that the guests were not many but only about 12; but that it was necessary that everything set before them be perfect, and this an instant of time could diminish. For it might come about that Antony would ask for dinner immedi-ately, and after a little while, by chance, would postpone it and call for a cup of wine, or take up a conversation with someone. Because of this, he said that not one, but many suppers were prepared, for the precise time was hard to hit.

It was Julius Caesar who elevated feasting to new levels of notoriety, thanks largely to his political acumen and sense of innovation and organization. His political skills are evident in the first passage, which recounts his utilizing the public feast to win over the people while advancing his own career. The excerpt also points to the corruption of Roman electoral politics in the mid-first century BCE. Caesar's creative and organizational skills are apparent in the second passage, the only recorded instance of a four-fold triumph in Rome, which he held in 46 BCE (Beard). This excerpt is equally important for its hint of the numbers fed on this occasion. If we understand Plutarch's mention of dining couches (*triclinia*) to mean a set of three couches with each couch accommo-dating three diners, then this particular event was attended by close to 200,000 participants. We must imagine that the diners were scatted across the city on this occasion, happy to partake in the celebration in whatever available public space they could find. Indeed, we learn from other sources that Caesar was elaborately dressed on this occasion and that he feasted on lampreys, a delicacy that does not seem to have been provided to the population at large. Once again, the power of food to differentiate the haves from the have-nots was affirmed, this time within the dramatic spectacle of the Roman triumph (Donahue 2004b).

5.16. Plutarch, *Caesar* 5.8–9

He was lavish in his expenditures, and seemed to be exchanging heavy spending for a fleeting and short-lived fame, though in reality he was purchasing things of greatest value at a small price. It is said, accordingly, that before he entered upon any public office, he was 1,300 talents in debt.[7] When appointed curator of the Appian Way,[8] he spent huge sums of his own money upon it ; and again, during his aedileship,[9] he provided 320 pairs of gladiators, and by extravagant provision besides for theatre plays, processions, and public banquets, he washed away the memory of the liberality of his predecessors. He treated the people in such a way that every man was seeking out new offices and new honors with which to repay him.

5.17. Plutarch, *Caesar* 55.1–4

But when Caesar came back to Rome from Africa, first he delivered a boastful speech to the people concerning his victory, claiming that he had overtaken a country large enough to supply annually 200,000 Attic bushels of grain and 3,000,000 pounds of olive oil for the public treasury. Next, he celebrated triumphs, an Egyptian, a Pontic, and an African,[10] the last not for his victory over Scipio, but supposedly over Juba the king. At that time also Juba, a son of the king, a mere infant, was carried along in the triumphal parade, the most fortunate captive ever taken, since from being a barbarian and a Numidian, he came to be enrolled among the most learned men of Hellas. After the triumphs, Caesar gave generous gifts to his soldiers and entertained the people with banquets and spectacles, feasting them all at one time on 20,000 dining couches, and furnishing spectacles of gladiatorial and naval combats in honor of his daughter Julia, long since deceased.

Public feasts of the emperors

Octavian's defeat of Antony in 31 BCE and his subsequent rule as Augustus, Rome's first emperor, meant that the feasts of the Hellenistic monarch and the Roman dynasts now found a place at the imperial table. The Principate would last for nearly five centuries, and while the written sources for this vast stretch of time are by no means equal in terms of reliability or completeness, they nevertheless consistently include imperial eating and drinking as elements of historical significance. The emperor's public feasts were particularly important because they allowed for the display of imperial munificence to large numbers of people. The two selections below underscore how divergent these events could be, depending on the interests and personality of the sponsoring emperor. First, the poet Statius offers an account of a banquet for the *populus* of Rome provided by the emperor Domitian at the Colosseum to celebrate the Saturnalia, a festival held each December in honor of the god Saturn. Notable in this account are all of the elements that would have made for a memorable ancient feast: a large and enthusiastic crowd; the distribution of fine foods (dramatically delivered by means of ropes suspended above the gathered masses); legions of servants scaling the steps of the amphitheater to deliver additional fare; and the presence of the emperor himself. We should also keep in mind that Statius wrote poetry that was meant to cast the emperor and his policies in the best possible light, so an occasion of this sort provided an opportunity for flattery that could not easily be passed up (Donahue 2004b).

5.18. Statius, *Occasional Poems (Silvae)* 1.6.9–20; 28–34

> Dawn was scarcely stirring when already candied fruits were raining down from the line, this dew the rising East wind scattered: whatever was famous from Pontic nut groves, or falls from the fertile slopes of Idume;[11] that which devout Damascus grows upon its branches[12] or thirsty Caunus ripens,[13] falls freely in ample plunder; soft cakes and honey-cheese fritters, and Amerian fruit perfectly ripe,[14] and cake made with wine must, and bursting dates were showering down from a hidden palm.

> Behold, however, another crowd, no fewer than the spectators, handsome and well dressed, advances through all the tiers. Some carry baskets of bread and white napkins and more luxurious feasts; others dispense languorous wines: you would think that they were so many cupbearers of Ida.[15]

Later in the poem, Statius would have us believe that all the attendees were eating the same food, but this surely was not the case. The handsome servants mentioned above were no doubt delivering food to the elites. Moreover, the seating arrangements in the Colosseum were clearly segregated by class, an arrangement that would have reinforced, not diminished, social differences on this occasion. Even so, Statius' florid account helps us to recognize the creative possibilities that were open to the emperor when it came to providing largess for his people.

We find a very different kind of public feast held in Rome some 30 years earlier—Nero's infamous banquet on an artificial lake in 64 CE. Tacitus, a historian much interested in moral decline, offers this graphic account of heavy drinking and sexual license as evidence of Neronian depravities of all sorts (Champlin; Goddard, in Elsner and Masters). In Tacitus' view, such extravagance, especially when placed in the wrong hands, only increased narcissistic impulses while advancing the corrosion of social values.

5.19. Tacitus, *Annals* 15.37

> He himself, in order to convince the people that nothing was equally joyful to him, began to arrange banquets in public places and to utilize the entire city as his palace. The most celebrated feasts in terms of extravagance and notoriety were those arranged by Tigellinus, which I shall describe as a type, instead of repeatedly narrating the same tale of prodigality. He constructed, therefore, on the pool of Agrippa[16] a raft with a banquet on deck, and set in motion by other craft pulling it along. The vessels were decorated in gold and ivory, and oarsmen were catamites gathered according to their ages and their libidinous accomplishments. He had collected birds and wild beasts from diverse lands, and marine animals even from the Ocean. On the banks of the lake stood brothels, filled with women of high rank; and, opposite, naked harlots came into view. First came obscene gestures and dances; and then, as darkness advanced, the whole of the neighboring grove and surrounding houses began to echo together in song and to glitter with lights. Nero himself, defiled by every natural and unnatural lust, had left behind no vice by which he might live more corruptly ...

The Roman *convivium*

As we saw earlier, the Greek symposium, with its emphasis on supervised drinking, was the primary venue for transmitting traditional values among aristocratic men. It acted as a closed system in that it had a clear beginning and ending, and it involved an elaborate code of conduct and procedures (Murray). The Roman version of the symposium, which involved both eating and drinking, was the *convivium*. Filtered through the Etruscans of central Italy, the *convivium* featured the host and his invited guests at a meal that was popular among emperors and elites alike.

A characteristic feature of these gatherings was an intense concern with the rank and status of the participants. Granted initially by birthright, rank was socio-political standing. In imperial times the emperor enjoyed the highest ranking, followed by senators, equestrians, free citizens, freed persons, and finally slaves. (Rank was not necessarily permanent; promotion was possible, for example, through election to office or emancipation from slavery.) On the other hand, status was a reflection of one's power, based on accomplishment or influence with others of higher rank. Social standing was a complex combination of these factors combined with wealth.

Figure 10. Banquet scene depicting people eating and drinking at a *convivium* (feast) beneath a portico. Roman fresco from House of Triclinium, Pompeii, first century CE. Museo Archeologico Nazionale, Naples, Italy. Photo Credit: Erich Lessing/Art Resource, NY.

The emperor as host

The *convivium* allowed the host to create his own world by inviting guests of his own choosing to his table. For the emperor, this typically meant inviting senators and ambitious men of equestrian rank as a means of confirming his own prestige while allowing the invitees to enhance their own status by enjoying a meal in the imperial presence. Ancient biography opened up all of the emperor's actions for scrutiny, including his *convivia*, where his choice of food, guests, and setting provided valuable insight into his character. Not surprisingly, "good" emperors tended to show restraint in their eating and drinking, while "bad" emperors did not. Examples of the former behavior are evident in Suetonius' assessments of Augustus and that of Hadrian from the *Historia Augusta*.

5.20. Suetonius, *Augustus* 74

At such dinner parties he would sometimes arrive late and leave early, letting his guests start and finish without him. He used to provide a meal of three courses, six when he was in a very generous mood, with no great extravagance and a most cheerful atmosphere. For he used to draw into conversation the quiet guests or the ones who muttered under their breath, and he introduced music and actors, or even roving players from the circus and, more frequently, story-tellers.

5.21. Suetonius, *Augustus* 77

He was also by nature very sparing in his drinking of wine. Cornelius Nepos writes that in camp at Mutina[17] he was accustomed to not more than three drinks during dinner. Later in life, however often he indulged himself more freely, he did not exceed a pint or, if he did, he used to vomit. And he especially enjoyed Raetian wine,[18] but he did not drink it casually during the daytime. Instead of a drink, he used to take bread soaked in cold water, or a slice of cucumber, or the heart of a young lettuce, or an apple with more of an acidic wine flavor, either fresh or dried.

5.22. *Augustan History, Life of Hadrian* 22; 26

When senators came to his banquets he received them standing, and he always reclined at table dressed either in a Greek cloak or in a toga. The cost of a banquet he determined on each occasion, all with the utmost care, and he reduced the amounts that might be spent according to ancient law.[19]

At his banquets he always furnished, as the occasion required, tragedies, comedies, Atellan farces,[20] sambuca players, readers, or poets.

At the same time, the *convivia* of those emperors who were less popular could be portrayed in highly unflattering terms. In the first excerpt Dio reprises Vitellius' reputation for gluttony during his brief reign in 69 CE; in the second entry he recounts a ghoulishly creative but excessively cruel and manipulative dinner party staged by Domitian (Fredrick, in Boyle and Dominik), the last of the Flavian emperors in the late first century CE.

5.23. Cassius Dio, 64.2.1–3

Vitellius, addicted as he was to extravagance and licentiousness, no longer gave consideration to anything else, either human or divine. For indeed from the beginning he had been the sort to idle about in taverns and gaming houses, and to pursue dancers and charioteers zealously; and he used to spend inexpressible amounts on such pursuits, with the result that he had many creditors. At that time, and more so when he had set himself up in such great power, he acted with insolence, and he squandered money most of the day and night alike. Insatiately, he took his fill and continually vomited up everything, as if nourished by the mere passage of the food. And this method was all that enabled him to hold out, since his fellow banqueters fared very badly. For he was always inviting many of the foremost men as dinner companions, and many times they feasted him. In this context one of them, Vibius Crispus, uttered a very clever remark; having been absent from the feasting for some days because of illness, he said: "If I had not become sick, I surely would have perished." The entire time of his reign was nothing but drunkenness and riotous reveling. All the most costly foodstuffs were brought in from as far as the Ocean (not to say farther) and from both land and sea, and were prepared so expensively that even now certain cakes and other foods are named "Vitellian" after him. And yet, why should one recount each of these incidents, when it is agreed upon by all alike that during the period of his reign he spent 900,000,000 sesterces on dinners? All of the costly food items were soon lacking because of a shortage, and yet it was absolutely necessary that they should be provided. For example, he once prepared a dish that cost a million sesterces, which combined the tongues, brains, and livers of certain fishes and birds.

5.24. Cassius Dio, 67.9.1–6

At another time he feasted the foremost men among the senators and knights in the following fashion. He arranged a room that was as dark as possible on every side— ceilings, walls, and floor—and having prepared bare couches of the same color resting on the uncovered floor, he called in his guests alone at night without their attendants. And first he set beside each of them a slab in the shape of a gravestone bearing the name of each guest and also a small lamp, the kind that hangs in tombs. Next, handsome naked boys, also painted in black, entered like ghosts, and after encircling the guests with some frightful dancing, they settled themselves at their feet. After this, all the things commonly dedicated in offerings to the dead were also set before the guests, all of them in black and in dishes of a similar color. As a result, every one of the guests was both fearful and trembling and was ever expecting to have his throat cut, especially since there was great silence on everyone's part, as if they were already among the dead, and since Domitian himself conversed on all things relating to death and slaughter. At last he dismissed them; but he had removed beforehand their slaves, who had stood in the vestibule, and now handed over his guests to some other slaves, whom they did not know, and he conveyed them either in carriages or litters, filling them with far greater fear. And scarcely had each guest made it home and, as one might say, was beginning to catch his breath, when it was reported to him that someone had arrived from the emperor. Then, while they were fully expecting to perish from this, one person brought in the slab, which was of silver, then others in turn provided the dinner implements, fashioned out of very costly materials; and last of all (came) that particular boy, who had been the divine spirit for each guest, now washed and adorned … thus, after having spent the entire night in terror, they received the gifts.

Patrons and clients

We are well informed about other attendees at convivial feasts besides the emperor. One such group included patrons and clients. As a free man, a client (*cliens*) supported a social superior, his patron (*patronus*), in political and private life in exchange for favors. Typically, a client displayed respect for his patron by accompanying him on his daily business and by going to his house each morning to greet him (*salutatio*). For the patron, it was important to have as many clients as he could maintain as a way of advertising his prestige and political influence. In return, the client received benefits, such as a daily handout of food or money (*sportula*) and assistance in legal matters. While scholars have disagreed over the impact of clientage on Roman social and political life, this kind of exchange of goods and services between persons of unequal status nevertheless underscored the reality that power and rank was based on personal interactions at all social levels (Wallace-Hadrill).

Martial, a writer of witty epigrams in the first century CE, was especially fond of casting himself in the persona of a client mistreated by his cheap and insolent patron. While the patron–client paradigm allowed Martial to be clever and humorous, the stinginess of the patron's dinner, as evident in the next two passages, points to larger concerns over social disequilibrium and the ease with which food and drink could be manipulated to exacerbate such differences in rank and status.

5.25. Martial, *Epigram* 2.19

Zoilus, do you think a dinner makes me happy? And then, Zoilus, that a dinner of yours makes me happy? The guest whom a dinner of yours makes happy, Zoilus, ought to beg on the slope of Aricia.[21]

5.26. Martial, *Epigram* 1.59

The dole at Baiae provides me with 25 sesterces.[22] What is that kind of poverty doing amid luxury? Give me back the murky baths of Lupus and Gryllus. When I dine so badly, Flaccus, why should I bathe well?

Such parsimony was all the more painful because the client typically received fare that was inferior to that of his social superiors, as Martial would have us believe in the excerpts below. To be sure, satisfaction at the dinner table could never be assured for those who had to rely on the hospitality of others.

5.27. Martial, *Epigram* 3.60.3–10

You take oysters fattened in the Lucrine lake, I cut my mouth sucking a mussel from its shell; you get mushrooms, I get swine fungi; you take a turbot, but I brill. A golden turtledove with fattened rump fills you up, a magpie dead in its cage is set before me… Ponticus, … let's eat the same meal.

5.28. Martial, *Epigram* 12.48

If you serve mushrooms and boar as if everyday fare and don't think that these are the objects of my prayers, so be it; but if you believe that I am made wealthy and you want to be designated as my heir because of five Lucrine oysters, good-bye. "Yet it's a fine dinner." Very fine, I confess, but tomorrow it will be nothing, or rather today, or rather right now, it will be nothing; a matter that the luckless sponge on a doomed broomstick knows of,[23] or some dog or other, or a pot by the roadside,[24] this is the result of mullets and hares and sow's udder—that, and a pasty complexion and feet that play the torturer. No Alban drinking party would be worth it to me,[25] no Capitoline and Pontifical banquets.[26] If a god himself should make me a gift of nectar, it would turn to vinegar and the treacherous, flat wine of a Vatican jar. Feastmaster, seek out other guests whom the proud despotism of your table might reel in. As for me, let my friend invite me for improvised scraps. I like a dinner I can return.

Women

An important distinction between the *convivium* and Greek *symposion* was that women could participate in the Roman meal, although it is not unusual to find banquets in the literary sources attended by males only. Women are said to have been seated at dinner during the Republican period, but to have reclined at table (on reclining, see more below) along with men by the time of the emperors. Indeed, dinner posture itself was a critical feature of the dining ritual and is now recognized as being encoded with various meanings (Roller).

The male bias of our sources makes it difficult to assess the extent to which women actually participated in the meal. In the passage below Juvenal would have us believe that women were garrulous and disruptive attendees. As a satirist he exaggerates, of course, yet it is equally hard to imagine that women played no role at all in this setting. It is perhaps best to believe that the nature and extent of their participation differed according to their rank and status and the preferences of the host.

5.29. Juvenal, *Satire* 6.434–42

But that woman is more intolerable, who, when she has begun to recline at dinner, praises Vergil, pardons the dying Dido,[27] and ranks the poets and compares them, placing Vergil in the one scale and Homer in the other. The grammarians give up, the rhetoricians are overwhelmed, the whole crowd grows silent; neither lawyer nor auctioneer will speak, nor another woman; so great flows the power of her words, that you would say that all the pots and bells were being struck together.

At the same time, women often appear at the intersection of food and sex. The topic is treated in greater detail at the end of this chapter. In the context of *convivia* the sources portray love affairs (Yardley, in Slater), while the emperors sometimes treated female invitees as sexual prizes to be taken away from the festal table. In the first excerpt below Suetonius provides a graphic example of the latter in the case of the troubled emperor Caligula. The second passage, advising guests not to ogle the wives of other men, is an actual inscription found on the dining room walls of the Casa del Moralista at Pompeii. It was a reminder of the kind of proper behavior that we may assume was not always practiced.

5.30. Suetonius, *Caligula* 36

Beyond his incest with his sisters and his notorious passion for the prostitute

Pyrallis, there was scarcely any woman of rank whom he did not approach. These he typically invited to dinner with their husbands, and as they passed by the foot of his couch, he would inspect them carefully and deliberately in the manner of buying slaves, even lifting up the face by his hand of anyone who looked down in modesty; then as often as it pleased him he would leave the dining room, sending for the one who pleased him best, and returning soon afterward with the signs of his indecencies still evident, he would openly praise or berate his partner, recounting one by one the good and bad features of her body and her performance. To some he personally sent a bill of divorce in the name of their absent husbands, and he ordered it thus to be entered in the public records.

5.31. *Corpus Inscriptionum Latinarum (CIL)* 4.7698b

Keep your horny leering and enticing glances away from other people's wives; decency should be on the tip of your tongue.

Parasites

The parasite was a low-status character of Greek and Roman comedy, who endured the abuse of his social superiors. At first he was known in Greek as a *kolax* ("toady," "flatterer"); alternatively, however, he was called a *parasitos* (hence "parasite" in English), which, in its original religious sense, meant "fellow diner," but came to mean "sponger." The goal of the parasite was to acquire whatever he could for free from the wealthy, especially a dinner. In exchange, he provided flattery, simple services, and a willingness to endure humiliation. Given his dubious livelihood, the parasite earned the condemnation of philosophers, moralists and satirists alike. In the first passage Lucian, a second-century satirist who wrote in Greek and displayed a keen eye for social commentary, provides a stinging assessment of the *kolax*, the flatterer, whom he blames for inflating the ego of the rich man at Rome. This was no doubt true, but so too was the reality that eating in antiquity always involved haves and have-nots, and such disparities were essential to maintaining social hierarchy at the dinner table and beyond. In the second excerpt it is not clear that the character Iortus is a parasite but his humorous observation is notable for the lengths to which flattery might go in an effort to win the favor of the dinner host. In the final passage, Martial humorously presents a certain Selius as a flatterer *par excellence*.

5.32. Lucian, *Wisdom of Nigrinus* 22

"Far more foolish, however, than the rich are those who visit them and flatter them. They get up in the middle of the night, run around the city in circles, have doors closed in their faces by household slaves, and endure hearing themselves called dogs, flatterers, and similar names. Their thanks for this cruel round of visits—the tiresome dinner—is the source of many misfortunes. How much they eat up, how much they drink contrary to their judgment, and how much they say that was not necessary to have been said! In the end they go away, either finding fault or being aggrieved, either complaining about the dinner, or accusing the host of insolence or pettiness. They fill the alleyways, vomiting and fighting at the brothels. Most of them go to bed by daylight and give the doctors a reason for making their rounds. But some—what is strangest—do not have the time to be ill!

Yet I hold that the flatterers are far worse than those whom they flatter, and that they are all but to blame for the arrogance established in others. When they admire their possessions, praise their gold, fill up their doorways at daybreak and go up and speak to them as if they are slave masters, what are the wealthy supposed to think? If by a common resolution they refrained but a short time from this voluntary servitude, don't you think that the opposite would happen, that the rich would come to the doors of the poor and beg them not to leave their happiness unseen and unattested and their beautiful tables and great houses unprofitable and unused? For they do not like being rich so much as they like being congratulated for it."

5.33. Plutarch, *On Mores (Moralia), Fragment 180*

At Maecenas' banquet alongside his couch there was a rectangular table of the largest size and of unsurpassed beauty; as one might expect, others found various ways to praise it. Iortus, at a loss to speak of its marvelous nature, in a moment of silence, remarked, "But, there is something you have not noticed, my dear fellow guests: it is round and very circular." So then, as was fitting, laughter broke out at this piece of pure flattery.

5.34. Martial, *Epigram* 2.27

When Selius casts his nets for a dinner and praises you, bring him with you, whether you are reciting or pleading a case. "Way to go!" "A killer!" "A quick strike!" "Cunning!" "Well done!" "Lovely!" "That's what I was waiting for!" You've got your dinner, now shut up!

Cooks and dinner slaves

Cooks prepared the meals for free families and for the guests of the wealthy. In larger households there was an established hierarchy among kitchen slaves, especially when it came time for staging a formal dinner. There were slaves who assisted with invitations and others who managed food supplies and performed the actual cooking of the meal. Slaves could also provide entertainment while they served the guests by singing, dancing, and reciting poetry. There was even a slave who tasted the food to prevent the emperor from being poisoned (D'Arms, in Slater).

In the first excerpt Horace utilizes the philosopher Catius as his mouth-piece to emphasize the importance of cleanliness by focusing on filthy slaves (Gowers). He is writing satire, of course, so we must allow for a degree of hyperbole. Moreover, we lack the testimony of slaves to provide an alternate account. Nonetheless, Horace reveals some of the social antipathy directed against the dinner slave. Such abuse was also frequently directed toward the cook as the one responsible for the meal itself. Dissatisfaction with the meal could easily lead to physical violence, as the passages from Martial suggest.

5.35. Horace, *Satire* 2.4.78–87

It really turns your stomach to see a slave with greasy hands from some food he has pilfered pick up a cup, or to find a coating of old filth inside an antique bowl. Brooms, place mats, sawdust—how much do these simple items cost? When you neglect these things, it's a great disgrace. Do you scrape mosaic floors with a muddy palm broom and throw dirty coverlets on couches covered with fine cloth? Do you forget, since neatness is both inexpensive and easy, that you're more justly blamed for lacking that one quality than any fancy item found only on the tables of the wealthy?[28]

5.36. Martial, *Epigram* 3.13

While you don't wish to carve up the fish or the fowl, and you are more sparing with the boar than with your father, Naevia,[29] you blame the cook and cut him up, as if everything that he brought in was indigestible.[30] I'll never get indigestion[30] this way.

5.37. Martial, *Epigram* 3.94

You say that the hare is undercooked and you call for the whip; Rufus, you prefer to slice up your cook rather than your hare.

Seating arrangements

Concerns with rank and status found full expression in the seating arrangements of the *convivium*, where the realities of social differentiation were reflected in the positions of the guests themselves. At the typical dinner party sets of three couches were arranged around a serving table, which held the food and drink delivered by the waiting slaves. Guests, three to a couch, reclined on their left elbow while taking food with their right hand. The host was in charge of determining the seating, which was usually arranged according to the rank and status of the invitees, with the guest of honor enjoying the most favorable position in relation to the host. Any household members who were present would recline in the positions of lowest status. Slaves, owing to their servile rank and to the fact that they were busy preparing and delivering the food, did not recline with the guests (Dalby 2003, s.v. "triclinium").

Seating arrangements were tricky business. The host who seated his guests properly might expect to enhance his social status by staging a successful dinner; he who overlooked this element, however, flirted with social disaster while putting his own reputation at risk. It is not surprising, therefore, that we find Plutarch debating the question of whether a host should determine the seating or leave it up to the guests themselves. In fact, Plutarch includes an entire work, entitled *Table Talk*, within his *Moral Writings*, which treats dining and dinner arrangements. It is further proof that Greek intellectuals like Plutarch and Athenaeus recognized dining and dinner arrangements as a cultural practice that would be of interest to their readers during the Roman period. The irony of this particular dialogue is that all the interlocutors agree that friendship and enjoyment is the goal of a dinner, yet there is no agreement on how best to achieve it. In this passage the guest Lamprias maintains that attendees should be able to learn from each other and that this is best achieved by seating people with opposite interests next to each other.

5.38. Plutarch, *On Mores (Moralia)*, *Table Talk* 1.2.618d–f

… of such a kind do I wish to make our dinner party, not seating together rich man with rich man, nor young man with young man, nor magistrate with magistrate, nor friend with friend. This arrangement is stagnant and inefficient toward the establishment and advancement of good fellowship; but supplying what is suitable to the man who lacks it, I bid him who is eager to learn to recline with the learned man, the gentle man with the man who is hard to please, the young man who is fond of listening with the old man who enjoys talking, the reticent man with the braggart, the calm man with the man who is prone to anger. And if by chance I observe a wealthy and generous dinner guest, I shall lead to him from some corner a poor and honest man, so that just as from a full vessel into an empty one, a certain kind of outpouring may take place. But I shall forbid sophist to recline at table with sophist and poet with poet:

"For beggar is jealous of beggar and poet of poet."[31]

Risk and reciprocity

While seating arrangements were important, so too was the reputation of both the host and the invitee. To be sure, risk was always present, as invitations could be declined or guests could be uninvited. Perhaps the biggest risk of all was that the host's dinner might be a social failure. We have to wonder if these were the kinds of concerns on Aesop's mind when he declared that a piece of bread eaten in peace is better than a banquet partaken in anxiety. At any rate, we observe some of these tensions in this next excerpt, in which Pliny expresses his exasperation at being stood up by an invitee who has opted for a better meal.

5.39. Pliny the Younger, *Letter 1.15* (To Septicius Clarus)

Who are you, to accept my invitation to dinner and not show up? The judgment is pronounced: you shall pay my costs in full, and this is no small amount. The dinner was all prepared: one lettuce each, three snails, two eggs, wheat cake, and honey wine chilled with snow (for you will pay for this too, surely among the first items, seeing that it melts in the dish), olives, beetroots, gherkins, onions, and countless other delicacies. You would have heard comic actors, a reader, or singer, or all three (it depends on my generosity). But you preferred oysters, sow's innards, sea urchins, and Spanish dancing girls at the house of a stranger. You'll pay for this—I'm not saying what it is. You have acted with cruelty: you have been spiteful, perhaps to yourself, certainly to me, but yes to yourself! How much we would have relaxed and laughed and learned! You can eat more magnificently at many houses, but nowhere more cheerfully, more simply and more casually. In sum, try me; and then, if you don't prefer to decline invitations elsewhere, you can always make excuses to me.

Finally, these dinners featured an element of reciprocity, as the guest was expected to repay the favor by inviting the host to a dinner party of his own. In this way, the *convivium* operated as a kind of gift exchange. In addition to confirming social status, this was an important way of providing goods and services in a pre-industrialized ancient economy.

Dining spaces of the emperor and the wealthy

As we saw in the case of the Saturnalia feast at the Colosseum (5.18), it is unlikely that all orders of society ate at the same tables; rather, that this was an example of distortion characteristic of poetry produced during the Domitianic regime. This should not distract us, however, from a very significant feature of feasting, namely, the importance of setting in private contexts, especially the dining room (*triclinium*). Whether at the emperor's palace atop the Palatine Hill in Rome or elsewhere, the dining room itself played a crucial role in helping to advertise status and to transmit social values to the guests (Fredrick, in Boyle and Dominik). Concerning the emperor's dining room, we know that Domitian's new palace, completed in 92 CE, contained oval-shaped pools of water that flanked each side of the dining hall. The room itself measured over 900 square meters and soared to a height of nearly 33 meters. Moreover, bold use of colored marbles, a fashionable trend among wealthy Romans of the time, added to the overall splendor of the dining area. Statius makes this clear during Domitian's reign in a poem he may have recited at the palace itself during the banquet (Coleman).

5.40. Statius, *Occasional Poems* (*Silvae*) 4.2.18–31

> A majestic edifice, huge, remarkable, not with 100 columns but as many as might support heaven and the gods above, if Atlas[32] were relieved of his burden … There, Libyan mountain (Numidian yellow marble) and shining Ilian (Phrygian purple marble) are rivals, and much Syenite (Egyptian granite) and Chian,[33] and the rock (Carystian marble)[34] that contends with the grayish-green sea, and Luna (white Italian marble), chosen only to carry the columns' weight. The view extends far aloft; you could scarcely gain sight of the roof with wearied eye, you would think it the ceiling of a gilded heaven.

Furthermore, the imperial dining room served as a perfect setting for a particular form of fine dining—the emperor's formal dinner, known as the *cena recta*.

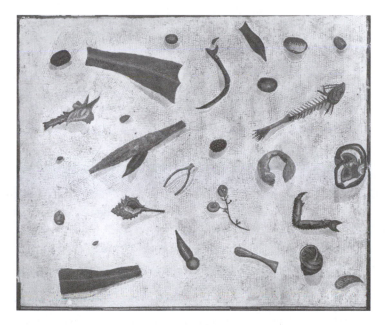

Figure 11. Mosaic of the Unswept Floor. Roman copy of a Greek original depicting the remains of a feast, second century CE. Museo Lateranense, Vatican Museums, Vatican State. Photo Credit: Alinari/Art Resource, NY.

Although the origins and Latin terminology of this dinner remain obscure, it was something more than the *convivium* and it was especially popular under Domitian, who deserves credit as one of the great innovators of the imperial dining experience. We are well informed about the *cena recta* thanks to Statius and Martial, who are keen to portray the emperor as a beneficent feast master. In this excerpt Martial claims that all classes dined together on this occasion. As we have seen, this is not consistent with the prevailing social realities, although it does underscore how welcome these occasions were for those who were invited.

5.41. Martial, *Epigram* 8.49

… so great, Caesar, are the banquets celebrating your laurels; our joys gladdens the gods themselves. Every knight feasts with you, and the people and the senators, and Rome shares an ambrosial feast with its leader. Though you promised great things, what greater things you have provided! You promised a handout (*sportula*), but you gave a formal dinner (*cena recta*).

Festal venues beyond the emperor's palace could be equally grand and dramatic. This excerpt recounts the famous meeting between Antony and Cleopatra in

41 BCE, when the queen met the Roman general at Tarsos in Asia Minor by sailing up the Cydnus River in her own luxury yacht (*thalamegos*). Athenaeus, citing the historian Socrates of Rhodes, provides a vivid description of the drinking party that she provided on board her ship. The emphases on color and smell add to the setting and to the glamour and mystique of the clever and generous Egyptian queen (Donahue 2012).

5.42. Athenaeus, *Sophists at Dinner* 4.147f–148b

In book three of his *Civil War*, Socrates of Rhodes, recording the banquet given by Cleopatra, the last queen of Egypt, who married the Roman general, Antony, in Cilicia, says the following: "Meeting Antony in Cilicia, Cleopatra arranged a royal drinking party in his honor, in which everything was of gold and inlaid stones and fashioned with exceeding skill; even the walls, he says, were hung with tapestries spun with purple and gold threads. And having spread 12 dining couches, Cleopatra invited Antony and his chosen comrades. He was astounded by the luxury of the display; smiling gently, she said that all these things were a present for him. She also invited him to come and dine with her the next day with his friends and officers. And then, when she put on a much better symposium, she made the first one seem paltry; and again she gave these items as gifts. As for the officers, she entrusted each one to take away the couch on which he had reclined, and even the sideboards and the spreads for the couches were divided up among them. And for their departure, she provided litters with attendants for the guests of high rank, while for the greater number she provided horses outfitted with silver-plated harnesses; and for all she offered Ethiopian slaves to carry the torches. On the fourth day she gave the payment of a talent for the purchase of roses, and the floors of the dining room were strewn with them to the depth of a cubit in net-like spirals spread over everything.

Among domestic dining space of the wealthy, detailed floor mosaics and elaborate wall paintings of mythological heroes and gods such as those found at various villae at Pompeii combined to create a visual rhetoric meant to transmit to the guests the sophistication and wealth of the host. In some instances these dining rooms grew in size over time. The hall at the House of Bacchus at Djemila in Roman North Africa had enough dining couches to accommodate nearly 50 diners (Ellis). Furthermore, it was not unusual for the wealthy to own several villas, each with multiple dining rooms meant to provide a range of dining experiences. As the owner of several estates, Pliny the Younger easily fitted into this category. This letter describes the most impressive of the several dining rooms located within his seaside villa south of Rome. Scholars have debated whether Pliny is describing an actual villa or is presenting a "rhetoric of self-stylization" (Bergmann) aimed at achieving lasting fame. Regardless, the passage is valuable for the insight it provides into the impulse of a wealthy Roman magistrate to create dining spaces that were memorable, dramatic, and evocative of his status and achievement.

5.43. Pliny the Younger, *Letter* 2.17.4–6 (to Gallus)

The house is large enough for my needs but not expensive to maintain. It opens into a hall, unpretentious but dignified, and then there are two colonnades, rounded like the letter D, which enclose a small but pleasant courtyard. This makes an excellent refuge in bad weather, being protected by windows and much more by the overhanging roof. Opposite the middle of it is a pleasant inner hall, and then a dining room, sufficiently lovely, which runs out toward the shore; and whenever the southwest wind drives the sea inland, the spray of the spent breakers lightly washes it. On all sides it has folding doors and windows no smaller than the doors, so that at the front and sides it seems to look out on to three seas; and at the rear it has a view to the woods and the mountains in the distance through the inner hall, the courtyard with the two colonnades, and the entrance hall.

Pliny was equally interested in providing a memorable dining experience for his family and friends at his estate in the upper Tiber valley north of Rome. Here he describes a device for delivering food to his guests amid his beautifully landscaped outdoor riding course. The Romans were fond of such contrivances. Varro spoke of revolving dinner tables and Nero even installed a revolving roof in his spectacularly elaborate palace, the Golden House (*Domus Aurea*). Here the curved dining seat is a *stibadium* or *sigma*, a semi-circular dining couch that was a variation of the *triclinium* arrangement.

5.44. Pliny the Younger, *Letter* 5.6.36–7 (to Domitius Apollinaris)

At the upper end (of the garden area) a vine shades a curved dining table of white marble; four small pillars of Carystian[35] marble support the vine. Water gushes out through little pipes from under the table as if pressed out by the weight of the people sitting there; it is caught in a stone cistern, and held in a finely worked marble basin regulated by a hidden device so as to remain full without overflowing. The appetizers and the heavier dishes are placed on the edge of the basin, while the lighter ones float about in vessels shaped like birds or little boats.

Table service and drinking implements

Closely related to space, of course, was dining furniture and accessories (Wilkins and Hill 2006). Of central importance was the dining couch mentioned earlier. This was an Eastern item that came to be well established in the symposiastic celebrations of men of status throughout the Greek cities by the end of the fifth century BCE, where it was known as a *kline*. The dining couch was equally important in Italy, where it was introduced to the Etruscans and other Italic peoples. Known as a *triclinium*, it gained even further prominence amid the Roman absorption of Hellenic luxury from the third century BCE onwards. Poorer people tended to recline on a straw mattress called a *stibas*.

Among other items, oil lamps to provide lighting, amphorae to bring wine into the *triclinium*, and shelving or furniture to store goods, were standard. Servants brought in the courses, circulated them among the guests and then removed them before the next dish was brought in. In terms of tableware, the *convivium* and *symposion* centered on individual service so that status boundaries could be maintained, while shared vessels became more common in the Roman world after the third century among dinners enjoyed by sub-elites (Hudson). As we have seen, our sources tend to be biased toward an elite population. Thus do we observe metal ware of gold and silver, such as we have seen already in the wedding feast of Caranus (no. 5.5). The Romans also admired fine metal ware. We get a strong sense of this in the *Satyricon* of Petronius, where Trimachio, the dinner host, utilizes a silver tooth pick and presents a silver skeleton to remind his guests of the fleeting nature of life. Of interest too are the finely wrought serving pieces as seen in this item made of Corinthian bronze, an alloy highly valued by ancient connoisseurs.

5.45. Petronius, *Satyricon* 31.8–11

A very sumptuous appetizer was brought in. Everyone had reclined to eat, with the exception of Trimalchio alone, whose place of honor as host was being reserved in the modern fashion. But I was speaking of the appetizers. A donkey made of rare Corinthian bronze had been set up with two panniers, one holding green olives, the other black. Flanking the donkey were two side dishes, both engraved with Trimalchio's name and the weight of the silver, while little bridges soldered on to the plate were holding dormice[36] dipped in honey and rolled in poppy seed. And sizzling sausages had been placed on top of a silver grill, while beneath the grill were plums with pomegranate seeds.

Venues and victuals among the people

At home

Eating and drinking spaces were not restricted solely to the *domus* of the wealthy, of course. The Greek house of an ordinary citizen was a simple structure of one or two levels. Kitchen space was typically to be found on the ground floor, although cooking could take place on portable braziers both inside and outside of the home. Often more elaborately decorated was a room to receive guests, typically men—hence the name *andron* to designate this space. It was here that the dining couches were arranged, usually five, seven, or 11 in number, with pebble mosaics sometimes decorating the floor. In the next excerpt Lysias, who produced speeches for defendants in the Athenian courts of the fifth century BCE, confirms the simple upper-story *andron* of Euphiletus, charged with the murder of his wife's lover. Euphiletus has traded spaces with his wife to allow her to take care of their newborn child more easily. Much work has been done in recent years to understand better the role of domestic space such as this, especially its relationship to the rest of the house, the household, and the potential symbolic role of spatial organization (Nevett).

5.46. Lysias, *Against Eratosthenes* 9; 22–3

I must tell you, gentlemen (for I am obligated to give you these details) that my dwelling consists of two floors, the upper level equal in size to the lower, with the women's quarters above and the men's below.

Sostratus was my close friend. After sunset I met him as he came home from the country. As I knew that, arriving at that particular time, he would find no one at home, I invited him to dinner. We came to my house, climbed to the upper room, and ate dinner. When he had eaten well, he left me and departed; I went to bed.

Taverns and inns

The most popular Italian equivalent of the simple Greek house was the multi-story urban tenement building (*insula*) from Rome and Ostia. The literary tradition typically characterizes the apartments (*cenaculae*) contained within these structures as crowded and dangerous. Not all of these units were of low quality, however, although challenges still remain in accurately estimating the living conditions of these *insulae*, and of non-elite domestic space in general (Rawson). Most importantly for our purposes, the occupants of these urban apartments did not typically cook indoors but instead purchased food and drink at *thermopolia*, (lit. places where hot drinks are sold) neighborhood bars scattered across the city that served items such as lentils, meat, cheese, and mulled spice wine (*calida*), the ancient equivalent of modern fast food. The reputation of these establishments was poor. Plautus speaks of them as gathering spots for lowly Greeks, while Dio records that in 41 CE the emperor Claudius once ordered that such places be closed altogether, a move suggesting that anxieties about public order remained a real concern for the emperor.

5.47. Plautus, *Curculio* 288–95

And as for those Greeks dressed in their *pallium*,[37] who walk around with their heads covered, who stroll about with their clothing stuffed with books and

Figure 12. Roman wine bar/café (*thermopolium*), Via dell'Abbondanza (Street of Abundance), Pompeii, Italy. Photo Credit: Gianni Dagli Orti/The Art Archive at Art Resource, NY.

handouts of food, they loiter about; like runaway slaves they trade stories with each other, they block your path, get in your way, stroll about with their smart ideas; you always see them drinking in a bar when they have stolen something— they drink hot drinks with their heads muffled, solemn, and tipsy do they go about—if I bump into them, I'll beat the crap out of each one of them.

5.48. Cassius Dio, 60.6.7

And realizing that there was no point in forbidding the people to do certain things unless their daily life should be reformed, he abolished the taverns where they gathered and drank, and ordered that no boiled meat or hot water should be sold; and he punished some who did not obey in this matter.

Elsewhere, Dio records that Caligula once even put a man to death for selling hot water at a bar during a period of mourning for his sister (59.11.6). Furthermore, the *Augustan History* records that some emperors were supposedly so depraved as to have cook shops within the palace or to vandalize them when possible, as in the case of Verus, who served as co-emperor with Marcus Aurelius in the second century.

5.49. *Augustan History, Life of Verus* 4.5–6

Besides, he is said to have been so dissolute that after he returned from Syria he installed a cook shop in his home, and he used to head off to that place after Marcus' banquets and have as his attendants every sort of base person … And he used to hurl into the cook shops very large coins that would smash the cups.

Such taverns were also popular in Greek cities, especially Athens. Known as *kapeleia*, they sold wine, vinegar, and torches to light the way home at night, as well as something to eat. The *kapeleion* appears frequently in comedy but also in a variety of other texts, as indicated by the two selections below. The first is an inscription preserving a curse (perhaps of a disgruntled customer or a teetotaler?), which suggests that these establishments were quite numerous and that they were operated by people of low standing; the second is a forensic speech, the tone of which is typical of the elite bias against these taverns (Davidson). Most importantly, the *kapeleion* allows us to view an alternative to the aristocratic symposium that is so widespread in the sources.

5.50. *Inscriptiones Graecae (IG)* 3.3

I bind Callias, the taverner and his wife Thraitta,[38] and the tavern of the old bald man, and Anthemion's tavern near [...], and Philo the taverner. Of all these, I bind their soul, their trade, their hands and feet, their taverns ... and also the taverner Agathon, servant of Sosimenes... I bind Mania, the bar girl at the spring,[39] and the tavern of Aristander of Eleusis.

5.51. Isocrates, *Antidosis* 286–7

Yes, for you have made the most moderate of young men spend their youth in drinking, screwing, lazy living, and childish follies, to the neglect of pursuing with zeal anything to make them better men; whereas those who are of a baser nature spend their days in the kind of excesses that not even a decent servant would have dared to pursue in former times. Some of them chill their wine at the *Nine Fountains*,[40] others drink in taverns; others play dice in the gambling houses, and many hang around the places where the flute girls are trained.

Closely related to the tavern was the inn, which offered lodging, food, and drink for the ancient traveler. Like the tavern, the inn was held in low regard by ancient commentators. Here, Sidonius, the famous poet, diplomat, and bishop of Clermont (Auvergne), and a key figure in the transition of the Roman Empire to the early Middle Ages in fifth-century Gaul, offers a particularly unappealing assessment of the fare and atmosphere of the inn in a letter once written to a friend, whom he has just learned has been murdered by his slaves. Note too his disparaging view of the entertainments and behavior of the lower classes. In the second passage the physician Galen even suggests that certain innkeepers served human flesh. These comments reflect the prejudices and stereotypes of those who never frequented such establishments; we might suppose that the assessments of actual travelers would have been less critical.

5.52. Sidonius, *Letter to Lupus*, 8.11.3

But if these deny me lodging as already being booked up, go next to the doors of the bishops and, kissing the hand of the holy Gallicinus, beg for the freedom of a tiny room, so that, if I am deserted by the refusal of a home, I should not have to go in sorrow to damp inns and, again and again stopping both nostrils, groan because of the many smoky kitchens where, in dishes garnished with thyme, the red sausage emits odors amid the twin berries,[41] or where clouds of smoke mixed with the steam of pots reek amid the clattering of plates. Here, when a feast-day has begun to excite hoarse songs and to crackle with the delightful complaints of the jesters, then, then, stirred up by the Camena[42] of my drunken host, I, more of a barbarian than they, shall murmur strains more worthy of you.

5.53. Galen, *On the Powers of Food* 3 (trans. Grant, 155)

The similarity between the flesh of man and pig in taste and smell has been observed when certain people have eaten unawares human meat instead of pork. Such incidents perpetrated by unscrupulous restaurateurs and other such people have been witnessed in the past.

Community feasts

For the ordinary citizen the kitchen and cook shop were by no means the only venues to offer a meal. To be sure, there were any number of events that featured food and drink as part of their festivities. As we saw earlier in this chapter, the emperor's public feasts were popular, as were his more intimate gatherings at the imperial palace for those lucky enough to gain an invitation. Religious festivals in Greece and Italy were also a common source for feasting, as seen in Chapter 4. Yet another opportunity to eat and drink was to be found in the numerous community feasts that occurred throughout the year, especially in Italy and the Roman West. The most typical scenario involved a municipal notable offering a meal, cash for a meal, or a bit of honey cake and sweet wine for the towns-people, perhaps to mark a statue dedication in his honor or the completion of a public works project for which he or she had paid. Such occasions allowed benefactors to advertize their generosity and to enhance their social standing as part of the widespread practice of privately sponsored philanthropy known as *evergetism* in the Graeco-Roman world.

A particularly striking aspect of this phenomenon was that it provided those of sufficient means but of lesser social standing the same opportunity to bestow largess as their social superiors. The first passage is an inscription that records the benefactions of a freedman who was also a local priest of the emperor in two towns in municipal Italy during the second century CE. Awarded the honors of a local senator (decurion), at the statue dedication in his honor he provided various forms of largess for the people. Indeed, some freedmen, especially those who had acquired a particular expertise while enslaved, went on to become quite wealthy when emancipated. Recall the fictional Trimalchio of Petronius' *Satyricon* seen earlier.

5.54. *Corpus Inscriptionum Latinarum (CIL)* 11.5965

For C. Messius Zosimus, freedmen of Gaius, one of the priests of Augustus here and at Forum Sempronium, awarded the honorary status of a local senator by the senate of Pitinum Mergens, the local senators and urban plebs (set up this statue) on account of his service. At the dedication of the statue he gave to each senator 12 sesterces and to the plebs he gave [? sesterces and], banquets, and a distribution of meat.

[ ] indicates a gap in the text.

This next entry, also an inscription, reveals the benefactions of a certain Junia Rustica, a priestess of the town of Cartima in first-century Roman Spain. It is difficult to know with any certainty the source of her wealth or her degree of relative independence (Donahue 2004a), but her munificence is quite remarkable nonetheless. Most importantly, the text vividly confirms that women too were recognized as important benefactors of their communities throughout the Roman West during the Imperial period.

5.55. *Corpus Inscriptionum Latinarum (CIL)* 2.1956 = *Inscriptiones Latinae Selectae (ILS)* 5512

Junia Rustica, daughter of Decius, priestess for life and the first (to be so designated) in the town of Cartima, rebuilt the public porticoes ruined by age, gave a parcel of land for the baths, paid the public taxes on the town, set up a bronze statue of Mars in the forum, gave as a gift at her own expense porticoes at the baths on her own property with a fish pond and a statue of Cupid, a public feast and a show being provided at her own expense. After remitting the cost, she also dedicated the statues decreed to her and to her son, C. Fabius Junianus, by the local council of Cartima, and she did the same thing for a statue to her husband, C. Fabius Fabianus.

A final inscription underscores an essential feature of community feasting—the quality of a meal, or the amount of cash for a meal, was often tied to the social status of the recipient. In the most common scheme, local senators received the best meal or most funds for a feast, followed by the local priests or members of various *collegia*, and then the townspeople. Once again, we witness the unmistakable Roman concern with rank and status, as the local community adhered to the same social conventions at table as did the emperor at Rome.

Here at Rudiae (modern Lecce in Apulia in southern Italy) a certain Marcus Tuccius Augazo, who lived during the time of the emperor Hadrian in the second century CE, has dedicated a statue to his son and has set up an endowment of 80,000 sesterces, the interest from which (typically c. 5 percent) was to provide a distribution of meat every year on his son's birthday. The value of the gift depended on the status of the recipient. This endowment, while generous, is far short of other known foundations, which were funded at levels as high as 250,000 sesterces. Finally, we have no idea of how many townspeople were fed on this annual occasion, but we can be sure that this gift would have been especially welcome, as meat was not normally part of the ancient diet (see Chapter 3).

5.56. *Corpus Inscriptionum Latinarum (CIL) 9.23 = Inscriptiones Latinae Selectae (ILS) 6472*

... M(arcus) Tuccius Augazo (set up this statue) for his excellent and most devoted son, at the dedication of which he promised in his son's memory 80,000 sesterces to the townspeople of Rudiae, so that every year on the birthday of his own son the interest from which (amount) might be divided for a distribution of meat at 20 sesterces each for the local councilors, 12 sesterces each for the priests of Augustus, ten sesterces each for the priests of Mercury, and also eight sesterces per person for the people. The location (for the statue) has been decreed by the town council.

Collegia

Collegia were organized societies of various sorts, most commonly formed around a common trade or the cult of a particular god or goddess (Perry, in Peachin). An integral component of urban life in cities and towns throughout the Roman empire, the *collegium* served the needs and interests of a colorful array of craftsmen and laborers as well as clerical and administrative groups of all sorts. Many of these associations banded together under the nominal tutelage of a deity to ensure a proper burial for their members through monthly collections. Moreover, these groups shared a common interest in dining together, a reality best reflected in the way they often described themselves, whether as "the college of messmates" or "drinking buddies." This terminology suggests conviviality and perhaps more importantly the need to seek temporary relief from the routine of daily life through common celebration.

This well-known text, the "Statute of the College of Aesculapius and Hygia," (Rome, 153 CE) records the gifts, including a banqueting structure and endowments for eating and drinking, for the group's 60 members. This portion of the decree lists seven gatherings per year, a generous number considering that the total does not include other probable opportunities for banqueting, such as the group's monthly business meeting or the occasional banquet to celebrate the birthday of a patron or benefactor. Once again, note the emphasis on rank within the group as a determinant of the level of benefits conferred. The elected leader of the group and the patrons receive the largest share of food or money, followed by dues-exempt members, curators, and finally the rank-and-file membership. In this way, access to food and drink could be regulated to reinforce the social hierarchies essential for confirming one's place in the group. As we have seen, the task was made that much easier by food, which, by its very nature as a critical commodity in ancient preindustrial society, could be manipulated to advertise more effectively than any other substance the social difference between one person and the next.

5.57. *Corpus Inscriptionum Latinarum (CIL)* 6.10234 = *Inscriptiones Latinae Selectae (ILS)* 7213

... so that they might distribute a handout on 19 September, the most blessed birthday of our holy Antoninus Pius,[43] father of our country (thus): in the temple of the holy ones in the shrine of blessed Titus, 12 sesterces for Caius Ofilius Hermes, the chief office holder in the college, or he who will be in office at that time; 12 sesterces for Aelius Zeno, father of the college; 12 sesterces for Salvia Marcellina,[44] mother of the college; eight sesterces each for the dues-exempt members; eight sesterces for each curator; four sesterces for each regular member. Also it was decreed that on 8 November, the founding date of the college, they distribute to those present from the interest written above at the Hill of Mars in our meeting house 24 sesterces for the chief office holder, 24 sesterces for the father of the college, 24 sesterces for the mother of the college, 16 sesterces for each dues-exempt member, 16 sesterces for each curator, (and) bread worth three asses; nine measures of wine for the chief office holder, nine measures for the father of the college, six measures for each dues-exempt member, six measures for each curator, three measures for each regular member. Also that they distribute *strenae*[45] on 9 January as written above for 19 September. Also on 22 February, the day of Cara Cognatio,[46] at the Hill of Mars in the same place they distribute bread and wine just as written above for 8 November. Also on 14 March, in the same place a dinner, which Ofilius Hermes, the chief office holder, promised had to be granted every year to those present, or a handout, as he was accustomed to give. Also on 22 March, the day of violets,[47] in the same place a handout of bread and wine to be divided for those present, just as on the days written above. Also on 11 May, the day of roses,[48] in the same place a handout of bread and wine be divided for those present, just as on the days written above.

While the identity of the college in the previous excerpt is well known, we know far less about the drinker and his affiliation in the next passage. The reference to "common meal contributions" suggests a link with some sort of association, however, while the emphasis on drinking and drunkenness, presented much like that of the Anacreontea previously seen, underscores the vital role of drinking as a group activity.

5.58. *Greek Anthology* 5.135 (Loeb I, p. 193)

Anonymous, to his Jug

Round, well-molded, one-eared, long-necked, towering, babbling with your narrow mouth, cheery servant of Bacchus and the Muses and Cytherea,[49] sweetly-laughing, delightful treasuress of our common meal contributions, why then when I am sober are you full, and when I get drunk do you become sober? You do wrong to symposiastic friendship.

Food and sex

The chapter concludes with two distinctive but essential contexts for under-standing food and drink in their social dimension, that is, as they related to sex (McClure, in Boys-Stones et al.; Flemming, in Barchiesi and Scheidel) and to the Spartans (Cartledge). These two topics have attracted substantial attention, both ancient and modern. Consequently, the passages collected here can represent only a small portion of the available source material. Once again, the reader is advised to consult the "Suggested Readings" at the end of this chapter for additional resources.

Food and sex have always had much in common. They are essential to human survival, they provide comfort and physical gratification, but they also can induce feelings of guilt and shame. In the Roman world, the *convivium*, with its emphasis on eating, drinking, gender mixing, and handsome servants, provided a natural setting for sexual expression. As we have seen, a particularly lurid Roman example was Nero's famously debauched feast on the *Stagnum Agrippae*, which underscored not only food and sex, but also Tacitus' ability to convey the atmosphere of imperial oppression as it existed under a tyrannically excessive ruler (see 5.19). Among the Greeks, the symposium and its strong connections with heavy drinking was also closely associated with sexual activity. The next several passages provide a colorful cross section of this reality. The first excerpt comes from Plato's *Symposium*, a dialogue on the nature of love in which the participants decide to drink, but only moderately, since some were still hung over from the previous days' drinking. This atmosphere of moderation does not last for long, however, as Alcibiades, the talented but unscrupulous Athenian leader during the Peloponnesian War between Athens and Sparta, crashes the proceedings while still drunk from a previous celebration. Upon seeing Socrates amongst the invitees, Alcibiades recounts his earlier attempt— ultimately unsuccessful—to seduce Socrates at a meal he once provided for the famous philosopher. The dialogue thus plays with notions of drinking vs non-drinking, seduction vs refusal, and same-sex attraction within a lager philosophical inquiry into the nature and power of love.

The second excerpt recounts the attempt by Persian envoys to gain the submission of the Macedonians during Persia's war with Greece in the early fifth century BCE. The Macedonians themselves were hard drinkers, so it is not surprising that their scheme involves getting the Persians drunk amid the promise of sex before killing them. The story also provides Herodotus with an opportunity to underscore an important theme in his narrative—the dissolution and folly of the Persians and, by extension, the East, as compared to the rationality and superiority of the Greeks and the West.

The final entry, a fragment of the *Hippotrophos* (*Horse-Breeder*) of Mnesimachus also treats food and sex but in a more humorous way. The excerpt describes an attempt to seduce handsome boys through the longest surviving menu from Greek comedy, one that is especially notable for its numerous varieties of fish. The humor lies in the motivation of the host—a lot of food for a lot of sex—but also in the suggestion that a growing menu represents the growing passion of the host (Wilkins 2000).

5.59. Plato, *Symposium* 217D–219D

When he came the first time, he wished to leave as soon as he had eaten. At that moment I was ashamed and let him go. But the second time I devised a plan: after we had dined, I conversed with him deep into the night, and when he wished to leave, I made an excuse that it was late and convinced him to stay. So he rested on the couch next to me, on which he had been sitting at dinner, and no one else was sleeping in the room but us ... Well, gentlemen, when the lamp had been extinguished and the servants were sent away, it seemed to me that I must not address him with fancy words but to speak freely of the things I intended. So I shook him and said,

"Socrates, are you sleeping?"

"Why, no," he said.

"Do you know what I have decided?"

"What is the matter?" he asked.

"You seem to me," I said, "to be the only worthy lover I have had, and it appears that you are reluctant to mention it to me. This is my position. I consider it a great folly not to gratify you in this as in any other need you may have of either my possessions or my friends. Nothing is more important to me than reaching the highest possible excellence, and in this I believe I can find no more capable partner than you. So I should feel a far worse shame before thoughtful people for failing to gratify such a man than I should before the vast multitude of senseless people for gratifying him.

When he heard this, he replied in that dissembling manner so characteristic of him, "My dear Alcibiades, you are in no danger of being considered a fool if what you say about me happens to be the truth, and there is some power in me that would help you to become better; for then what a tremendous beauty you must see in me, greatly superior to your attractiveness. And if in observing this you are making an attempt for a mutual exchange of beauty for beauty, it is no slight advantage you are counting on, for you are trying to obtain real beauties in exchange for reputed beauties, and in reality are designing to exchange "gold for bronze." But, my dear friend, be more circumspect, you may be deceived and I may not be worth anything. Keep in mind, the intellectual sight begins to be sharp when the visual enters on its decline. But these things are still far away for you."

When I heard this I said, "This is what I've had to say; not a word differs from what I have been thinking. You thus need to consider for yourself what you think best for me and for you."

"Ah," he replied, "well said. In the time to come we shall consider and do what appears to be the best thing for both of us in this matter and in our other affairs."

Well, after I had exchanged these words with him and let my arrows fly, as it were, I fancied that he felt the wound. And so I got up and, not allowing him to speak another word, I wrapped my own coat around him—it was wintertime—drew myself under the cloak, wound my arms about this truly spiritual and wondrous man and slept the whole night … . know well, by the gods and goddesses, that when I awoke I had in no more particular sense slept a night with Socrates than if it had been with my father or older brother.

5.60. Herodotus, 5.20

… Alexander said to the Persians, "My friends, these women are at your service entirely, and you may go to bed with any or all of them as you please. You have only to say the word. Now, however, since it is nearly bedtime and, as I observe, you are well primed with drink, send these women away to take a bath—if it is agreeable to you—and after they have bathed you may have them back again." Having thus spoken, the Persians agreed, and Alexander himself, after telling the women to return to their quarters, dressed an equal number of smooth-chinned young men in their clothes, gave each of them a dagger, brought them back in, and said to the Persians: "Men of Persia, you have feasted, I think, to your heart's content. Everything we had, and everything we could find to give to you, has been yours; and now, we lavish upon you the greatest thing of all—our mothers and sisters—so that you may fully know that we honor you as you deserve, and furthermore that you may report to your king who sent you, that a Greek, the lord of Macedonia, entertained you royally, both with bed and board." When he had spoken, Alexander sat a Macedonian by the side of each Persian, as if the Macedonians were women. When the Persians attempted to touch them, they were killed.

5.61. Athenaeus, *Sophists at Dinner* 9.402e–403d

Mnesimachus provides the following in the *Horse-Breeder*. Come forth, Manes, from chambers roofed with cypress; go to the market place, near the Herms,[50] where the cavalry officers regularly resort, and the handsome pupils whom Pheidon is drilling in mounting and dismounting the horses. Do you know whom I mean? Well, tell them this—that the fish is cold, the wine is warm, the dough is dry, the loaves are crusted. The entrails are roasting, niblets have been snatched from the fire, the meat taken from its pickling juice; there's a slice of sausage, a slice of tripe, another of mince-meat, another of black pudding—all having their throats cut by the guests inside. They are emptying in gulps a mixing bowl of wine. Toasts to one's health are continuing. They're dirty dancing. They're thinking of sex. Everything is turned upside down indoors. Remember what I say, pay attention to what I tell you. Are you yawning? Look this way! How will you give the message? I will say it again for you now from the beginning. Tell them to come right away, and not to delay, and not to mistreat the cook, as there's fish that is boiled and fish that is baked and fish that is cold; and tell them of each menu item—bulbs, olives, garlic, cauliflower, squash, bean soup, fig leaf, vine leaf, slices of tuna, of sheat fish, dog fish, file fish, conger eel; a whole carp, a whole crow-fish, anchovy, mackerel, she tunny, goby, spindle fishes, a slice cut from the tail of one of the dog sharks, electric ray, fishing frog, perch, lizard fish, herring, forked hake, brincus, red mullet, piper, roach, lamprey, bream, mullet, labias, gilt head, speckled beauty, Thracian wife, flying fish, shrimp, squid, plaice, dracaena, polyp, cuttle fish, sea perch, cray fish, sole, small fry, needle fishes, grey mullet, sculpin, eel, bear crab—there is meat besides (the amount is not to be told)—of goose, pig, steer, lamb, sheep, boar, goat, cock, duck, magpie, partridge, thresher shark. And after dinner the quantity of good things there is marvelous. Everyone in the house is kneading, cooking, plucking, chopping, slicing, soaking, laughing, playing, jumping, dining, drinking, skipping, lying on their back, screwing. There are the solemn, gentle sounds of flutes; there is dancing and singing and rioting, and Arabian spice from the sacred sea dunes of Syria breathes forth. The nostrils are embattled from the solemn fragrance of frankincense, sage, myrrh, sweet flag, storax, marjoram, lindus, cindus, cistus, mint; such is the vapor filled with all good things that pervades the house."

Beyond convivial gatherings, the intersection of food, drink and sex could also be found in certain items thought to promote and/or increase sexual desire and/or performance. Much of our knowledge on this topic comes from medical authors such as Dioscorides and Galen (see Chapter 7), although references can be found across all genres. A wide range of food and drink, most commonly known as "aphrodisiacs" after Aphrodite, the Greek goddess of love and fertility, were believed to promote sexual potency (Dalby 2003, s.v. "aphrodisiacs"). Included among such items were mint and saffron, as well as barley, beans and bulbs. Among fruits, pomegranates were associated with fertility, while brides ate apples before consummating their marriage. Seafood, too, was popular, especially crayfish and eels, evidence that is consistent with the pictorial convention of sea creatures often appearing in erotic scenes. Athenaeus records a claim from Theophrastus of unusually powerful aphrodisiacs in the passage below.

5.62. Athenaeus, *Sophists at Dinner* 1.18d–e

Theophrastus (*HP* 9.18.9) says that there are aphrodisiacs strong enough to allow a man to have sex up to 70 times, and that they ejaculate blood in the end.

Food could also be made to look like male or female genitalia as in the passage below, which comes from Book 14, the *Apophoreta* ("things carried away") of the Roman poet Martial. These elegiac couplets were written as mottoes for items that could be taken home from banquets at the festival of the Saturnalia. Wine too was an aphrodisiac. Ovid makes this clear in the second excerpt, which emphasizes that the effectiveness of wine as a stimulant depended on the amount consumed.

5.63. Martial, 14.69

If you wish to satisfy your hunger, you may eat my Priapus; although you may gnaw at his very groin, you will be clean.

5.64. Ovid, *The Cures for Love (Remedia Amoris)* 803–10

You ask what I teach you about the gifts of Bacchus? Get ready to be enlightened very briefly by my warnings. Wine prepares your heart for love, unless you drink too much, and your mind stands still, immersed in lots of uncut wine. A fire is fed, and it is extinguished, by wind: a light breeze fans the flames, a heavier gust kills them. Either be sober or drink so much that it takes your cares away; if it's anywhere in between the two, it's harmful.

The Spartans: A special case

In many ways, the Spartans had much in common with other Greek city-states: they practiced polytheism; they based their economy on agriculture; and they utilized slaves, known as *helots*. They were also patriarchal in social and family relations and placed a high value on military bravery (Kennell; Cartledge). But the Spartans were also unique. First, they embraced kingship as their political model. Herodotus details in the first excerpt some of the rights and prerogatives that belonged to this office in the realms of eating and drinking.

5.65. Herodotus, 6.57

Such are their rights in wartime; in peacetime their rights are according to these features I provide. If any public sacrifice is offered, the kings shall be first to sit down and to be served at the banquet, each of them receiving a double portion of all that is given to each of the guests; they shall have the first libations, and the hides of the sacrificed animals. At each new moon and each seventh day of the first part of the month, a full grown victim for the temple of Apollo shall be given to each of them from the public supplies, and a bushel of barley meal and a Laconian quart of wine, and the best seats set apart for them at all of the games. To these it shall belong to appoint whatever citizens they might wish as officials to entertain foreign guests; and they shall choose the Pythians, each of them two. The Pythians are public messengers sent to enquire at Delphi, who eat with the kings at public expense. And if the kings do not come to the public dinner, two choenixes of barley meal[51] and a half pint of wine shall be sent to their houses, but when they come they will receive a double share of everything. They will have the same honor when private citizens summon them to dinner.

Sparta also played a highly intrusive role in the daily lives of its citizens. Boys who were deemed sufficiently fit were educated by the state from a young age to be soldiers in a system known as the *agoge*; girls too followed a rigid system aimed at producing healthy wives and mothers of soldiers. The result was totalitarian regulation that extended to one's personal appearance, marriage, and child rearing (Kennell; Powell). Many of these features were attributed from as early as the tenth century BCE to Lycurgus, a shadowy but revered lawgiver, who may or may not have been a historical figure. For our purposes, one of the most interesting institutions attributed to him was the *syssition*, the "dining group" or "group mess," to which every Spartan soldier was required to belong. Soldiers shared the same meal in groups of fifteen or so, an experience aimed at fostering the military virtues of loyalty and equality. In this setting younger members, by witnessing the behavior of older soldiers, became further socialized into the life of military service to the state. Plutarch, one of our main sources for the Spartans, elaborates on the importance of these values:

5.66. Plutarch, *On Mores (Moralia), Sayings of the Spartans* 226.4–6

4. Having determined to attack the prevailing luxury, and to do away with the rivalry for wealth, he established the common meals. And to those who sought to know why he had set these up, and had divided the citizens, when under arms, into small units, he said: "So that they may get their orders immediately, and, if they attempt anything revolutionary, the offence may be limited to a small number; and that there may be an equal portion of food and drink for all, and so that not only in drink or food, but in bedding or furniture or anything else whatsoever, the rich man may have altogether no advantage over the poor man."

5. Having made wealth unattractive, since nobody was able to make any use or display of it, he said to his close friends, "What a fine thing it is, my friends, to show in actual practice the true nature of wealth, that it is blind!"

6. He was careful that none should be allowed to dine at home and then go to the common meal filled with other kinds of food and drink. The rest of the unit

used to disparage the man who did not drink or eat with them, because they judged that he was lacking in self-control and was too weak for the common way of living. Moreover, the man who was detected paid a fine. As an example, Agis, their king, returning from a military campaign after a long time (he defeated the Athenians in battle), wished on this one day to dine at home with his wife, and sent for his allowance of food; but the military commanders would not send it. The next day, when the incident was disclosed to the ephors,[52] they fined him.

The sources reveal that the *syssition* was characterized by very limited and unappetizing fare. Athenaeus provides some insight into the menu (see also 6.6–6.8).

5.67. Athenaeus, *Sophists at Dinner* 4.141b–c

Everybody receives the same meat dish at all times, a piece of boiled pork; sometimes not even that, except a small bit of meat weighing at most a quarter pound; and besides this, there is nothing else other than the broth from this meat, enough to make a circuit through the entire group for the whole dinner; then perhaps an olive or cheese or a fig, or they might receive something in addition—a fish, or a hare, or a ring-dove, or something similar.

Clearly the items included here would have been insufficient as a diet for soldiers. We may suppose that state religious festivals and military campaigns would have provided additional sustenance, as would have stealing, for example, which the Spartans viewed as a sign of individual resourcefulness. The point is that we must be careful not to overstate the importance of the *syssition* as a meal, when perhaps its most important function was to build group solidarity and to educate younger Spartans in the ways of their elders. We must take a similar approach with Spartan drinking, which is also presented in idealized terms. Thus do we find the sources portraying the Spartans as moderate drinkers, who routinely forced their enslaved population, the helots, to drink undiluted wine and to act in vulgar and ridiculous ways as a reminder of the dangers of heavy drinking and of the base nature of servitude. To be sure, there is much debate among scholars as to how to interpret such distinctive evidence. Nevertheless, the Spartans provide a remarkable example of how a particular society utilized eating and drinking to reinforce specific social values, however unique or extreme these values might have been in comparison to the ancient norm.

Suggestions for Further Reading

Barchiesi, A. and Scheidel, W., eds. 2010. *The Oxford Handbook of Roman Studies.* Oxford.

Beard, M. 2007. *The Roman Triumph.* Cambridge, MA.

Bergmann, B. 1995. "Visualizing Pliny's villas." *Journal of Roman Archaeology* 8: 406–20.

Boyle, A. and Dominik, W., eds. 2003. *Flavian Rome: Culture, Image, Text.* Leiden.

Boys-Stones, G., Graziosi, B. and Vasunia, P., eds. 2009. *The Oxford Handbook of Hellenic Studies.* Oxford.

Burton, J. B. 1998. "Women's commensality in the Ancient Greek world." *Greece and Rome* 45: 143–65.

Carpentier, T. H. and Faraone, C. A., eds. 1993. *Masks of Dionysus.* Ithaca, NY.

Cartledge, P. 2003. *The Spartans: The World of the Warrior-Heroes of Ancient Greece.* New York.

Champlin, E. 2003. *Nero.* Cambridge, MA.

Coleman, K. M. 1988. *Silvae IV by P. Papinius Statius.* Oxford.

Dalby, A. 1996. *Siren Feasts: A History of Food and Gastronomy in Greece.* London.

—2003. *Food in the Ancient World from A to Z.* London.

Dalby, A. and Grainger, S. 1996. *The Classical Cookbook.* London.

Davidson, J. 1997. *Courtesans and Fishcakes; The Consuming Passions of Classical Athens.* London.

Donahue, J. F. 2004a. "Iunia rustica of Cartima: female munificence in the Roman west." *Latomus* 63: 873–91.

—2004b. *The Roman Community at Table during the Principate.* Ann Arbor.

—2012. "The floating feasts of Ancient Rome." *Proceedings of the Oxford Symposium on Food and Cookery 2011,* 95–104.

Dunbabin, K. M. D. 1993. "Wine and water at the Roman *convivium.*" *Journal of Roman Archaeology* 6: 116–41.

Ellis, S. 2000. *Roman Housing.* London.

Elsner, J. and Masters, J., eds. 1994. Reflections of *Nero: Culture, History, and Representation.* Chapel Hill.

Foss, P. W. 1994. "Kitchens and Dining Rooms at Pompeii: The Spatial and Social Relationships of Cooking to Eating in the Roman Household." Ph.D. thesis, University of Michigan.

Gold, B. and Donahue, J. eds. 2005. *Roman Dining: A Special Issue of the American Journal of Philology.* Baltimore.

Gowers, E. 1993. *The Loaded Table; Representations of Food in Roman Literature.* Oxford.

Grant, M., trans. 2000. *Galen on Food and Diet.* London.

Grocock, C. and Grainger, S., text, comm. and trans. 2006. *Apicius: A Critical Edition with an Introduction and an English Translation of the Latin Recipe Text Apicius.* Devon, UK.

Hudson, N. F. 2010. "Changing places: the archaeology of the Roman *convivium*." *American Journal of Archaeology* 114: 663–95.

Kennell, N. M. 2010. *Spartans: A New History*. Oxford.

Laurence, R. and Wallace-Hadrill, A., eds. 1997. *Domestic Space in the Roman World: Pompeii and Beyond. Journal of Roman Archaeology, Supplementary Series, no. 22*. Portsmouth, RI.

Murray, O., ed. 1995. *Sympotica: A Symposium on the Symposion*. Oxford.

Nevett, L. C. 2010. *Domestic Space in Classical Antiquity*. Cambridge.

Nielsen, I. and Nielsen, H., eds. 1998. *Meals in a Social Context: Aspects of the Communal Meal in the Hellenistic and Roman World*. Aarhus.

Olson, S. D. and Sens, A. 2000. *Archestratos of Gela : Greek Culture and Cuisine in the Fourth Century* BCE *: Text, Translation, and Commentary*. Oxford.

Peachin, M., ed. 2011. *The Oxford Handbook of Social Relations in the Roman World*. Oxford.

Powell, A., ed. 1989. *Classical Sparta: Techniques behind Her Success*. Norman, OK.

Rawson, B., ed. 2011. *A Companion to Families in the Greek and Roman Worlds*. Oxford.

Roller, M. 2006. *Dining Posture in Ancient Rome: Bodies, Values, and Status*. Princeton.

Salza Prina Ricotti, E. 1995. *Dining as a Roman Emperor: How to Cook Ancient Roman Recipes Today*. Rome.

Slater, W., ed. 1991. *Dining in a Classical Context*. Ann Arbor.

Steiner, A. 2002. "Private and public: links between *Symposion* and *Sussition*." *Classical Antiquity* 21: 347–79.

Wallace-Hadrill, A., ed. 1989. *Patronage in Ancient Society*. London.

Wilkins, J. and Hill, S. 1994. *The Life of Luxury: Europe's Oldest Cookery Book: Archestratus*. Devon.

—2000. *The Boastful Chef: The Discourse of Food in Ancient Greek Comedy*. Oxford.

—2006. *Food in the Ancient World*. Oxford.

Younger, J. M. 2005. *Sex in the Ancient World from A to Z*. London.

6

Eating, Drinking, and Fighting:
Food and Drink in the Military

War is the father of all things.
  Heraclitus, in H. Diels and W. Kranz, *Fragmente der Vorsokratiker* 22 B 53

Although a philosopher and not a soldier, Heraclitus is not far off in his assessment of ancient warfare. War was as common as it was calamitous in ancient Greece and Rome and because of this it played a significant part in shaping the social, economic, and political institutions of ancient society. The evidence reveals a world where wars were waged on both land and sea; were local, national or international in scope; and might last from a few hours to many, many years. The numbers of dead and wounded in any single battle ranged from modest to absolutely staggering.

Indeed, the sources themselves are full of fighting. Ancient history, literature, and art, along with material remains from weapons, forts, and camps all help us to recreate more completely the world of the ancient soldier, whether the hoplite fighter of the Greek phalanx, the infantryman of the Roman legion, or the shaggy-haired warrior of the Gallic tribes. Furthermore, to carry Heraclitus' statement one step further, if war was the father of all things, then it was provisioning that sustained it. To be sure, the task of providing sufficient provisions for the Greek and Roman military was both constant and daunting. As one measure of this reality, the nearly 300,000 soldiers of the Roman army in the second century CE might well have consumed annually about 100,000 tons of wheat at one kilogram of grain per person each day. By the early third century, the amount would have risen to 150,000 tons with a larger army (Campbell 2002). It is no wonder then that Vegetius, the Roman military writer of the fourth century CE, felt compelled to claim that an army unsupplied with grain and other necessary provisions risked being vanquished without striking a blow. We will be able to evaluate his statement more fully in the excerpts to follow, which will treat not only diet and provisioning but also food and drink in the realms of military strategy and discipline.

The military diet

The sources are replete with evidence of eating and drinking in a military context, an indication not only of the importance of militarism in antiquity but also of the critical need of adequately sustaining the ancient army. In order to accomplish this task, the ancients relied on a military diet that was based largely on grain but often supplemented by any number of additional items. Furthermore, while the fare may not have always been appetizing, the ancient soldier is generally considered to have been fed as adequately as, if not better than, his contemporary civilian counterparts. Indeed, perhaps the strongest indication of the ancients' expertise in military provisioning is that there is no record that the Roman army ever mutinied over food (Davies).

On active service

For soldiers on active service, provisions needed to be portable, calorie-rich, and easy to cook. Plato confirms this reality in the *Republic* while discussing campaign practices during Homeric times, when soldiers were responsible for their own provisions. Here it is interesting to note that the cooking equipment absent in Homer's day was to become more common later on. Furthermore, the emphasis on meat eating, a practice closely linked to elite status in epic poetry, was broadened to include additional items over time, as the passages from Aristophanes and Xenophon suggest below.

6.1. Plato, *Republic* 3.404C

> For you recognize that in the banqueting of heroes on campaign he [sc. Homer] does not feast them on fish, although they are at the coast on the Hellespont, nor on boiled meat, but only on roasted meat, which is what soldiers could most easily obtain. For everywhere, one may say, it is easier to use fire itself than to convey pots and pans along … Neither, as I believe, does Homer ever mention relishes. Is that not a thing that all men in training realize – that, if one is to keep physically fit, he must leave such things alone altogether?

This passage is from the *Acharnians,* a comedy written by Aristophanes in 425 BCE, the sixth year of the Peloponnesian War between Athens and Sparta. It reveals the range of foodstuffs available to the soldier and also confirms that he was still expected to provide his own initial supplies in the later fifth century BCE.

6.2. Aristophanes, *Acharnians* 545–51

The city would fill with the clamoring of soldiers … of roaring colonnades, of rations being measured out, the ship's oar furnished with its strap, of buyers of wine jars, of garlic, olive oil, onions in nets, garlands, anchovies, flute girls …

In addition to garlic, olives, onions, and anchovies, other items typically included figs, cheese, and cheap wine. Popular too was *opson*, a kind of prepared relish, often made of dried fish. Xenophon includes it among the soldier's rations in his *Cyropaedia* (*The Education of Cyrus*), a narrative about the Persian ruler Cyrus the Great as preserved in eight books.

6.3. Xenophon, *Education of Cyrus* 6.2.31

Concerning relishes it is necessary to take along such that are sharp, pungent, and salty. For these stimulate the appetite and offer the most lasting nourishment.

Roman soldiers on the march carried "iron rations," which typically included bacon fat, (*laridum*), which was more portable than oil; hard tack (*bucellatum*), a low-quality bread; and cheap wine (*acetum*), which could be mixed with water to form *posca*, a beverage inferior to vintage wine. Josephus reveals that legionaries carried a three-day supply of rations and a sickle to reap the crops (*BJ* 2.528). It was especially desirable that the soldier procured and milled his own grain whenever possible, for labor of his sort recalled the virtue of earlier times. Marius, the famous Roman general of the first century BCE, is generally credited with the innovation of soldiers carrying their own rations, as attested by Frontinus, the author of a Latin work on military strategy.

6.4. Frontinus, *Stratagems* 4.1.7

In order to reduce the number of pack animals that was especially impeding the army's march, Gaius Marius arranged for the utensils and food of the soldiers to be wrapped up in bundles and attached to forked sticks, so that the troops could readily carry them and easily rest. From this came the well-known epithet, "Marius' mules."

In a deliberate act of social leveling, emperors and generals often ate the same simple fare as the rank and file troops. This lesson was not lost on Caracalla, an emperor of the early third century CE, who is included in a history of the Roman emperors by Herodian, a Syrian who wrote in Greek during the second and third centuries.

6.5. Herodian, 4.7.5–6

> He used to eat whatever bread was readily at hand. He would grind enough grain for himself with his own hands and make a barley cake, which he would eat after baking it on charcoal. He did not indulge in any luxury and he used only the cheapest thing available to the poorest of his men. He claimed that he loved being called a fellow-soldier by them instead of the emperor.

Quality of the fare

All of the evidence cited above confirms that the provisions of the soldier on active duty were far from luxurious. Even so, criticisms of the military diet in the ancient record are rare, either in accounts of campaigns or in peacetime. While this may be due to chance, it is more likely a combination of the aristocratic bias of our sources and the conformist nature of military service. Given this situation, the following passages on the Spartan military are especially interesting (see also 5.65, 66, 67), not only as examples of unappetizing fare but also for the Spartan approach to this issue.

6.6. Plutarch, *Lycurgus* 9.4–5

> Thus it happened that such common and necessary accoutrements as couches, chairs, and tables were most skillfully made among them, and the Laconian *kothon* was especially well thought of by the soldiers, as Critias says. For its color hid the disagreeable appearance of the water, which they were often forced to drink, and its curving lips caught the muddy sediment and kept it inside, so that only the cleaner part reached the drinker's mouth.

The Spartans must also be cited for their strict and scanty diet, which they believed was essential for building character and courage. Scholars now believe that such evidence of cultural distinctiveness had largely diminished by the fifth century BCE. In the first passage below Plutarch provides evidence of the notoriously unappetizing Spartan black broth as part of his biography of Lycurgus, the legendary legislator of Sparta. Elsewhere, he is more specific in explaining that it consisted of pork cooked in its own blood and seasoned with salt and vinegar. In the second excerpt he offers the Spartan rationale for their strict diet.

6.7. Plutarch, *Lycurgus* 12.7

> Of their dishes the black broth is held in the highest regard, so that the older men do not even ask for a helping of meat but leave it to the young men, while

for themselves they have broth poured out for their meals. And it is said that one of the kings of Pontus even bought a Spartan cook in order to have this broth, but after having tasted it he was displeased. And the cook declared: "O king, this broth is to be savored by those who have bathed in the Eurotas River."[1]

6.8. Plutarch, *On Mores (Moralia), Customs of the Spartans* 237.13

This was the reason for the starvation diet. It was scanty for the reasons given, and so that that the youths should never become used to being filled up, but to being able to go without food; for thus, the Spartans thought, the youths would be more useful in battle if they were able to toil on without food, and they would be more disciplined and more abstemious if they lived a very considerable time at small cost. And to endure the plainest diet, so as to be able to consume any food that came to hand, they thought made the youths' bodies more vigorous because of the scanty diet, and they believed that this practice caused the bodies, repressed in any impulse towards heaviness and girth, to grow tall, and also to make them handsome; for they believed that a spare and lean condition resulted in suppleness, while a condition based on too much food was against it, because of excess weight.

Sources of supply

Local communities and allies

Turning to the sources of supply for the fighting army, Herodotus' portrayal of the requirements of the vast Persian army of Xerxes as it made its way westward to fight the Greeks in the Persian Wars of the early fifth century BCE is especially noteworthy. Although Herodotus may have overestimated the size of the Persian forces elsewhere in his account, here he clearly reveals the measures that cities were forced to take in order to supply the army en route. In the second passage, Thucydides describes the reception granted to the Athenian expeditionary forces on their arrival in Sicily in 415 BCE during the Peloponnesian War. The reaction of individual cities was based on support or fear of Athens. In the third passage Xenophon reveals how well fed his troops were in the villages of Armenia as recorded in the *Anabasis*, an account of the Greek-assisted expedition of the younger Cyrus against his brother, the king of Persia, in the late fifth century BCE. Such treatment was not typically the norm, and it may help to explain why Xenophon provides such a detailed account. The final passage offers a bit of a twist, as it records the food and drink provided by certain towns for the Greek general Themistocles as his reward for cooperating with the Persians during their war with the Greeks in the early-fifth century BCE.

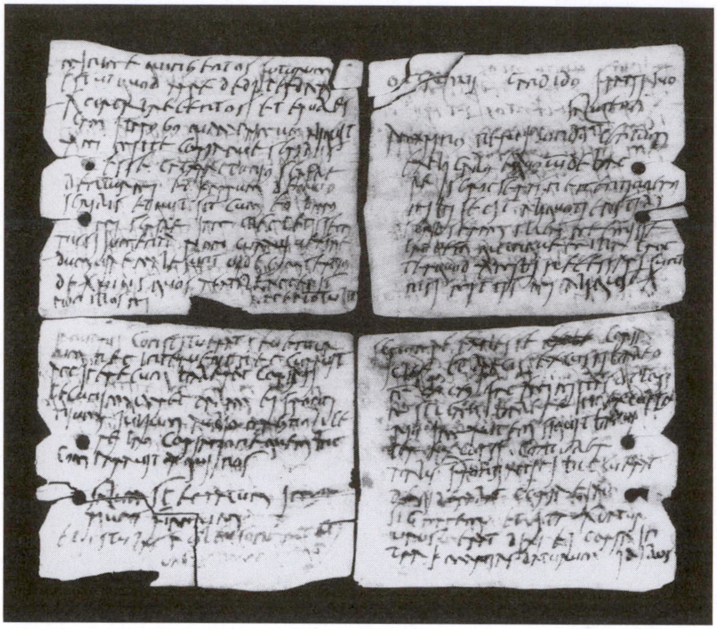

Figure 13. Writing-tablet with a letter from Octavius, an entrepreneur supplying goods on a considerable scale to the army at the fort in Vindolanda, Roman Britain. Food items typically would have been among these supplies, late first or early second century CE. © The Trustees of the British Museum/Art Resource, NY.

6.9. Herodotus, 7.119

As soon as the inhabitants got word from the announcement of the heralds, they divided up the corn among themselves in their cities and for many months together they ground it to wheaten and barley meal. Moreover, they fattened up the finest cattle that money could buy; and they maintained poultry and waterfowl in cages and in ponds for entertaining the army; and they prepared vases and drinking cups of gold and silver and all else that was required for the table service. These latter were made for the king himself and for those who dined with him; for the rest of the army, only the food was arranged.

6.10. Thucydides, 6.44

And when the entire force reached the Iapygian peninsula and Tarentum and wherever they severally found the chance to make land, they sailed along the Italian coast – some of the cities not receiving them with a market nor allowing them into town, although offering them water and anchorage. Tarentum and

Locri did not even supply them with the latter. They came to Rhegium, a promontory of Italy and now they gathered there and set up camp outside the city in an area sacred to Artemis, since they were not permitted inside. In that place the people of Rhegium provided them with provisions and then, drawing up their ships on shore, they rested.

6.11. Xenophon, *Anabasis* 4.5.30–3

On the next day Xenophon took the village chief and set out to Cheirisophus. Whenever he passed a village, he would make a detour to visit the troops stationed there, and everywhere he found them being well entertained and in high spirits; and there was no place from which the men would let them go until they had served them breakfast, and there was no place where they did not serve on the same table, lamb, kid, pork, veal, and poultry, along with many loaves of bread, some of wheat and some of barley. And whenever a man might wish to drink to another's health out of good fellowship, he would draw him to the mixing bowl of wine, and then one had to bend over and drink from it, gulping greedily like an ox. To the village chief they offered the opportunity of taking whatever he wanted. He refused for the most part to accept anything, but whenever he noticed any one of his kinsmen, he always drew him toward himself. When they reached Cheirisophus, Xenophon found his men in their quarters, crowned with wreaths of hay and served by Armenian boys in their foreign dress; and they were pointing out to the boys what they should do, as if they were deaf and dumb.

6.12. Cornelius Nepos, *Themistocles* 10.2–3

Themistocles made many promises to the (sc. Persian) king, of which the most welcome was, that if Artaxerxes would agree to follow his advice, the king's army would conquer Greece. Then, after receiving many gifts from the monarch, he returned and took up residence at Magnesia; for the king had given that city to him, with the information that it would provide him with bread (the annual revenue of the district was 500 talents), also Lampsacus to supply him with wine, and Myus to furnish relish.

Allies too could prove to be reliable suppliers, as Livy, in his history of Rome, reveals in his portrayal of the Carthaginian general Hanno in Italy during the Second Punic War in 212 BCE.

6.13. Livy, 25.13

Hanno set out from the land of the Brutii with his army, avoided the camps and consuls of the enemy, who were in Samnium, and when he was now approaching Beneventum, pitched camp on high ground three miles from the city itself. Then he ordered grain to be brought into camp from allied peoples all around, among whom it had been collected in the summer; and he provided a convoy to escort these supplies.

Foraging and pillaging

In longer campaigns, when the army might be cut off from supply lines in enemy territory, plundering became a necessity. This strategy could be dangerous, however, since foraging parties risked being attacked and captured. This excerpt reveals the potential hardships of foraging in enemy territory, in this instance involving the Roman army in Parthia (modern day Iran) under the emperor Caracalla in the third century CE.

6.14. *Augustan History, Severus* 16

And so with summer now ending, Severus invaded Parthia, drove out the king, and arrived at Ctesiphon; and at about the start of the winter season he took the city, because in those regions it is better to wage war during the winter, although the soldiers live on the roots of plants and so contract diseases and illnesses. For this reason, although he could go no further, since the Parthian army was blocking the way and his men were suffering from diarrhea because of their being unaccustomed to the food, even so he persisted, captured the city, put the king to flight, slew a great multitude, and acquired the name "Parthicus."

In this passage, Onasander, who compiled in Greek a work on conventional military wisdom in the first century CE, instructs the general to keep his army on the move so as not to diminish unnecessarily their provisions in any one place. Military manuals of this sort are important for revealing strategy and tactics, which evolved gradually over time and the importance of command superiority, which remained perhaps the single most important factor in determining victory. In the subsequent passage, Tacitus' account of pillaging Roman soldiers reveals that Onasander's advice was not always followed.

6.15. Onasander, *The General* 6.13

When his army has been recruited to full strength, the general must not settle down and delay, either in his own territory or in subject territories or in lands of an ally; for he will exhaust his own crops and will hurt his friends more than his enemies. Instead, he should lead out his forces as quickly as possible, if affairs at home are in good order. He will have bounteous provisions from the enemy's country, if it is fertile and prosperous; but, if it is not, at least he will not be hurting a friendly territory and he will also have more gains from injuring the enemy.

6.16. Tacitus, *Histories* 4.22

The commanders of the legions, Munius Lupercus and Municius Rufus, began to strengthen the ramparts and walls of their camp in order to meet the threatening war that was rising from many quarters. The buildings erected during the long peace, which in fact had grown into a town not far from the camp, they tore down, for they did not wish them to be of use to the enemy. But they paid too little attention to supplies being conveyed into the camp. They allowed the troops to pillage, so that in a few days the recklessness of the soldiers exhausted what would have met their requirements for a long time.

At other times, pillaging could prove to be quite fortuitous, as in this excerpt, where Greek mercenaries come upon the stores of the Mossynoecians, who lived in the eastern part of northern Anatolia (modern Turkey).

6.17. Xenophon, *Anabasis* 5.4.27–30

The Greeks, in plundering the strongholds, found supplies in the houses, as the Mossynoecians described them, of bread in heaps from last year's grain, while the new grain was laid away with the straw, most of which was spelt. They also found slices of dolphin preserved in jars, and in other vessels dolphin blubber, which the Mossynoecians used in the same way as the Greeks use olive oil; and on the upper floors of the houses there were many flat nuts without any clefts.[2] By boiling and baking these nuts into loaves, they made the bread that they used most. The Greeks also found wine, which by reason of its roughness appeared to be sharp when drunk unmixed, but when mixed with water was fragrant and pleasant.

Failure of provisions

Finally, the inability to supply an army properly might even account for the failure of an entire campaign, as Thucydides claims concerning the defeat of the Greeks in the Trojan War, as recorded in his *Histories*. Although his claim tells only part of the story, the importance of proper provisioning cannot be ignored. The second passage comes from the *Alexander Romance*, composed by an unknown author several centuries after the death of Alexander the Great. The excerpt is typical of the fantastical and dubious nature of this work, whose chief aim is to celebrate the heroism and ingenuity of Alexander. Nevertheless, this incident is reminiscent of Alexander's deadly march through the Gedrosian desert in the fall of 324 BCE, when similar acts of desperation were required. More importantly, the excerpt reminds us of the peril that could result from the failure of supplies.

6.18. Thucydides, 1.11

> The cause was not so much a shortage of men as it was a lack of money. For it was a shortage of supplies that prompted them to lead out a smaller force, of such a size as could be expected to live off of the land while fighting. And when they arrived and were victorious in battle –clearly they were, for they could not otherwise have built walls around their camp – even then they did not seem to utilize their whole army there, but to have turned to farming in the Chersonese and to plundering because of a lack of supplies. On this account, because the Greeks were scattered, the Trojans found it easier to hold out against them by force during those ten years, being adversaries to those who were periodically left in camp. But if the Greeks had gone all together with a plentiful supply of food and waged war continuously, without relying on farming and foraging, they would have easily won in battle and captured the city, since they endured, even with forces that were not united but were only available occasionally on the spot; whereas, if they could have sat down and besieged Troy, they would have overtaken it in less time and with less trouble.

6.19. Pseudo-Callisthenes, *Alexander Romance* 124 (trans. Wolohojian)

> When the soldiers' food supply was exhausted, he ordered them to slay the horses and to eat them. Although they complied with the order out of necessity, they did so noisily and bitterly, as though he had done that

purposely so that they would have no hope for the future. So when they abandoned military regulations and the customary precautions, the king himself came forward publicly to them and said: "I am not at all unaware, soldiers, that the horses which I ordered slain and used for food would be more valuable than anything else for battle. But since there was a double difficulty upon us, either to eat them and live or spare them and die with or before them, I presume to say that I picked the better solution and avoided the worse. Therefore, I promise you that when the gods help us to conquer a nation, and fill up on their abundant foodstuffs, this calamity over the horses will never happen again. I could probably find other soldiers in the place of those lost in this famine, but now where will I be able to find Macedonians?"[3]

The military diet in peace time

The diet of the army during peacetime is best approached through the Roman evidence. It would have consisted of grain, bacon, cheese and most likely vegetables and sour wine, as well as salt and olive oil. A fixed amount (*ad victum*) was deducted from each pay installment to pay for these goods, with the soldier paying for additional items out of his own funds. Special days in the military calendar would have provided the soldier with an even greater variety of food, as apparent in the first passage, which records the food made available to soldiers and the populace during the triumphal parade of a victorious Roman general. Beyond special occasions of this sort, commanders would have typically enjoyed better fare than the rank and file on a daily basis, a practice evident in the second passage, an inventory most likely attached to the *Praetorium* (command headquarters) at Vindolanda in Britain, the site of a Roman fort in the third century CE. Note the variety of meats, suggesting that meat eating in the military was common when rank and circumstances allowed.

6.20. Athenaeus, *Sophists at Dinner* 4.153c

Whenever they hold a banquet in the temple of Heracles in Rome and he who is celebrating a triumph at the moment serves as the host, the preparations for the feast are themselves Herculean; for much honeyed wine is poured, and the food consists of big loaves of bread, stewed smoked meat, and generous roasted portions of the beasts that have just been sacrificed.

6.21. *Vindolanda Papyri* (Bowman and Thomas 191)

...] denarii, [...], spices [...], roe-deer [...], salt [...], young pork [...], ham [...], in [...], wheat [...], venison [...], in [...], for preserving [...], roe-deer [...]. Total, denarii [...]. (2nd hand) Total, denarii 20+. (1st hand) cereal [...], denarii [...]

Supplying an army in peacetime was complex, as supplies had to be obtained from multiple sources. Civilians in the provinces were major contributors, most typically providing goods through requisitions or compulsory purchase at a fixed price. Lands and shops near the fort were another potential source, as were the tag-along merchants and suppliers who were a common sight, especially at Roman military installations. Not to be overlooked too were family and friends as well as extortion.

Critical task for the leader

Before surveying a selection of these sources on supply, we must recognize that proper provisioning was so important as to be recognized as a fitting theme in those didactic works concerned with portraying the ideal king or general. Dio Chrysostom, a Greek orator and popular philosopher of the first century CE, makes this clear in the passage below, which is notable for its use of food in two vivid similes. Note how these similes underscore the delicate balance between discipline and excess, a reality that every king or general needed to recognize, if he was to be successful.

6.22. Dio Chrysostom, *First Discourse on Kingship* 28–9

For a ruler who disdains the military and has never or infrequently seen those who endure dangers and hardships in support of his kingdom, but incessantly flatters the useless and unarmed masses, is just like a shepherd who does not know those who help him to keep watch, never offers them food, and never shares the watch with them; for such a man tempts not only the wild animals, but even his own dogs, to prey upon the flock. On the other hand, he who weakens his soldiers by not drilling them or encouraging them to work hard and, at the same time, neglects the greater populace, is like the captain of ship who harms his crew with too much food and midday sleep and pays no attention to his passengers or his ship as it goes to ruin.

Compulsory purchase

As Tacitus describes in this laudatory account of his father-in-law, while the latter was governor of Britain in the late 70s CE, compulsory purchases were open to corruption. This passage reveals that not only did the natives have to pay for grain that they did not want and never actually received, but also that they left it in the granary as part of the tribute they paid to Rome.

6.23. Tacitus, *Life of Agricola* 19.4

> He made the requisition for grain and tribute less onerous by equalizing the burdens; he abolished all the profit-making schemes that were more grievous than the tribute itself. For truly, the natives used to be forced to go through the mockery of stationing themselves at locked granaries, to purchase grain beyond what they needed, and to redeem their obligations at a price. Back roads and distant districts were named in the governor's proclamations, so that the tribes with winter quarters close by (sc. the granaries) delivered (sc. the grain) to remote and difficult to reach areas, until a thing that was easy for everybody became a source of profit for the few.

Traveling merchants and suppliers

Merchants and suppliers who accompanied the traveling army were also a potential source of supplies. They were not an official part of the army, however, but were driven by profit, and so could often be found selling luxury items to the soldiers. Those in command frowned upon this practice as weakening army discipline (see more at nos. 42–5). This is evident in the actions of Metellus in the war with Jugurtha, a North African rebel in the late first century BCE, as recorded by the Roman historian Sallust.

6.24. Sallust, *War with Jugurtha* 45.2

> For in the first place he is said to have removed inducements to laziness by an edict that no one should sell bread or any other cooked food within the camp, that camp followers should not attend the army, and that no private soldier should have a slave or pack animal in camp or on the march; and he set a strict limit on other practices of this sort.

Appian, a compiler of narratives in Greek of various Roman wars, depicts the famous Roman general Scipio as even more harsh in his attempts to restore army discipline in Spain in the second century BCE.

6.25. Appian, *Wars in Spain* 85

When he arrived, he drove out all traders, prostitutes, soothsayers and diviners, whom the soldiers were unceasingly consulting because they were demoralized by defeat. For the future he forbade the importing of anything not necessary, even a victim prepared for purposes of divination. He also ordered all wagons and their non-essential contents to be sold, and all pack animals, except such as he himself allowed to remain. For cooking utensils it was only permissible to have a spit, a brass kettle, and a single cup. Their provisions were limited to plain, boiled and roasted meats. They were forbidden to have beds, and he (sc. Scipio) was the first to sleep on straw.

Extortion

The widespread oppression of civilians by soldiers was an unfortunate fact of military life in antiquity, especially in the Roman world, where a military presence, both large and small, could be found from Spain to the Euphrates. As this passage reveals, local officials, in this instance in Egypt in the mid 130s CE, were aware of such abuse, although it proved difficult to do much about the situation here or elsewhere. We can suppose that the illegal requisition of food was among the abuses mentioned below.

6.26. *Papiri greci e latini (PSI)* 446=*Select Papyri II, no. 221*

And thus it has come about that private citizens are offended and abused and the army is criticized for greediness and injustice.

In this excerpt it is not certain whether the troops speaking to John the Baptist were Roman soldiers or those belonging to King Herod, but it is clear that the situation was no better in Judaea during the first century CE.

6.27. *Luke* 3.14 (*New Oxford Annotated Bible*)

Soldiers likewise asked him, "What about us?" He told them, "Don't abuse anyone. Denounce no one unjustly. Be satisfied with your pay."

The *Augustan History* frames food extortion in the context of excessive punishment, as these two passages confirm. While much of this source is pure fantasy, illegal requisitioning remained a problem throughout Roman history.

6.28. *Augustan History, Avidius Cassius* 4.1

And since we have begun to speak of his severity, many indications of his cruelty rather than his strictness are evident. For, in the first place, soldiers who had seized anything from the provincials by force he crucified on those very locations where they committed the crime.

6.29. *Augustan History, Pescennius Niger* 10.5–6

Likewise, for the theft of a single cock he gave an order that the ten comrades of the same maniple[4] who had shared the bird which one of them had stolen, should all be beheaded; and he would have carried out the order had not the entire army petitioned him to such a degree that there was fear of a mutiny. And when he had spared them, he ordered that the ten who had feasted together on the stolen bird should pay the provincial who owned it the price of ten cocks.

Family and friends

Family and friends were another source that allowed the soldier to supplement his diet beyond that which was provided by the army. In this papyrus fragment, written in Greek, Claudius Terentius, a legionary stationed in Alexandria in the early second century CE, writes to his sister requesting her to send olyra, a type of grain, and the oil of radishes, which could be used like olive oil. Since Terentianus likely would have received enough food in his regular rations, we are left to wonder whether he needed these items for a special celebration or if he had simply wasted his pay on other items.

6.30. *Papyri, Univ. of Michigan (P. Mich.)* 474

Take every step to supply me with two *ceramons*, of the largest size, of olyra, and an *artab* of radish oil. I sent the marjoram to you with the oil.

Strategy

That food and drink could be used for strategic purposes in ancient warfare is well documented in the sources. As the following passages reveal, strategic use of food included eating at the proper time, starving out the enemy, and subterfuge. First, it was critical not only that soldiers were sufficiently fed but also that they ate at the appropriate time of day, as Onasander writes.

Eating at the proper times

6.31. Onasander, *The General* 12.1

If encamped opposite the camp of the enemy, the general should not neglect the proper time at which to serve meals. For if he thinks that it lies with him to lead out his troops to battle whenever he wishes, he may set a meal time for his troops at whatever time he wishes. But if he should happen to have come into such a great difficulty, because of the terrain, or the weakness of his camp, or for some other reason, so that it is left up to the strength of the enemy to attack whenever they wish, and to force his army to seize their weapons and draw up for defense, he should not hesitate to announce the first meal at sunrise, lest the enemy, by a prior attack, force his men to fight while still hungry. On the whole, this matter must not be considered of trifling importance, nor should a general neglect to pay attention to it; for soldiers who have eaten sensibly, so as not to put too great a burden on their stomachs, are more hearty in battle; often times armies have been overcome for just this reason, their strength fails them due to lack of food – that is, whenever the fighting is decided not in a critical moment, but when the battle persists for the entire day.

Starving out the enemy

In terms of specific strategies, imposing famine upon the enemy was particularly favored. Vegetius makes this clear in the two passages below.

6.32. Vegetius, 3

It is a mark of supreme skill to distress the enemy more by famine than by the sword.

It is much better to defeat the enemy by imposing starvation, surprise or terror upon him than by general actions, since in the latter instance luck often plays a greater role than bravery.

Cities in antiquity attempted to avoid this fate, however, by keeping reserve stocks of food, as Philon, a Greek engineer and writer on mechanics in the latter half of the third century BCE, records in his *Siegecraft*. When this was not possible, they attempted to deceive the enemy about their supplies, as Frontinus describes in two separate instances. For more on deceptive strategies, see 6.40, 41.

6.33. Philon of Byzantium, *Siegecraft B1–2*

It is proper to keep in reserve in public storage and in private homes other foodstuffs that will not perish, such as pearl barley, wheat in sheaves, chick peas, lupines, *hippace*,[5] lentils, sesame, poppy seeds for preparing medicines, and millet too; in addition, there should be bread made from dates. The wealthy citizens should keep meat that has been dried or preserved in wine sediment, or other salted meat. For they make no trifling contribution to nourishment and strength, and are completely sufficient by themselves, and do not require dressing or salt. Legumes should also be on hand, completely grilled, but if not, in their raw state; others should be soaked in olive lees, for in this way they do not decay.

6.34. Frontinus, *Stratagems 3.15.6*

The Milesian commander, Thrasybalus,[6] when his soldiers were suffering in a long siege conducted by Alyattes, who was hoping he could starve them into surrender, ordered that all the grain should be collected in the forum in preparation for the arrival of envoys from Alyattes; and he arranged banquets at the same time and provided luxurious feasts throughout the city. In this way he convinced the enemy that they had an abundance of provisions with which to endure a long siege.

6.35. Frontinus, *Stratagems 3.15.1*

The Romans, now in dire famine when the Capitol was besieged by the Gauls,[7] threw bread at the enemy. They created the impression that they were well stocked with food, and thus held out until Camillus[8] arrived.

Despite such efforts, strategies to bring about hunger and thirst persisted, and might include tampering with the water supply. Appian's account of Hannibal's troops cut off from water during the Punic Wars and Frontinus' portrayal of Cleisthenes contaminating the enemy's water supply at Kirra provide vivid evidence of how this strategy played out in actual battle.

6.36. Appian, *Punic Wars 8.7.40*

The town of Cilla was nearby and next to it was a ridge well suited for a camp. Hannibal, conceiving the idea of seizing the hill, sent forth some men to mark out his camp, and immediately started to march forward as though he were already in possession of it. But since Scipio had anticipated him and had seized it beforehand, Hannibal was cut off in the middle of a plain without water, and he spent all night digging wells. His army, persevering in the sand, obtained with difficulty a little muddy water to drink, and so they spent the night without care for their bodies, with no food, and with some of them still in their armor. Observing this, Scipio moved against them at dawn while they were weary from marching and from lack of sleep and water. Hannibal was agitated, since he did not wish to commit to battle in these circumstances. Yet he realized that if he should remain in that place, his army would suffer badly from lack of water, while if he should retreat, he would revive the morale of the enemy, who would press him hard and inflict heavy losses on him. For these reasons it was necessary for him to fight.

6.37. Frontinus, *Stratagems* 3.7.6

Cleisthenes of Sicyon ruptured the water pipes leading into the town of Cirra;[9] soon, when the inhabitants were afflicted with thirst, he restored the supply contaminated with hellebore. When they used this, they were so weakened by diarrhea that Cleisthenes captured them.

Frontinus also records the practice of increasing the population of the besieged city in order to reduce its supplies, a strategy once implemented by Alexander II in his war against an anti-Macedonian coalition in Greece in the third century BCE. Alternatively, once a city was besieged, novel methods of providing supplies might be called for. Frontinus again, is instructive, this time in the case of Hannibal's capture of Casilinum during the Second Punic War in 216 BCE.

6.38. Frontinus, *Stratagems* 3.4.5

When Alexander[10] was about to besiege Leucadia, a town rich in supplies, he first captured the forts on the border and allowed all the people from these to flee to Leucadia so that their provisions might be used up more rapidly because of the increased numbers.

6.39. Frontinus, *Stratagems* 3.14.2

When Hannibal was besieging Casilinum, the Romans sent jars of wheat downstream on the Volturnus River to be picked up by the besieged. When Hannibal prevented this by stretching a chain across the river, they scattered nuts on the water. These floated down on the current to the town and this food nourished the allies in their time of need.

Subterfuge

Food and food implements could also play a role in military strategy by concealing weapons and communications. Aeneas Tacticus ("the Tactician"), a Greek military writer of the fourth century BCE, illustrates this stratagem in the following passages.

6.40. Aeneas the Tactician, 29.6–7

And in baskets of chaff and of wool, small rimless shields and small round shields were hidden; and others even smaller in baskets full of raisins and figs, as well as hand knives hidden in jars of wheat and dried figs and olives. And unsheathed daggers were likewise imported in ripe gourds, pushed down along the stems among the seeds of the gourd.

6.41. Aeneas the Tactician, 31.10–13

Communications are also are delivered in this manner. Take a pouch equal in size to a flask large enough for your needs; inflate it, tie it tightly, and let it dry out; then, in ink mixed with glue, write on it whatever you wish. When the writing is dry, deflate the pouch and press it into the flask, allowing the mouth of the pouch to protrude from the mouth of the flask. Then inflate the pouch inside the flask in order to stretch it as much as possible, and filling it with oil, cut off the part of the pouch that comes over the top of the flask, fitting it in the mouth as inconspicuously as possible, and, corking the bottle, carry it openly. Hence, the oil will be visible in the flask but nothing else. When it reaches the appropriate party, he will pour out the oil, inflate the pouch, and read the writing. And washing it off with a sponge and writing on it in the same way, let him return it.

Food, drink, and military discipline

Excessive eating and drinking was always a threat to military discipline (*disciplina militaris*). In extreme cases it could even lead to death, as when Alexander the Great, in a drunken rage, murdered his commander Clitus while on campaign in the East. This incident, as well as others involving heavy drinking in the military, receives greater attention as an issue of health in Chapter 7. In the meantime, we know of various methods that were

Figure 14. Detail of Alexander the Great, renowned general and prodigious drinker, from the Battle of Issus. Roman floor mosaic, originally from the House of the Faun in Pompeii, Italy, c. first century BCE and believed to be a copy of an early third century BCE Hellenistic painting. Museo Archeologico Nazionale, Naples, Italy. Photo Credit: Scala/Ministero per i Beni e le Attività culturali/Art Resource, NY.

employed to discourage disruptive and dangerous behavior of this sort, most notably, the banishing of luxury items and linking punishment to specific foods.

Luxury items banished

One way to discourage profligate behavior among the rank and file was for military leaders to restrict the soldiers' access to camp followers and luxury items, especially after a defeat. Limiting the troops to grain, meat, and vegetables, the items most reminiscent of ancient military virtue, was thought to incite the proper fighting spirit. Recall Scipio Aemilianus imposing severe restrictions at Numantia and Metellus acting in similar fashion in the war against Jugurtha (see 6.24, 6.25).

Helpful in this regard are the sayings of kings and commanders, a common-place of ancient literature, which, although difficult to verify, nevertheless are revealing in their emphasis on the commander's need to set the proper example for his men concerning eating and drinking. In this passage Plutarch records those sayings attributed to Epameinondas, the famous general and statesman of Thebes in the fourth century BCE.

6.42. Plutarch, *On Mores (Moralia), Sayings of Kings and Commanders, Epameinondas 4–6*

4. He was so thrifty in his way of living that once, when he was invited to dinner by a neighbor, and found there was a provision of cakes and rich fare and perfumes as well, he left at once, saying, "I thought that this was a sacrificial meal and not a display of arrogance."

5. When the cook rendered his accounts to the officers of the expenses for several days, Epameinondas showed irritation only at the great amount of olive oil. As his fellow-officers expressed their surprise, he said it was not the matter of expense that bothered him, but that he had taken so much oil into his body.

6. While the city was celebrating a holiday, and all were busy with drinking and parties, Epameinondas, as he was walking along unkempt and lost in thoughts, met one of his close friends. Amazed, the friend inquired why it was that he alone was going about in that state. Epameinondas said, "So that all of you may get drunk and have a holiday."

Food and punishment

Food could just as easily be linked to the punishment of soldiers. Augustus decimated cowardly cohorts, that is, he executed every tenth man selected by lot, and he would substitute unappealing fare for troops who had performed unsatisfactorily.

6.43. Suetonius, *Augustus.* 24.2

He dismissed the entire tenth legion in disgrace because of insubordination and others too, who arrogantly demanded their discharge, he dismissed without the rewards of recompense earned through service. If any cohorts gave way in battle, he decimated them, and fed barley[11] to the rest.

Polybius, whose *Histories*, written in Greek, record the rapid and dramatic rise of Rome during the Republican period, provides additional historical context when he describes the practice whereby ten percent of those who deserted their posts were chosen at random to suffer *fustuarium* (beating to death with sticks) as an efficient means of punishment and of striking fear in the hearts of the soldiers. The passage below continues with the punishment of those not selected for death.

6.44. Polybius, *Histories* 6.38

The remaining ones receive rations of barley instead of wheat and are ordered to encamp outside the camp in an undefended spot. Therefore, the danger and the fear of drawing the fatal lot hangs over everyone equally, since it is uncertain on whom the lot will fall. And since the public humiliation of receiving barley rations comes to everyone equally, this custom is best calculated to inspire fear and correct the fault.

In a particularly severe imposition of *disciplina militaris*, the emperor Galba deliberately starved to death a soldier who had sold his rations for profit in the later first century. Since the integrity of the military food supply system was paramount, especially when food was scarce, it was necessary that the punishment in such cases be severe. Of course, we have no account of the troops' reaction to such punitive measures, but they surely would not have been pleased.

6.45. Suetonius, *Galba* 7

When provisions were very scarce during a foray and a soldier was accused of having sold for 100 denarii a peck of wheat left over from his rations, Galba forbade anyone to help the man when he began to lack food, and the soldier starved to death.

Suggestions for Further Reading

Barrett, J., Fitzpatrick, A. P., and Macinnes, L., eds. 1989. *Barbarians and Romans in North-West Europe from the Later Republic to Late Antiquity*. Oxford.

Bowman A .K. and Thomas, J. D. 1994. *The Vindolanda Writing-Tablets (Tabulae Vindolandenses II)*. London.

—2003. *The Vindolanda Writing-Tablets (Tabulae Vindolandenses III)*. London.

Brice, L. L. and Roberts, J., eds. *Recent Directions in the Military History of the Ancient World*. Claremont, CA.

Campbell, B. 1984. *The Emperor and the Roman Army*. Oxford.

—1994. *The Roman Army, 31 BC–AD 337: A Sourcebook*. London.

—2002. *War and Society in Imperial Rome: 31 BC–AD 284*. London.

—2004. *Greek and Roman Military Writers: Selected Readings. London.*

Cool, H. E. M. 2006. *Eating and Drinking in Roman Britain*. Cambridge.

Davies, R. W. 1971. "The Roman military diet." *Britannia* 2: 122–42.

—1989. *Service in the Roman Army*. Breeze, D. and Maxfield, V.A., eds. New York.

Erdkamp, P. 1998. *Hunger and the Sword: Warfare and Food Supply in Roman Republican Wars (264–30 BC)*. Leiden.

—2007. *A Companion to the Roman army*. Malden, MA.

Gilliver, C. M. 2001. *The Roman Art of War*. Gloucestershire.

Hanson, V. D. 2000. *The Western Way of War: Infantry Battle in Classical Greece*. Berkeley.

Le Bohec, Y. 2000. *The Roman Imperial Army*. London.

Kinzl, K. H. ed. *A Companion to the Classical Greek World*. Malden, MA.

Phang, S. E. 2008. *Roman Military Service: Ideologies of Discipline in the Late Republic and Early Principate*. Cambridge.

Roth, J. P. 1999. *The Logistics of the Roman Army at War (264 BC–AD 235)*. Leiden.

Sage, M. M. 1996. *Warfare in Ancient Greece: A Sourcebook*. London.

Southern, P. and Dixon, K. R. 1996. *The Late Roman Army*. New Haven.

Van Wees, H. 2004. *Greek Warfare: Myths and Realities*. London.

Wesbter, G. 1998. *The Roman Imperial Army of the First and Second Centuries A.D.* Norman, OK.

Wolohojian, A., trans, and intro. 1969. *The Romance of Alexander the Great by Pseudo-Callisthenes*. New York.

Eating, Drinking, and Living Healthy: Food, Drink, and Medicine

For although we do not invariably make use of other resources, life without
food is impossible, whether we are healthy or ill.

Galen, *On the Properties of Foodstuffs* 1.1

Ancient medicine is a vast specialty that continues to attract new interests and approaches. Consisting of works ranging from philosophy and physiology to semiotics and therapeutics, ancient medicine provides a range of materials that is remarkably useful, despite the fact that much of ancient medical literature has disappeared (Nutton). Even so, new sources continue to emerge. The corpus of antiquity's most famous and prolific physician, Galen of Pergamum, for example, now totals some three million words, as scholars continue to discover or translate his works for a new generation of readers.

Given these realities, our focus in this chapter must necessarily be limited to a modest selection of sources that will help us to understand the strong connection that existed between food and health in the Graeco-Roman world. Several themes will become apparent, including: the therapeutic power of all kinds of foods; the close relationship between medicine and cooking; and the self-help nature that characterized much of ancient medicine. Underscoring all of these aspects is the uncertainty that remains concerning the extent to which ordinary people sought dietary advice, or took it when provided. Indeed, there is no shortage of material, and the reader who wishes to explore the topic more deeply is encouraged to consult the various works listed at the end of the chapter. In the meantime, some modern comparative examples will provide an entranceway to the topic.

We would be hard pressed to find a cultural force as pervasive in modern life as our preoccupation with dieting. It is estimated that more than 100 million people are on diets each year in America, with the typical dieter making four to five attempts to lose weight per year. Best-selling books enthusiastically promote the latest fad diets, while morbidly obese contestants compete for the title of the "biggest loser" in weight-loss dramas packaged for prime-time television. One recent estimate has put the annual revenue of the U.S. weight-loss industry, including diet books, diet drugs, and weight-loss surgeries, at a staggering $20 billion. Closely tied to dieting, of course, is the emphasis on those foodstuffs best suited for a healthy lifestyle. Do you wish to find the best food and drink for breakfast, snacking, or exercising? How about for stronger teeth, a sharper mind, or a healthier colon? To be sure, the amount of information, whether based on careful science or on making a quick buck, is staggering and it has much to tell us about modern notions of health and wellbeing.

As obsessive as all of this may sound, it is not entirely new. Already by the fifth century BCE the Greeks were beginning to embrace the notion that bodily processes, health, and disease were not subject to the arbitrary assistance of the gods but could be explained in the same way as other natural phenomena and that, as part of this thinking, food and drink played a critical role in maintaining health. In fact, in its broadest sense the ancient Greek word for "diet" (*diaita*) meant not only eating choices but also a way of life that included proper attention to exercise, sexual activity, hygiene, and sleep (Conrad). It is easy to see that modern society shares a similarly holistic view of diet and health. Furthermore, as in the modern world, the image of the body in antiquity was a cultural construct, which meant that it informed the community about the relationship between the eater and his or her eating habits. A direct link between body image and diet was thereby established, which, in turn, compelled Greek physicians to place great emphasis upon physical activities (Nadeau, in Erdkamp).

Diet and regimen in Greek medicine

We first witness this "new medicine" in the corpus of writings attributed to Hippocrates of Cos, who is recognized as the most famous physician of antiquity and the founder of rationalist medicine. The works contained in this corpus, written mainly between 420 and 350 BCE and largely assembled around Alexandria in 280 BCE, are too varied by date and viewpoint to belong to a single author. Even so, some of these writings likely belong to Hippocrates himself, who was probably a contemporary of Socrates. What is most essential for our purposes is the major presumption in the corpus that health and illness were related to the notions of balance and imbalance in the body. This belief, found only in *Nature of Man* and not elsewhere in Hippocrates, was tied to a more complex theory that recognized four essential fluids, or bodily "humours"— bile, phlegm, blood, and black bile—as essential to health. Each humour was linked to a certain season (bile/summer, phlegm/winter, blood/spring, black bile/autumn), making it mandatory for one to adjust his diet in order to counteract the effects of the environment on the body. So, for example, hot, dry foods were better in the winter, which was cold and wet, whereas, cold, moist, and easily digestible foods were preferred in summer when it was hot and dry. The key to this system was maintaining the proper balance among the humours by removing whatever was in excess and by building up whatever was deficient in the body through the administration of certain foodstuffs.

This paradigm was not the only model in antiquity that attempted to explain illness and health in rationalist terms, yet it nevertheless possessed significant explanatory capacity and was capable of almost limitless variation (Conrad). At the same time, the fact that the Greeks "got it wrong" concerning the humoural system should not diminish our admiration for their pursuit of scientific

Figure 15. Hippocrates, b. 460 BCE, Greek physician, and Galen, b. 129 CE, Roman physician and philosopher. Fresco, thirteenth century. Anagni Cathedral, Italy. Photo Credit: Alfredo Dagli Orti/The Art Archive at Art Resource, NY.

knowledge. Instead, it underscores the reality of science as a process of constant discovery through which theories are modified or discarded as new knowledge becomes available. In this way ancient medicine had its limitations, but the same can be said of modern medicine, which awaits answers to mysteries like autism and cancer—answers that only additional research and experimentation can provide.

An important concept too in this system was cookery, or concoction. This was the result of a belief common among most ancient physicians, which held that foods were absorbed through the vessels after they had been ingested and then transformed into liquid in the stomach (Wilkins and Hill). Digestion, therefore, was a form of cooking, and through a process of trial and error man was able to determine those foods that were easier to digest and concoct. Hippocrates provides additional perspective on these matters:

7.1. Hippocrates, *Ancient Medicine* 3.36–54

> So from wheat they produced bread, after crushing, stripping it of its hull, and milling, sifting, kneading, and baking it; and from barley they produced cake. They tested foods that they boiled or baked, and they mixed in many other things, combining the strong and unmixed with the weaker components in order to adapt these foods to man's constitution. They believed that pain, disease, and death would come from foods that were too strong for the human constitution to assimilate once eaten, while nourishment, growth, and health would result from that which could be assimilated. What more deserving or fitting name could be given to this discovery and research than medicine, in that it has been discovered with the health, preservation, and nourishment of man as its goal, instead of that manner of living that brought pain, disease, and death?

Equally important was the strongly held belief that foods contained certain powers (*dunameis*) that could be utilized to maintain health in addition to the nourishment value (*trophe*) of food for the body. We find this critical principle on display in *Regimen* and *Epidemics*, two works that help to place Hippocratic principles on health and wellbeing in a broader context. In the first passage, note that the ancients grasped two principles that are critical to the modern dietary regimen as well—the importance of exercise and the need for portion control (even though the concept of calories was still unknown in antiquity and the emphasis on rich meats would not be a feature of many modern dietary schemes).

7.2. Hippocrates, *Regimen in Health 4*

Fat people who wish to become thin should always exercise on an empty stomach, and sit down to eat while they are winded and before they have cooled down; and beforehand they should drink diluted wine that is not very cold. Their meats should be seasoned with sesame, sweet spices, and such things. And let the meats also be fat. In this way they will satisfy their hunger with a minimum amount of food. They should eat just one full meal a day, refrain from bathing, lie on a hard bed, and walk about with light clothing as much as possible. Thin people who wish to become fat should do the opposite of these things, and in particular they should never exercise on an empty stomach.

While *Regimen* dealt with lifestyle, *Epidemics* consists of seven books that record observations of the doctor-authors during their itinerant travels in northern Greece. The meaning of the title is ambiguous, as it could mean either "of the people (demos)," or "sojourning in a place," (deme); hence, the subject could be the illnesses occurring in a given time and place, or the visits of the doctor in an area. The work itself includes a broad range of maladies—from heartburn and headaches to kidney, liver, and uterine ailments—and their accompanying remedies as found in food and drink. *Epidemics* is also important because, although there are drug recipes concerning gynecology, there is no Hippocratic text dedicated to pharmacology, so this as close as we can come to the topic (Wilkins and Hill).

The first text below recalls the remedy contained in the modern saying "the hair of the dog that bit you," as it calls for a good dose of uncut wine for the drinker who is hungover. The second passage discusses more serious afflictions—kidney and bowel disease. Both of these texts are typical of the ancients' emphasis on observation and therapy instead of aetiology. In this way, the ancients were less interventionist than practitioners of modern medicine. Furthermore, such evidence confirms a therapeutic reliance on simple foodstuffs, including wine, grain, and olive oil, which, as we saw earlier, formed the basis of the ancient Mediterranean diet. It is not so surprising then that they appear frequently in a medicinal context as well. The ancient reliance on items of this sort serves as a reminder of their popularity but also underscores two important realities of the "new" medicine of the fifth century BCE: namely, that regimen and dietetics were aimed at making the patient the master of his own health (Holmes, in Boys-Stones et al.); and that medicine remained largely self-help and agrarian in nature, factors that compelled the patient to seek out and utilize whatever local remedies were available (Hanson, in Potter).

7.3. Hippocrates, *Epidemics* 2.6.30

If the patient has a headache from a hangover, give him a half pint of uncut wine to drink. For other head pains, have him eat very warm bread dipped in uncut wine.

7.4 Hippocrates, *Epidemics* 7.115

Clonegus, in Abdera, suffered from a kidney disease. Little by little, he painfully urinated much blood. Furthermore, he had trouble with a dysenteric bowel. He was given goat's milk early in the morning and a fifth part of water, and they were boiled to a total of three cups. And in the evening he was given roasted bread as a main dish, beets or cucumber, and thin red wine. And he was given ripe cucumber. When he adhered to this regimen, his intestines became stable, and his urine became clear. But he did drink milk until the urine returned to normal.

In addition to the writings of the Hippocratic corpus, food and drink intersected with health and healing within sanctuaries dedicated to Asclepius, the main Greek god of healing. The sick and the dying would travel to these centers (considerable distances in some cases) to seek cures by going to sleep in the temple (incubation) in the hope that the god would appear to them in a dream and cure them. Many cities and towns in the classical period had sanctuaries dedicated to this god; some centers, such as those at Pergamon, Kos, and Epidaurus, achieved reputations that attracted pilgrims from across the ancient world.

Pilgrims would typically leave inscriptions, which purported to be a record of the cures they received from this god at a particular temple site. The records of these cures, known as *iamata*, have often been dismissed for their fantastic nature, yet they are important for the light they cast on the nature of these healing cults (Dillon). For our purposes, *iamata* are especially significant as evidence for food and drink that was gathered and administered by the patients themselves in a manner similar to the prescriptions written by the doctor. This is the case in the next excerpt from Lebena, an important healing temple of Asclepius on the island of Crete during the first century BCE. Dreams are not mentioned in the records from here but the sick were clearly cured while they slept. Note that the list of foodstuffs shows a growing familiarity with medicine, or at least how a medical prescription might sound for someone who incubated in such a temple (Wickkiser).

7.5 *Inscriptiones Creticae (IC) I xvii 17*

To Asclepius.

Poplios Granios. According to command.

I had a persistent cough for two years, and I was expectorating for the whole day, when the god took in hand to cure me.

He gave me salad rocket to take after fasting, and Italian pepper to drink; fine meal with hot water, then a powder from the ashes of the altar with holy water; then an egg and pine resin; next, black pitch, next, the iris plant with honey, then an apple.

(The rest of the inscription is fragmentary.)

Diet and regimen in Roman medicine

Few medical writings survive from the centuries between the time of the Hippocratic corpus and the first Roman emperors. Even so, we are informed in a broad range of areas, including: medical theory, with several theorists important enough to be mentioned by Galen in the second century CE; scientific method and zoology, especially as pioneered by Aristotle; anatomy, physiology, and vivisection, most notably at Alexandria; and different methodological approaches to medicine espoused by various sectarian groups. Evidence for a continued emphasis on regimen and dietetics into the Roman imperial era is clear from the surviving works of the two most prominent medical writers of the period, Celsus and Galen.

Celsus, active during the reign of the emperor Tiberius (14–37 CE), was not a physician but an educated Roman who felt compelled to acquire medical knowledge for the good of his household and friends. His only surviving work, the seven-book *De Medicina* (*On Medicine*), contains a detailed treatment of food and drink. Here we find a scheme that also embraced the humoral system by detailing the ease with which foodstuffs could be digested, the nourishment they provided, and whether they heated or chilled the body. Essential to this system was the need to classify as strong or weak a broad range of foodstuffs, including meat, vegetables, fish, fruit, birds, and wine. At the same time, there was certainly room for flexibility, as Celsus strongly believed that each man had to follow his own ideas rather than what he had found to be true by actual fact (*On Medicine* 2.33.6).

Sometimes this scheme produced unusual results. In the following excerpt we find that Celsus favored fatty pastry as very nourishing, presumably because of the honey and cheese it contained. The assessment is at odds with modern theories of nutrition, which place a greater emphasis on fruit and vegetables instead of carbohydrates; nonetheless, it is typical of the ancient dietary regimen and the enduring predilection for grain.

7.6. Celsus, *On Medicine* 2.18.2

And so it is necessary to know that all pulses, and all breadstuffs made from grain, are the strongest kind of food (I call strongest that which has the most nourishment). To the same class of food belong: all domesticated quadruped animals; all large game, such as the wild she-goat, deer, wild boar, wild ass; all large birds, such as the goose and peacock and crane; all sea monsters, among which is the whale and such alike; also honey and cheese. Hence, it is no wonder that pastry made of grain, lard, honey, and cheese is very strong food.

Celsus was equally concerned with the treatment of disease, especially fevers, to which he devotes much of his third book. Here we find a general statement on treating fevers. Its emphasis on liquid food can also be found in Hippocrates.

7.7. Celsus, *On Medicine* 3.6.10

For patients with a fever liquid food is best, or whatever is closest to fluid, and that of the lightest possible variety, barley gruel especially; and if there have been high fevers, that mixture should be very thin. Honey separated from the comb may also be added in the proper proportion to give the body more nutriment; but if it upsets the stomach, this is unnecessary, as also is the gruel itself. But in its place either crumbled bread or washed spelt groats in hot water can be given …

Galen on food and drink

The importance of food and drink in maintaining health is most fully addressed by Galen, a towering figure in the study of ancient medicine (Mattern). Both a philosopher and a physician, Galen was born of a wealthy family in Asia Minor and rose spectacularly from gladiator doctor in the East to court physician of the emperor Marcus Aurelius in Rome, where he spent most of his career until his death in 216 CE. Galen thought of himself as a Greek first rather than a Roman, and much of his thinking was based on Greek medical and philosophical principles. An ambitious polymath and prodigious author, he has left us more material than any other writer in antiquity; we know that he authored over 350 works, although many have not survived.

In matters concerning diet Galen essentially promoted the medical principles of Hippocrates to an elite and well-educated Roman audience. For Galen, diet was more than just food and drink but included sleep, physical activity, and the environment. Even so, he was enormously interested in food and drink, and he produced several large works on foodstuffs and their role in health. A striking feature of Galen's dietetics is his deep interest in food itself. In fact, he provides the most comprehensive survey of foods available in his own time, having acquired this knowledge through a lifetime of personal observation and travel throughout the Roman Empire. This is evident, for example, in his discussion of radishes in the excerpt below, which is also notable for displaying Galen's interest in the differences in diet among urban and rural inhabitants of the Graeco-Roman world. Note here that city dwellers ate radishes as an appetizer but county folk, likely out of necessity, paired them with bread to make more of a meal. Galen found such social observation fascinating, although it is often difficult to assess why he included such material, other than perhaps to emphasize to his educated readers the general boorishness of rural dwellers (Powell).

7.8. Galen, *On the Powers of Food*, 2 (trans. Grant, 152)

> Those who live in the cities, for the most part, only eat these (sc. radishes) raw as a starter with fish sauce to relax the bowels, but some people pour vinegar over them. Those who live in the country often serve them with bread, rather like the other natural accompaniments, among which are fresh oregano, nose-smart, thyme, savory, pennyroyal, serpyllum, green mint, catmint, pellitory, and rocket.

Like Hippocrates, Galen linked the properties of foods to the four humours of the body and their various constituent qualities. Since the body got its nourishment from food and all foods had their own properties and powers—some foods were moistening or drying, others provided coolness or heat—it followed that food and drink could affect the body, especially its vital fluids. By matching foods to what the body required, the physician could address both good and bad health. This practice of listing foods and placing them according to their strengths, weaknesses, and digestibility differed little from other ancient writers on food and diet. This passage on snails is typical of these features; through its inclusion of recipes it also is typical of Galen's belief that the physician also had to be a good cook.

7.9. Galen, *On the Powers of Food*, 3 (trans. Grant, 157)

Like testaceans, they (sc. snails) contain a juice that relaxes the stomach, and so some people, after seasoning them with olive oil, fish-sauce, and wine, use the resulting stock as a laxative for the bowels. If you want to use the flesh of this creature only as food, first boil it in water before transferring it to fresh water, then boil it once again in this water, season it and boil it a third time until the flesh becomes really soft. Prepared like this it will check the stomach, yet still furnish the body with sufficient nourishment.

Finally, while a modern dietician would approve of most of Galen's recommendations (Nutton), we must not forget that bias was inevitable. Recall at 5.53 Galen's remark that it was difficult to tell the difference between swine flesh and human flesh and that innkeepers would take advantage of this and serve the latter to their customers. The comment seems to be based not on scientific observation but on second-hand information and the ancient practice of understanding certain behaviors in terms of social rank and class. Equally important to recognize were the limitations of scientific understanding and technology in antiquity, as mentioned earlier concerning the humoural system. In this passage, Galen's reveals his low regard for fruit since it contains little nourishment in terms of energy (calories). We might suppose, however, that this assessment may have been partly rooted in the difficulties of keeping fruit fresh in a warm Mediterranean climate where refrigeration was non-existent.

7.10. Galen, *On the Properties of Foodstuffs* 2.7.570 (trans. Powell, 76)

Generally speaking then, you should understand, as a general principle regarding fruits edible to man, that the nutriment that the moist ones produce and deliver to the body is moist and thin. From which it follows, absolutely, that such nutriment passes through the system and goes rapidly through the body as a whole, being quickly evacuated both in the urine and through the skin. This is why all such foods have been properly described by physicians as poorly nutritive.

Women, children, and slaves

We are not as well informed about the diet of women, children, and slaves as we are about the men to whom ancient writings on the topic are generally directed. The surviving testimony tends to confirm their status as marginalized people whose nutritional needs did not receive as much attention as those of the male elites who exerted control over them. Even so, the surviving evidence is compelling, and helps us to reconstruct the dietary regimen of these groups with some degree of confidence.

In general, the life of a slave was brutal, cruel, and often short. Medical care, perhaps furnished only when slaves were to be sold, was minimal (Nutton). In terms of diet, slaves were fed bland and scarcely nutritious food. Earlier (3.36) we learned of the rations of wine that Cato granted for his farm slaves. Here, we see the food allowances he offered to these same slaves. We might imagine that these items were fairly typical of those provided by the frugal estate owner of the second century BCE, who depended heavily on slave labor. Notice too that Cato adjusted the amounts of food on the basis of the nature of the work to be done. This demonstrates that owners of slaves working in strenuous occupations such as farming and mining realized the need for striking a balance between economizing on the slave's diet and ensuring that the calories provided were sufficient to accomplish the work at hand.

7.11. Cato, *On Agriculture*, 56; 58

Food rations for the slaves: four measures[1] of wheat in winter, and in summer four and a half for the field hands. The overseer, the housekeeper, the foreman, and the shepherd should receive three. The chain gang should have a ration of four pounds of bread[2] through the winter, increasing to five when they begin to work the vines, and dropping back to four when the figs ripen.[3]

Relishes[4] for the slaves: store all the windfall olives you can, and later the mature olives, which will yield very little oil. Issue them sparingly and make them last as long as possible. When they are used up, issue fish-pickle[5] and vinegar, and a pint of oil per month per person. A modius of salt per year per person is sufficient.

By comparison, the diet of women and girls was more important, but perhaps only marginally so. For girls, the emphasis was on ensuring that they passed through puberty at the right time on the way to a fertile marriage. Consequently, their diet had to be carefully regulated by avoiding meat and other strong foods, as well as wine. Exercise was also important for warming the body. Xenophon relates that this was the rule in areas beyond Sparta:

7.12. Xenophon, *Constitution of Sparta*, 1.3

> The girls who are destined to become mothers in other states are raised in the accepted manner and live on the simplest food with a very limited amount of luxury fare.

With women, we witness something of a paradox in that they were in charge of managing food resources within the household but often received less at meal times due to social conventions that emphasized female moderation in eating, drinking, and sexual activity. Furthermore, women themselves often perpetuated these inequalities by passing them on to their own daughters as part of the social code of acceptable female behavior (Nadeau, in Erdkamp). Given these circumstances, it is not surprising that we find men overseeing the diet of women within the parameters of the humoural system. Here, Rufus of Ephesus, a Greek physician of the first century CE, demonstrates such a concern. His fragmentary writings are preserved in a compilation of excerpts from other medical writers in the ancient world by Oribasius, a Greek medical writer and the personal physician to the emperor Julian in the fourth century.

7.13. Oribasius, *Uncertain Books*, 37=*Corpus Medicorum Graecorum* VI. 2.2. 109. 26–8

> As everyone would agree, women's bodies are wetter and colder. So it is fitting that a hotter regimen be given to them, so that the regimen might balance the excesses of their temperature.

As Rebecca Flemming has noted, such a diet would have avoided cold and wet foods such as fish in favor of those that were hot and dry, such as honey. Eating in moderation was also critical, as was a short period of rest after eating. Physical activity, massages, mineral baths, and voice exercises were also desirable. In all of this evidence regimen was essentially corrective, and the diet and regimen of males remained the standard reference point. It is important to remember, too, that we cannot know how frequently advice of this sort was put into practice or how far it was disseminated throughout ancient society (Garnsey).

Children faced significant obstacles when it came to health and diet. One in three children died in the first year of life, while one in two did not survive past the age of ten, as deficiencies in hygiene, sanitation, medical care, and nutrition took a heavy toll (Parkin and Pomeroy). This was especially the case in urban areas and among the poorer classes. The following excerpt preserves the regimen for an infant as recorded by Mnesitheus, a Greek physician of the fourth century BCE whose works on diet were known to Galen and Athenaeus. His emphasis on grain, while not surprising, would have been insufficient if not combined with other foodstuffs and it would have contributed to deficiencies such as lack of height and malnutrition later in life (Garnsey).

7.14. Oribasius, *Uncertain Books*, 37=*Corpus Medicorum Graecorum* VI, 2.2, p. 135=Bertier, *20 (37H)*, 175

Regimen for young children. Excerpts from the works of Mnesitheus of Athens.

The nurse must utilize a bath, bathing the child at length and using lukewarm water. During the first year, she must do this three times a day: in the morning after exercise; then at mid-day; and thirdly, in the evening. After this time, she must remove the warm mid-day bath and replace it with an anointing of oil. Do not feed the child immediately after the bath, but wait. Do not give him anything to chew, but very fine wheaten flour that has been boiled or wheaten meal or crushed millet. It is necessary for all of these things to be boiled properly for a long time, and to give soft grain to a child, especially when his bowels are relaxed. On the other hand, if he is constipated, one should boil flour with honey mixed in. And if that does not work, one must draw up a mixture of chickpea and terebinth resin.[6] If a cough or a cold should arise, in this case it is wrong to provide a treatment with honey. One must bathe the child in plenty of hot water, without forgetting his head, and make him eat a lot of honey and gently press his tongue with one's finger. In this way the child vomits a lot of mucus.

Finally, community feasts (5.54–6) provide another opportunity to gauge the diet of children. Here the quality of the fare depended upon a number of factors, but most especially the generosity of the sponsor(s). Accordingly, children might sometimes enjoy a full banquet along with the adult beneficiaries, at other times they might only receive measures of nuts and wine. These two inscriptions, dated to the time of the emperors, confirm this range of possibilities in municipal Italy.

7.15. *Corpus Inscriptionum Latinarum (CIL)* 11.3206

For Marcus Ulpius Thallus, a well-deserving freedman of Augustus,[7] Flavia Inventa, his wife, and Ulpia Procula, his daughter, gave a feast to the decurions,[8] the Augustales[9] and the plebs, and to their wives and children. A place was set up for this statue by a decree of the decurions.

7.16. *Corpus Inscriptionum Latinarum (CIL)* 10.5853 = *Inscriptiones Latinae Selectae (ILS)* 6271

... It is desirable if (sc. the aediles[10]) have offered to plebeian boys without distinction of free status a scattering of nuts in the amount of 30 modii[11] and a serving of drinks from six urns of wine according to their status.

Food for travellers

Given that making adjustments to one's diet was a basic principle of ancient medicine, it follows that dietary rebalancing was also required for the traveler exposed to variable environmental conditions. As Dalby has noted, Diocles of Carystus, a Greek dietary writer of the fourth century BCE, suggested barley meal with salt for those traveling by foot in the summer, but no food or drink before mid-day for those traveling in winter. Travelers often carried their own foods, which were lighter and more compact than regular daily fare—hence, barley meal might be favored over bread, and traveler's spiced wine (*conditum viatorium*) over a regular vintage, since it could be added as a concentrate to whatever beverage might be available (Dalby 2003, s.v. "traveller's food). Similarly, those traveling by sea also had to adjust their diet. In this fragment, Dieuches provides remedies for seasickness, which would have been a common ailment in antiquity. Some modern remedies still rely on thyme as found here, although ginger, which is known for settling the stomach, is now more popular for those seeking natural remedies. Dieuches' reliance on wine in various forms would not find similar support in modern remedies.

7.17. Oribasius, *Synopsis*, V, 33, t. V, p. 231, 7–232, 13 ed. Daremberg=Bertier, 19, 257

Regimen for people who sail. Extract from the works of Dieuches.

It is neither easy nor useful for those who sail for the first time to inhibit vomiting. For it is often more advantageous to vomit. After vomiting, one should not eat much, or anything, but take either lentils with vinegar, well cooked, with a little pennyroyal, or bread crumbled in fragrant wine mixed with water. Drink a little bit of wine weakened with a lot of water or some vinegar wine or some mead. One must cook the lentils, and then, when softened, finely crush them, dry them out, and then deposit them in an earthenware container. If the vomiting continues for a long time, one must cut back some more on the food and drink a little bit, either some vinegar mead with water, in which one has soaked some thyme, or some pennyroyal and some water with fine barley flour that has been grilled, or some fragrant wine, also with flour. In order to remove unpleasant odors on the ship one must breathe in quinces or thyme or pennyroyal …

Pharmacology

The body of collected knowledge about the therapeutic properties of any substance used for healing was known as *materia medica* in antiquity, more generally as pharmacology in a modern medical context. Hippocrates discussed more than 250 drugs in his treatises *Aphorisms* and *Prognostics*, along with diet and diseases. At the end of the fourth century, Theophrastus, considered by historians as the "father of botany," detailed medicinal herbs and herbal concoctions for physicians in his *History of Plants* (*Historia Plantarum*) (Jashemski, 2002, 1999). Galen, too, showed much interest in the topic, copying many works on drugs that would otherwise be lost and attempting to explain drug therapies within the context of the humoural system.

Most important, however, was Dioscorides of Anazarbus, who, in his *Books on Materia Medica* (*De materia medica libri*), described some 600 pharmaceuticals in the fullest account of drugs and drug lore of Greek, Hellenistic, and early Roman imperial times. As one of the most influential herbal books in history, the *Materia Medica* remained popular into the European Renaissance and it laid the foundation for the beginnings of modern pharmacology. Dioscorides' work is typical in showing the overlap in ancient thinking between food and drugs, an inevitable consequence in a world where, in the absence of synthetic remedies, foodstuffs had to play a major role as substances for healing. The following passages, which tout the efficacy of wheat, radishes, and roses, respectively, offer but a glimpse of the range of products utilized as remedies for a wide array of afflictions.

7.18. Dioscorides, *De Materia Medica* 2.107 (trans. Beck, 2.85, 129–30)

Puroi, Greek, *Triticum,* Latin, wheat

1. Wheat is excellent for health use if it is new, fully ripe, and quince-yellow in color; next to this one ranks "three-month" old wheat, which some call *setaneios*.[12] When eaten raw, wheat breeds round intestinal worms, but if chewed, then plastered on, it benefits those bitten by dogs. Bread made with the finest wheat flour is more nutritious than bread made from coarse meal, and bread made from *setaneios* meal is lighter and easy to digest. *Setaneios* meal is plastered on with juice of henbane as a remedy for rheums of the tendons and for intestinal flatulence, and it removes birthmarks with vinegar and honey.

2. Its bran, when boiled with sharp vinegar and plastered on warm, gets rid of leprosies and it is a useful plaster for all incipient inflammations; when boiled with rue broth, it stops breasts from swelling with clots of milk and it is suitable both for those bitten by vipers and for colicky. Dough made from its meal, being able to warm and to draw, thins especially the calluses on the soles of the foot and with salt it ripens and opens the other growths and abscesses. Meal made from *setaneios* wheat, when plastered on with either vinegar or wine, is a fit remedy for venomous animals; boiled as one boils glue then used as a lozenge, it benefits those who spit blood, and when boiled with green mint and butter, it is good both for coughs and for roughness of the trachea. Also the fine meal of this wheat, when boiled with a mixture of hydromel or with water mixed with oil, disperses all inflammations. The bread, too, boiled with hydromel or even uncooked, relieves all inflammations when plastered on, because it softens a great deal and it gently cools when mixed with some herbs or juices.

3. Bread that is old and dry, either by itself or combined with something or other, controls diarrhea, but fresh wheat bread, soaked in brine and applied as a plaster, treats old lichen-like eruptions of the skin. A spoonful of thinned down and tepid glue, the kind they make from fine wheat flour and very fine meal for gluing books, is suitable to swallow for people who spit blood.

7.19. Dioscorides, *De Materia Medica* 2.137 (trans. Beck, 2.112, 140–1)

Raphanis, Greek, *Raphanus sativus* Latin, radish

1. The radish, too, causes flatulence, it is tasty, it is not good for the stomach, and it causes belching. It is diuretic and warms, and it eases the bowel if taken after meals, helping digestion rather nicely; but if eaten before meals, it buoys the

food. Eaten before meals, it is suitable also for people who plan to vomit, and it sharpens the senses. Taken boiled, it helps those with a chronic cough and those who produce a thick substance in their chest. But its peel, taken with vinegar and honey, is more emetic; it is suitable for those with edemata, and when used as a poultice, it is suitable also for spleen disease. With honey, it stops spreading ulcers, it removes black eye, it helps those bitten by vipers, it restores hair on bald spots, and with meal of darnel it clears birthmarks. It does also help people who choke from mushrooms and it draws down the menses.

2. Its seed is emetic, diuretic, reduces the spleen when taken as a drink with vinegar. It helps people with sore throats, if they use it in a gargle boiled with warm vinegar and honey; it helps with the bite of the asp when drunk with wine, and it strongly demarcates gangrenes when plastered on with vinegar.

The wild radish, which the Romans call *armoracium*, has leaves resembling those of the cultivated, tending rather towards the leaves of charlock, but its root is thin, long, and somewhat sharp. Both the root and the leaves are boiled to eat as potherbs. It warms, it is diuretic, and it is very hot.

7.20. Dioscorides, *De Materia Medica* 5.35 (trans. Beck, 1.99, 70)

roda, Greek, *rosa* Latin, rose

1. Roses cool and contract, but the dried ones contract more. You must extract the juice from roses that are young, cutting off with shears the so-called onyx;[13] this is the white part on the petal, then you must squeeze and pound in a mortar the rest until it is compressed into a ball, and thus store it for eye ointment. The petals are dried in the shade, being turned frequently lest they become moldy.

The expressed juice from dried roses that were boiled in wine is effective for headaches, hurting eyes, earaches, hurting gums, anal pains, and for pains of the uterus when smeared on with a feather brush and when used as a wash.

2. The roses themselves, chopped up without being squeezed, are good when plastered on for inflammations of the hypochondrium, for excess of fluids in the stomach, and for erysipelas. Ground up fine when dry, they are sprinkled on the inside of thighs,[14] and they are mixed with lip salves, with wound medications, and with antidotes. They are also burned to use in paints for eyelids and eyelashes. The flower found in the middle of the roses, dried and laid on, is good for discharges from the gums. Rose hips control diarrhea and spitting of blood when drunk.

Drinking and drukenness

We have seen throughout this source book the significance of wine in the Mediterranean diet. It was the daily drink of all classes in Greece and Rome and it was also a key feature of the Roman (*convivium*) and Greek (*symposion*) drinking party, one of the defining social institutions of aristocratic life. Given that wine played such an important role in Mediterranean antiquity, it will be useful to conclude this chapter by exploring briefly a topic that has largely escaped scholarly attention, the role of heavy drinking and drunkenness as a physical and moral health issue among the Greeks and Romans. To be sure, the topic was not unknown among the ancients. Theophrastus and Aristotle, for example, both wrote treatises on drunkenness. Although neither of these works has survived, drinking, especially heavy drinking and its attendant problems, was clearly of interest, and there is no shortage of accounts from additional sources to help us understand this phenomenon.

Before presenting a sampling of the evidence, two features are worth bearing in mind. First, the ancient Greeks and Romans were not familiar with the modern understanding of alcoholism as "a primary, chronic disease with genetic, psychosocial, and environmental factors influencing its development and manifestations," as defined, for example, by the American Medical Association. As we shall see, the ancients clearly understood the physical and mental effects of heavy drinking, yet there is nothing in the sources to suggest that they recognized it as a disease with genetic factors. Second, heavy drinking prompted strong objections from across the ancient world, whether from philosophers or from those who appropriated the topic in order to malign their political enemies. Such denunciations characterized heavy drinking as a moral failure or defect of character, not as a physical ailment. Even though the Greeks and Romans may not have characterized heavy drinking and drunkenness as a disease in the modern sense, the highly detrimental effect that heavy drinking had on physical and mental health and, by extension, the social health of the community, is a recurring theme in the sources and therefore makes it worthy of consideration.

Physical and mental effects of drinking

The following passages all share an awareness of alcohol use as causing both physical and mental changes in the imbiber. Several of the excerpts are in the form of aphorisms that provide ironical but useful perspectives on the issue;

Plutarch, on the other hand, compares the transformational paradigm of drinking to the changes that the political leader had to undergo in order to be successful. The final two passages, both from Homer, underscore the physical harm or violence that could result from heavy drinking.

7.21. Lucilius, *Remains of Old Latin* 3.132

The bottom of the wine holder was turned upside down, and so were our thoughts.

7.22. Athenaeus, *Sophists at Dinner* 14.613b

When the wine goes down into the body, evil words float to the surface.

7.23. Homer, *Odyssey* 14.463–6

"For the crazy wine bids me, which allows the very thoughtful man to sing much and to laugh softly, and makes him spring up to dance and also elicits a word better left unsaid."

7.24. Athenaeus, *Sophists at Dinner* 14.613b

And so the comic poet Clearchus says in *The Corinthians*: "If it turned out that those who get drunk every day had a headache before they drank the uncut wine, none of us would ever drink. But as it is, taking our pleasure first, before the pain, we arrive too late to get the good."

7.25. Plutarch, *On Mores (Moralia), Precepts of Statecraft* 799b–c

For any attempt by the statesman to bring about by himself at the beginning a change of character and nature in the people will not easily be achieved, nor is it safe, but it is a thing that requires a lot of time and great power. Just as wine in the beginning is controlled by the character of the drinker but quietly, as it heats up his whole body and becomes mingled with it, itself forms the character of the drinker and changes him, just so it is necessary that the leader, until he has built up his political strength by his reputation and by trust, must accommodate himself to the disposition of the people as it is set before him and make that the goal of his efforts, recognizing by what things the people is pleased and led by nature.

7.26. Athenaeus, *Sophists at Dinner* 13.607c–d

Moreover, people who wish very earnestly to be sober keep a close watch on this ideal up to a certain point in their drinking bouts; then, when the spirit of the wine insinuates itself, they display every indecency; this happened not long ago when the delegation from Arcadia visited Antigonus.[15] For they were eating breakfast in a very dignified and graceful way, as they believed, not glancing at any of us, not even one another. But as the drinking continued and there entered, among other entertainments, those Thessalian dancing girls, who, according to their custom, danced naked in loincloths, the men could no longer behave themselves, but got up from their dining couches and shouted at the sight they were witnessing as something marvelous; and they praised the king as a blessed man because it was possible for him to enjoy these things, and they went on to commit very many other indecencies similar to that.

7.27. Homer, *Odyssey* 11.60–5

"Son of Laertes, sprung from Zeus, resourceful Odysseus, the evil doom of some spirit and unlimited wine did me in. Having lain down to sleep in Circe's palace, it did not occur to me to come down again by way of the long ladder, but I fell straight down from the roof. My neck snapped from my spine, and my soul went down to the house of Hades."[16]

7.28. Homer, *Odyssey* 21.295–8

Wine even made a fool of the centaur,[17] famous Eurytion, in the palace of great-hearted Pirithous when he visited the Lapiths. And when he had made his mind crazy with wine, in his madness he brought troubles upon the house of Pirithous.

Philosophical reaction

Calls for moderation in drinking resounded from philosophers who embraced a variety of schools or approaches. We have already witnessed some of this sentiment from Philo Judaeus, the Graeco-Judaic philosopher of Alexandria during the second century CE (see 4.45). Seneca and Lucretius (see Chapter 2, "Food for thought") add two more perspectives in the following excerpts. As an advocate of Stoicism, a philosophy whose ethical scheme recognized virtue as the law of the universe and right conduct as the path to happiness, Seneca viewed drinking as nothing more than bringing to the surface unchecked lust and arrogance and a humiliating lack of control over bodily functions—all in direct opposition to the life of virtue. For Lucretius, author of a treatise that brought the tenets of Greek Epicureanism to a Roman audience, wine overcame the soul of the drinker, thereby providing evidence for the kind of change that proved the mortality of the body, and hence the absence of any afterlife.

7.29. Seneca, *Epistle* 83.20–1

Drunkenness takes over our spirit, and whatever vice is used to hiding emerges. Drunkenness does not create vices, but it draws them out; at such times the lustful man does not even wait for the bedroom, but without delay gives free rein to as much as his own passions have sought; at such times the unchaste man proclaims and advertises his malady; at such times the impudent man does not restrain his tongue or his hand. The haughty man grows in arrogance, the ruthless man in cruelty, the slanderer in spitefulness. Every vice is given free play and steps forward. Add to that, the ignorance of who we are, the halting and poorly spoken words, the unsteady glance, the shaky step, the spinning head, the very ceiling moving about as if a hurricane were swirling about the whole house, the tortures of the stomach when the wine produces gas and our very bowels swell.

7.30. Lucretius, *On the Nature of Things* 3. 476–86

Moreover, why, when the sharp power of wine has penetrated into a man, and its fire has been dispersed and spread through the veins, does heaviness come upon the limbs, do his legs impede him as he staggers, does his speech become slurred, his mind become soaked, his eyes swim, shouting, sobbing, and brawls swell up, and now all the rest of such things follow? Why do these things exist, unless it be that the violent fury of wine is accustomed to confuse the spirit while in the body itself? But if anything can be confused and hindered, this indicates that, if some cause a little more compelling should work its way in, the thing would perish, and be deprived of its future life.

Top topers of antiquity

Anacharsis, a philosopher from Scythia (a multinational region of central Eurasia in classical times) in the sixth century BCE is reported to have said that the vine bore three kinds of grapes: the first of pleasure; the next of intoxication; and the third of disgust (Diogenes Laertius *Anacharsis* 103). To be sure, antiquity's heaviest drinkers were well acquainted with all three of Anacharsis' grapes, as confirmed by accounts of their alcohol-fueled follies and the outrage that their actions often provoked. It is too simple to say, however, that individuals, especially elites, simply drank to excess because they could and that ancient authors were keen to report it in a manner similar to the way in which the tabloid press sensationalizes the missteps of modern celebrities. As the following excerpts will reveal, the cultural context of the drinker is important for us to understand, as are the motivations and interests of the authors who are doing the reporting, and it is only by considering these aspects that we can hope to reach a more informed understanding of this phenomenon.

Turning first to women, modern anthropology and archaeology have revealed much about female drinking. In many societies women were expected to drink less than men, to behave differently from men while drinking or intoxicated, to prefer different drinks of alcohol than men, or to drink in different places than men (Dietler). Some of these features also characterized female drinking in antiquity, although we are not nearly as well informed in this area as we are for ancient women in general, including commensality. What we do know is that women drank with men in a variety of settings and circumstances, including elite *convivia*, public banquets, and religious festivals. At the same time, due largely to an unrelenting focus on drunken women, the literary record is at odds with this evidence. This is not entirely surprising, given that men were doing the writing and that notions of masculinity were traditionally linked to the practice of men drinking with other men, as the Greek *symposion* and other evidence has made clear.

Given these realities, women, especially drunken women, were an unwelcome challenge to the established order of male–female relationships and to public and private decorum. Closely related to these beliefs was the male expectation that a women's behavior was to be above reproach at all times. The forces behind this expectation, especially among the Romans, were complex; they involved a fear of adultery but also a desire for moderation achieved through repeated legislation aimed at limiting excessive displays of wealth from the second century BCE onwards. Such measures proved to be unsuccessful.

The three selections included here focus on the male response to female drinking, especially excessive drinking. In the first selection Athenaeus reprises some of the traditional protections in place to control female drinking while revealing much about traditional behavioral expectations and levels of independence for women. For those women who did choose to imbibe, they became easy targets for the moralist and satirist alike, whose scathing denunciations are captured in the subsequent selections of Seneca and Juvenal.

7.31. Athenaeus, *Sophists at Dinner* 10.440f

Among the Romans, so says Polybius in the sixth book, women are not allowed to drink wine; but they drink something called *passum*. This is made of raisins, and when drunk it resembles the sweet wine of Aegosthena, or like the Cretan; therefore, they use it to counteract the urgency of thirst. But it is not possible for a woman drinking wine to escape unnoticed; for, in the first place, the woman does not have control over wine; besides this, she must kiss her own and her husband's relatives, down to cousin's children, and do this every day as she sees them. Finally, she is on her guard, since the chances of meeting make it uncertain whom she will encounter. For the matter is such that if she should take a small sip, there is no need of false accusation.

7.32. Seneca, *Epistle* 95.21

… in rivaling the freedom of men, women have also rivaled the troubles of men. They stay out late at night no less than men, and drink no less, they challenge men in both wrestling and in drinking uncut wine; equally do they vomit from distended stomachs and they mete out again all of their wine by throwing up; equally do they gnaw on ice, as a relief to their burning gullet.

7.33. Juvenal, *Satire* 6.419–33

She frequents the baths by night and at night time she orders her oil flasks and her quarters to be moved there; she loves all the hustle bustle and sweat of the bath; when her arms have fallen, fatigued by the heavy barbell, the skillful anointer presses his fingers on her genitals and forces her loins to shout with satisfaction. Meanwhile, her unlucky guests are overcome with sleep and hunger. Finally she appears with a face flushed, thirsty enough for the entire three-gallon wine holder laid at her feet, from which she throws down another pint before her dinner to create a raging appetite; then she brings it all up again and pounds the floor with the vomit of her insides. Streams run over the marble pavement; the golden basin stinks of Falernian, for she drinks and vomits like a big snake that has fallen into a vat. Then her husband, disgusted, controls his anger by closing his eyes.

Among men, the evidence is as colorful as it is revealing. Alcibiades was an Athenian general whose shifting allegiances during the Peloponnesian War against Sparta in the fifth century BCE, combined with his charismatic but dissolute personality, made him a fascinating subject of many genres, including Thucydides' history of the war, the biographies of Plutarch and Cornelius Nepos, and Plato's philosophical dialogue on love, the *Symposium*. This excerpt captures much of Alcibiades' personality as the drunken trickster, a feature that was especially important to Plutarch as a biographer who believed that an anecdote such as this often told more about a man's character than his exploits in politics or battle. It is equally important to note that Alcibiades' heavy drinking did not prevent him from achieving political and military prominence during the Peloponnesian War, a phenomenon that is discussed more fully in the Roman evidence below.

7.34. Plutarch, *Alcibiades* 4.1.5

> This man happened to be a lover of Alcibiades, and, entertaining some friends, asked Alcibiades also to the dinner. He declined the invitation, but after having drunk heavily at home with some friends, he went in drunken procession to the house of Anytus, stood at the door of the men's chamber and, gazing at the tables full of gold and silver beakers, bid his slaves to take half and carry it home for him; he did not deem it worthy to go in, but after he did this he was off. As a result, the guests were displeased and said that Alcibiades had treated Anytus insolently and arrogantly. "But fairly and kindly," said Anytus; "he could have taken everything, he has left us half."

Theopompus and Arrian both wrote histories that included the exploits of the Macedonian generals, Philip and his son, Alexander. Theopompus, a contemporary, was able to maintain a critical distance from father and son, while Arrian, writing several centuries later, was a strong admirer of Alexander. Although separated by time and temperament, both historians confirm the tradition that characterized the Macedonians as heavy drinkers. Part of this tradition was cultural, as drinking, along with hunting and fighting, was one of the activities that had helped to unite the Macedonian king with the nobles upon whom he relied for support. Alcohol, then, played a key role in helping to consolidate and legitimize political power. At the same time, the inclusion of heavy drinking served as a cultural marker that helped to distinguish the Macedonians as "other" or "different" from the Greeks to the south (Carney). The first passage highlights Philip's deep attachment to drinking and debauchery; the second chronicles one of the saddest chapters in Alexander's life, the murder of Clitus, one of his most capable and long-serving commanders. Alcohol abuse became a growing problem for Alexander in his final years and it surely contributed to his death at the age of 32 (O'Brien).

7.35. Athenaeus, *Sophists at Dinner* 10.435b–c

Philip, father of Alexander, was another lover of drink, as Theopompus records in the twenty-sixth book of his *Histories*. And in another part of his history he writes: "Philip was crazy and prone to dangers, partly by nature and partly because of drink; for he was a heavy drinker, and frequently he was drunk when he entered into battle." And in the fifty-third book, after recording the events at Chaeronea and telling how Philip had invited to dinner the Athenian ambassadors who had arrived, he says: "When they had departed, Philip immediately sent for some of his companions, and he ordered them to call the flute-girls, Aristonicus the harp-singer, Dorion the flute-player, and all the rest who were accustomed to drink with him; for Philip led around such persons with him everywhere, and he was always equipped with many accoutrements for a drinking-bout and a party. For since he was a drink-lover and intemperate and a buffoon in character, he surrounded himself with many musicians and comedians. And so, after drinking the whole night through, and getting very drunk and committing every folly,[18] he dismissed all the others and made them depart, while he reveled with the Athenian ambassadors until sunrise."

7.36. Arrian, *Anabasis* 4.8

At this point, since the time is right, I will relate the tragedy of Clitus, son of Dropides, and its effect upon Alexander, even if the incident took place a little later. The story is as follows. The Macedonians observed a day sacred to Dionysius, and Alexander offered sacrifice each year on that day. They say that he neglected Dionysius on that occasion but made a sacrifice to the Dioscuri; for some reason he had it in mind to sacrifice to them. The drinking was excessive (and indeed Alexander had made innovations toward the more barbaric when it came to drinking), but in the course of the drinking bout talk arose about the Dioscuri, how Tyndareus was robbed of their birth and how the twins were remitted to Zeus. And some of the company, in flattery of Alexander—the sort of men who have always harmed, and will never stop destroying, the interests of kings—declared that, in their opinion, Polyduces and Castor were not to be compared with Alexander and his achievements; others in the drinking bout did not even leave Heracles untouched: they said it was only envy which stood in the way of living men and deprived them of their due honors from their friends. Clitus, however, had made it clear for some time past that he was aggravated by Alexander's change to a more barbaric style and by the words of his flatterers. Now, urged on by the wine, he would allow them neither to disrespect the divine power nor to diminish the deeds of the heroes of old, nor to confer an undeserved gift upon Alexander. Moreover, in his view the accomplishments of Alexander were not as great and wonderful as they were touting; and Alexander had not achieved them by himself but a great part of the deeds belonged to the Macedonians. Alexander was deeply distressed by his words. I do not approve of his speech, but I think it sufficient amid such drunkenness to keep one's opinions to oneself, nor to cause offence with the same flatteries as the others. But when some in attendance recalled Philip's deeds, saying with complete injustice that he had accomplished nothing great or wonderful, again with the thought of trying to win Alexander's favor, Clitus, no longer able to contain himself, paid honor to the achievements of Philip, and compared Alexander's deeds to his; he was, by now, very drunk and, among much else, he taunted Alexander with the reminder that he had saved his life when the cavalry battle had been joined with the Persians on the Granicus River. And raising up his right hand haughtily, he cried, " This is the hand, Alexander, that saved you on that day!" Alexander could no longer tolerate Clitus' drunkenness and insolence, and he leapt up in anger against him, but he was restrained by his fellow drinkers. Clitus did not ease off with his insults. Alexander shouted out, calling for the Guard. Since no one answered, he said that he had been brought to the same place as Darius, when he was led as a captive by Bessus and his followers,[19] and that he had nothing left but the name of a king. His companions could no longer hold him back; springing to his feet, they say he snatched a spear from one of the attendants and struck Clitus dead.

Our final two excerpts point to the complexities of decoding drunkenness in a Roman setting. Cicero's depiction of Antony is unrelenting but consistent not only with other accounts of Antony' drinking habits but also with the orator's goal in the *Second Philippic* of delivering a fierce invective against the man who had tried to bestow the kingship on Julius Caesar. Cicero himself, however, was not above reproach on this issue. He could blithely overlook the heavy drinking of others when it did not suit his purposes, for example, as in his defense of M. Caelius Rufus (*Pro Caelio*) in 56 BCE on a charge of poisoning brought against him by the sister of one of Cicero's most hated political enemies. Clearly, it could be just as effective to employ heavy drinking as a political weapon as it was to reprise it as a failing of character and a breach of decorum—hence the importance of political context and authorial intent.

7.37. Cicero, *Philippic* 2.25.63

But let us pass over these things, which are of a more robust improbity; rather, let us speak of the most worthless kind of inconstancy. You with that gullet of yours, with those lungs, with that gladiator-like strength of your whole body, had put away so much wine at Hippias' wedding that you were forced to vomit in the sight of the Roman people the next day. Oh, a disgusting thing, not only to see, but also to hear of! If, amid those enormous draughts of yours, this had happened to you in the middle of dinner, who would not think it disgraceful? But at an assembly of the Roman people, while conducting public business, a master of the horse, for whom it would be disgraceful to burp, vomited and filled his own lap and the whole tribunal with remnants of food stinking of wine!

We already know something of Seneca's Stoic beliefs, so his recognition of Piso's drunkenness is not so surprising. What is interesting here though is that Piso and Cossus, despite their tippling, were still held in high enough esteem to be entrusted with positions of authority in Roman government. As John D'Arms noted (D'Arms, in Murray and Tecusan), this suggests that, although breaking decorum by heavy drinking was to be discouraged among the ruling elites, when it did occur, the ranks perhaps closed "in protective solidarity" around one of their own. Thus, the excerpt reveals much about the aristocratic value system of the Romans and the ways in which it could be negotiated to maintain the status quo when challenged by potentially problematic behaviors. It also confirms that intoxication was a permissible mode of comportment for reinforcing social identity among certain groups.

7.38. Seneca, *Epistle* 83.14–15

Lucius Piso, the director of public safety at Rome, was drunk from the very time he was appointed. He used to spend the greater part of the night at banquets; he used to sleep until almost noon; this was his morning routine. Even so, he applied himself most attentively to his office, which included the guardianship of the city. Even the deified Augustus entrusted him with secret orders when he placed him in command of Thrace, which he conquered. Tiberius, too, trusted him when he set out for Campania, when he left behind him in the city many matters that aroused both suspicion and hatred. I think that because Piso's drunkenness turned out well for the Emperor, he appointed Cossus as prefect of Rome, a man of authority and restraint, but so steeped and soaked in wine that once, at a meeting of the senate, where he had come after a banquet, he was overcome by a sleep from which he could not be aroused, and was carried away. Nevertheless, to this man Tiberius wrote many orders in his own hand, orders which he believed ought not to be entrusted even to his own ministers. Cossus let no secret slip out, whether personal or public.

Suggestions for Further Reading

Beck, L., trans. 2005. *Pedanius Dioscorides of Anazarbus, De Materia Medica*. Hildesheim.

Bertier, J. 1972. *Mnesithée et Dieuchès*. Leiden.

Boys-Stones, G., Graziosi, B., and Vasunia, P., eds. *The Oxford Handbook of Hellenic Studies*.

Carney, E. D. 2007. "Symposia and the Macedonian elite: the unmixed life." *Syllecta Classica* 18: 129–80.

Conrad, L. I., Neve, M., Nutton, V., Porter, R., and Wear, A. 1995. *The Western Medical Tradition, 800 BC to AD 1800*. Cambridge.

Dalby, A. 2003. *Food in the Ancient World from A to Z*. London.

Dietler, M. 2006. "Alcohol: anthropological/archaeological perspectives." *Annual Review of Anthropology* 35: 229–49.

Dean-Jones, L. 1994. *Women's Bodies in Classical Greek Science*. Oxford.

Dillon, M. 1994. "The didactic nature of the Epidaurian Iamata." *Zeitschrift für Papyrologie und Epigraphik (ZPE)* 101: 239–60.

Erdkamp, P., ed. 2012. *A Cultural History of Food in Antiquity*. London.

Flemming, R. 2000. *Medicine and the Making of Roman Women: Gender, Nature, and Authority from Celsus to Galen*. Oxford.

French, R. K. and Greenaway, F. *Science in the Early Roman Empire: Pliny the Elder, His Sources and Influence*. London.

Garnsey, P. 1999. *Food and Society in Classical Antiquity*. Cambridge.

Grant, M. 2000. *Galen On Food and Diet*. London.

Grmek, M. D. 1989. *Diseases in the Ancient Greek World*. Baltimore.

—1998. *Western Medical Thought from Antiquity to the Middle Ages*, trans. A. Shugar. Cambridge, MA.

Jashemski, W. F. 1999. *A Pompeian Herbal: Ancient and Modern Medicinal Plants*. Austin.

—2002. *A Natural History of Pompeii*. Cambridge.

King, H. 2001. *Greek and Roman Medicine*. Bristol.

Kinzl, K. H., ed. *A Companion to the Classical Greek World*. Oxford.

Mattern, S. 2013. *The Prince of Medicine: Galen in the Roman Empire*. Oxford.

Murray, O., ed. 1990. *Sympotica: A Symposium on the Symposion*. Oxford.

Murray, O. and Tecusan, M., eds. 1995. *In Vino Veritas*. Rome.

Nutton, V. 2005. *Ancient Medicine*. London.

O'Brien, J. M. 1992. *Alexander the Great: The Invisible Enemy*. London.

Parkin, T. and Pomeroy, A. 2007. *Roman Social History: A Sourcebook*. London.

Potter, D. S., ed. *A Companion to the Roman Empire*.

Powell, O. 2003. *Galen, On the Properties of Foodstuffs (De Alimentorum Facultatibus)*. Cambridge.

Riddle, J. 1985. *Dioscorides on Pharmacy and Medicine*. Austin.

Scarborough, J., ed. 1987. *Folklore and Folk Medicines*. Ann Arbor.

Singer, P. N., trans. 1997. *Galen: Selected Works*. Oxford.

Wickkiser, B. 2008. *Asclepios, Medicine, and the Politics of Healing in Fifth-Century Greece*. Baltimore.

Wilkins, J. and Hill, S. 2006. *Food in the Ancient World*. Oxford.

Wilkins, J., and Whitmarsh, T. 2009. *Galen and the World of Knowledge*. Cambridge.

Notes

Chapter 2

1 A name that recalls Iris, the messenger god.

2 Dionysius, god of wine and wine making, ecstasy, and the theater.

3 Wine was typically cut with water in antiquity according to various ratios depending on the wishes of the drinkers. This mixture is strong.

4 A drinking buddy who can speak of poetry (Muses) and love (Aphrodite), for example.

5 The Tiber is called Maecenas' paternal river because he was born in Etruria, where the Tiber was traditionally considered an Etruscan river.

6 A reference to the applause Maecenas received at the Theater of Pompey upon his recovery from an illness in 30 BCE. It is poetic exaggeration to claim that the ovation was heard as far away as the Vatican hill.

7 The food and drink of the gods.

8 The reference is to hand washing before a meal. See Wilkins, *Boastful Chef*, 113.

9 Text is uncertain.

10 Imaginary herbs.

11 Additional fictitious herbs, especially suggesting physical ailments (e.g., *halitosis*, bad breath).

12 Petro is a derogatory term for a country yokel.

13 A *plethron* is about 100 feet.

14 A wine of high quality thought to have originated in Thrace.

15 One of the titles of the Greek god Apollo, especially as the god in charge of the oracles at Delphi.

16 The reading is uncertain.

17 The species is uncertain.

18 The man accused by Anytus was Socrates.

19 Aufidius is unknown.

20 A Greek wine.

21 A statue of Apollo was located in the Forum of Augustus. The Arabarch is perhaps an allusion to Julius Alexander, a Jewish prefect of Egypt, 67–70 CE.

22 *Iliad* 24.602.

23 *Iliad* 19.225.

24 The Rhine River.

25 Tacitus is not suggesting that this was Roman policy but rather a weakness of the barbarian races.

26 "Strong-wine-spoiler to Funnel-Master." Humorous and fictitious names, the latter of which refers to an intemperate drinker who would insert a funnel into his mouth, through which he would unceasingly pour wine.

27 A cook's name in comedy. See, e.g. Athenaeus, *Sophists at Dinner*, 9. 377d

28 The *Stoa Poecile*, or Painted Porch, where Athenians came to hear Zeno, and this is why the adherents were called men of the Stoa, or Stoics (Diogenes Laertius 7.1.5).

29 Spurrina was the augur who warned Caesar that his life was in danger shortly before he was assassinated. Favonius is the west wind, which heralds in spring. Cicero is teasing his friend by saying that Spurrina has predicted trouble for Rome if Paetus fails to resume attending dinners by springtime.

30 If the date of the letter is correct, this is the *lex Aemilia* of 115 BCE, which sought to prohibit certain foods and food preparations at dinners. According to the elder Pliny (*HN* 8.57 [223]), prohibited luxury items included mice, rats, stuffed (or force-fed) dormice, mussels, and birds that came from foreign lands.

31 Lentulus was augur in 57 BCE. This is the only clue we have to the date of this letter. *Cenae* of this sort were common at certain *rites de passage* (see 4.28–38).

32 Part of a mill used to grind grain into bread.

33 These were native Latin comedies as opposed to *comoedia palliata*, which were translated or adapted from the Greek.

34 The reading is uncertain.

35 The overbearing wife of Trimalchio.

36 The reading is uncertain.

37 Habinnas' arrival is perhaps meant to recall the late and drunken arrival of Alcibiades in Plato's *Symposium*, which was a convention of sympotic literaure.

38 The *cena novendialis*, a feast offered on the ninth day after the funeral. See, e.g. Tacitus, *Annales* 6.5.

39 This was the 5 percent tax charged for freeing a slave.

40 Condemned to Hades for killing their husbands, they were forever sentenced to filling up with water a jar with holes in the bottom.

41 Ancient books were written on sheets of papyrus, which the reader had to unroll as he read.

42 See note 14 above.

43 The swallow. Procne, the daughter of Pandion, King of Athens, was changed into a swallow while fleeing from her husband, Tereus.

44 A variant of fish sauce, used widely for its saltiness.

45 Considered a delicacy in ancient Rome, where they were raised in special enclosures (*gliriria*) and served as an appetizer or as a dessert (dipped in honey with poppy seeds).

46 Resin from a fennel-like plant thought to aid in digestion and frequently called for as a spice in Roman recipes. Its culinary role was similar to that of the onion in English cooking. See Dalby (2003), s.v. "asafoetida," "silphium."

Chapter 3

1 According to Hesiod, one of the Titans, the children of the primeval couple Uranus and Ge in Greek mythology. The Romans identified Cronus with Saturn.

2 I.e. in the Golden Age, when Saturn ruled.

3 A sticky substance used to capture small birds.

4 A triple gateway that formed part of the ancient Servian Wall of Rome, presumed to be located near the Forum Boarium.

5 *Frag. Hist. Graec.* 1.462 Mueller. A Greek scholar, historian and grammarian of the second century BCE.

6 See 18.3. From *ardor*, an ancient name for "spelt," because grain was the chief prize given to the conqueror, and wreaths of grain adorned his temples.

7 *puls*, i.e. porridge.

8 Any food that was originally eaten with *puls*, and later with bread, was called by this name, including meats, vegetables, etc.

9 The term used is *offam*, which first meant a hardened lump of porridge and later came to mean a "cake."

10 I.e. in annual salary.

11 I.e. Cyperus dissipates his earnings just like grain is reduced to flour dust.

12 A bread of low quality, perhaps closer to the modern cracker or biscuit, which was especially popular among soldiers because it was cheap and durable.

13 In mid-September.

14 In fact, Longus presents this story as a guide's explanation of a painting he saw while hunting on Lesbos.

15 Nearly nine gallons.

16 A *medimnus* was about a bushel and a half.

17 Presumably because of its bad wine.

18 A *iugerum* is about two-thirds of an acre.

19 The term here, *arbustum*, also means trees around which vines were trained.

20 For feeding livestock.

21 A *quadrantal* was the equivalent of about 6 gallons.

22 I.e. "cut around."

23 See note 18 above.

24 One *urna* was the equivalent of half of an amphora, or about three and a half U.S. gallons. One amphora equals about 6.85 U.S. gallons.

25 Modern Faenza, about 20 miles southwest of Ravenna.

26 Along the Adriatic coast of Italy.

27 The Stoic philosopher Lucius Annaeus Seneca.

28 One *culleus* equals 20 amphorae, about 137 U.S. gallons.

29 Ceretanum, or a "wine from Ceret" in Spain, which would have been known to Columlella, a native of the country. It was an early sherry.

30 See note 24 above.

31 One sestertius equalled 4 denarii. A loaf of bread was about two denarii.

32 The yield is significant, although a century earlier Varro reported grain yields of 10 to 1 in some parts of Italy (*Res Rust.* 1.44.1–2) and 15 to 1 in Etruria, north of Rome.

33 An ancient Sabine town of Italy, now Mentana.

34 Region of Irpinia in southern Italy settled by the Aminei in Roman times. This wine is known today as Fiano.

35 See 3.32 above.

36 Roman liquid measure equivalent to about one pint.

37 Singular *congius*, equal to six sextarii, or one-eighth of an amphora.

38 The Saturnalia was a festival held each December in honor of the god Saturn (see 5.18). The Compitalia, a festival also held in December, honored the spirits that guarded and protected the boundaries of property. *Compita* were crossroads, the intersection of property boundaries.

39 The skull-capped brothers are Castor and Pollux, often depicted in felt caps. Their temple was near the southeastern end of the Forum. The nine posts were pillars similar to barber poles, which advertised the many taverns in this part of the city.

40 Egnatius' part of Spain, Celtiberia, was known for its long-haired rabbits.

41 The name means "Pleasure" in Greek.

42 Cytherea claimed to be the birthplace of Aphrodite, goddess of love, beauty and pleasure.

43 Because it was uncut by water.

44 As the leader of the drinking party, Postumia would have called the toasts and determined the strength of the wine. She is a hard drinker, the implication being that she drinks like a man. Although she may have been present on this occasion, it is also possible that Catullus is simply invoking her as a model to be followed.

45 The poet addresses the waters directly to raise the emotional tone. In this instance, they would have ruined the wine by diluting it, although cutting wine with water was the standard practice.

46 sc. the drinking cup as it is raised.

47 The wine is pure because it is uncut by water. Thyone was the mother of Dionysius, god of wine. Born as Semele, she was beloved by Zeus, who was compelled to destroy her after Hera, his wife, discovered the illicit affair. Dionysius rescued her from the Underworld under the name Thyone and introduced her among the immortals.

48 A legendary king of Athens whose grandfather (with whom *Ererchtheus* was often identified) was the son of Hephaestus, the Greek god of fire, and the Earth.

49 So as not to damage any of the equipment.

50 A sixth of a congius, which was an eighth of an amphora; a pint.

51 The watery part that flows out in pressing olives.

52 I.e. Olympia.

53 Officials who undertook the census of the people and exercised general supervision over the conduct of citizens.

54 Publilius Syrus, a former slave, was known for the pointed social commentary of his mimes, a form of drama that was acted out without words and was popular in the first century.

55 See Chapter Two, note 46.

56 Sirius, the Dog-star, whose rising in July was associated with extreme heat.

57 Hermes, the messenger god, but also the god of luck and wealth, hence the patron of fishermen in antiquity.

58 Ascanius, the son of Aeneas, founded Alba Longa, which was near the Alban Lake and was also the location for the flame of Vesta, which the Trojans had brought from Troy. A larger temple of Vesta was found at Rome.

59 I.e. Agamemnon; the use of an illustrious Homeric name to emphasize Domitian's supreme kingship.

60 About a bushel and a half.

61 I.e. the *medimnus* could hold only 9,999 of these figs.

62 For an alternative explanation of the Baian bean as derived from Old French or Old Norse, see Grocock and Grainger, 219, note 2.

63 *liquamen*: fish sauce; *caroenum*: a sweet wine boiled down; *passum*: raisin wine, made from semi-dried grapes.

64 Prefect of the city: the chief magistrate of Rome under the emperor; by this time he presided over the senate and supervised the officials responsible for the city's food supply and public works.

65 The son and successor of Satyrus, Leucon ruled over the Bosporus from 393 to 353 BCE. In thanks for these services, the Athenians had given him citizenship, voted a golden crown for him, and granted him an exemption from the public services and from paying customs at the Piraeus. Of his three sons, Spartocus and Paerisades succeeded him as joint rulers.

66 Demosthenes' figures are generally accurate and find corroboration in other ancient sources.

67 As the controller of grain at Athens (an office that Demosthenes himself held), Callisthenes received so much grain from Leucon that he was able to make 15 talents for the treasury by selling the surplus elsewhere after he had met the needs of Athens.

68 The Papian-Poppaean Law penalized the childless; full Roman citizenship included the right to vote; privileges of mothers with four children included freedom from having to submit to the protection of a man and the power to receive inheritances. The legal sources add that these privileges applied to anyone who owned a ship with a capacity of at least 10,000 *modii* (about 70 tons) and who used this ship to bring grain to Rome for at least six years.

69 A municipal priesthood that was especially attractive to freedmen during the imperial period.

70 Modern Lyons. Located at the confluence of the Rhône and Saône, the city featured an important shipping and commercial quarter.

71 Modern Pozzuoli. Located north of Naples, it handled a large proportion of grain imports to Rome.

72 The fact that these freedmen were named after Nereus, an old sea god, and Palaemon, a younger marine deity, suggests that they too were involved in maritime trade.

73 This symbol, common in epitaphs from ancient Gaul, might be connected with the preparation of a new tomb, which would have been dedicated while the work was still in the hands of the stonemason, who originally carved out the stone block with his adze.

74 A magistrate in charge of the marketplace (*agora*) in Greek cities.

75 A sub unit of a tribe.

Chapter 4

1 Italian deity identified with Bacchus, god of wine.

2 Most likely the consul of 33 BCE, the year in which Horace received the gift of his Sabine farm from Maecenas.

3 A ladle for filling goblets with wine. One hundred cyathi would be far more than one would be expected to drink, and this is part of the poem's playful humor.

4 Upon the death of Heracles, his children came to Athens as suppliants who carried branches in their hands in order to escape the wrath of the tyrant Eurystheus.

5 A common slave name in Greek New Comedy of the third and fourth centuries BCE.

6 The ten officers, one from each of the tribes in Athens, who managed the sacred rites, seeing to it that the victims were without blemish.

7 One of the cult titles given to Athena, in this case as the deity of health and healing.

8 *Prytaneis* were executives of the citizen assembly in Athens for part of the calendar year.

9 In Athens maidens who carried on their heads baskets containing sacred objects in procession at the feasts of Athena, Demeter, and Bacchus.

10 Athena as protectress "of the City" (Polias) of Athens.

11 Athena as goddess "of Victory" (Nike) in war and wisdom.

12 The potters' district in Athens.

13 *hekteus*: about 8.7 liters.

14 See note 6 above.

15 The anniversary of the dedication of one of the three temples of Fortune on the Quirinal Hill in Rome.

16 The anniversary of the dedication of the temple of Magna Mater on the Palatine Hill in Rome in 191 BCE. Circus games were held in her honor from April 4–10.

17 The anniversary of the dedication of the temples of Jupiter Victor, vowed in 295 BCE, and Jupiter Libertas, vowed in 246 BCE.

18 This festival was marked by the sacrifice of a pregnant cow (*forda*) to Tellus, the earth, when the land was full with new crops.

19 This festival included the sacrifice of a pregnant sow, the release in the Circus Maximus of foxes carrying burning torches, and horse races. It also involved a *lectisternium*, a banquet for the gods whose images were placed on a couch (*lectus*). Supervised by priests, it included public participation and was meant to please the gods and avert pestilence or enemies.

20 A rural festival associated with the foundation of Rome. See 4.21.

21 Many ancient authors claimed that the Vinalia was a festival to Jupiter, yet Venus was also linked to it. Two temples to Venus Erucina (Venus as worshipped in Sicily as Eryx) were likely dedicated on April 23, in 215 and 181 BCE.

22 This festival involved the sacrifice of a dog and a sheep to propitiate the deity Robigo, the personification of mildew, which could be harmful to the growing wheat.

23 Household deities who were invoked most often in domestic rituals.

24 A reference to the prytaneis (see note 8 above).

25 The Spartan name for the *syssitia*, the public messes.

26 In the Athenian calendar, roughly equivalent to July.

27 Zeus as protector of the phratry.

28 A Greek goddess, mother of Artemis and Apollo as the result of a love affair with Zeus.

29 One of the tribes in which a Roman citizen was enrolled.

30 A religious official who observed and interpreted omens.

31 See Chapter Five, note 9.

32 One of the two leaders of the local town council elected every five years in the year of a census and of higher rank than other local officials.

33 A hoopoe, a colorful bird known for its distinctive feathers that was popular in antiquity.

34 Selene, goddess of the moon.

35 An ass, the same animal that the Christians were frequently charged with worshiping.

36 The Egyptian god often represented in art with ram's horns.

37 Exod. 12.15–20, 34–9.

38 Deut. 5.15; Levit. 25.4.

39 Dio Cass. 37.18–19.

40 A reference to M. Cornelius Fronto, a North African by birth who became a prominent teacher and rhetorician in Rome in the second century. His *Speech against the Christians* does not survive.

Chapter 5

1 I.e. the vine.

2 One of the sea-breams, usually caught by hook and line but sometimes by traps or by hand.

3 Nearly 300 tons.

4 Some scholars read the text as "120."

5 A mandrake (mandragora) is a plant closely related to belladonna. It can cause delirium and hallucinations if ingested in sufficient quantities. Mandrake was a common ingredient in medicine and magic spells from ancient times through the Middle Ages.

6 Gorgias was a contemporary orator and rhetoric teacher known for his ornate style.

7 Perhaps more than 3,000,000 sesterces. By comparison, the cost of bread was one or two sesterces.

8 Office for which Caesar volunteered in 66 BCE. He spent vast amounts of borrowed money on improving the Appian Way, the most important and well known of all Roman roads. This experience allowed him to build ties with many local communities and to acquire valuable expertise in construction and engineering.

9 Aediles were responsible for maintaining public buildings and regulating public festivals. Like many aspiring politicians during the Roman Republic, Caesar utilized this office to win public favor among the people by spending heavily on these activities.

10 Also included was his conquest of the Gauls, bringing the number of his triumphs to four.

11 Dates from Pontus and Palestine.

12 Plums from Syria.

13 Figs from Asia Minor.

14 Apples and pears from Ameria.

15 A reference to Ganymede, a handsome boy from Mt. Ida near Troy who, according to ancient myth, was abducted by Zeus in the form of an eagle to be the cupbearer at feasts of the gods on Olympus.

16 The *Stagnum Agrippae*, a large artificial lake or pool in the Campus Martius. As a large open area for the mustering of troops, the Campus Martius also served as an important site for public entertainment in Rome.

17 A battle fought in northern Italy at the site of modern Modena in 43 BCE in which Octavian helped to defeat the army of Marc Antony. Twelve years later Octavian would defeat Antony a final time at Actium and subsequently rule as Augustus, Rome's first emperor.

18 Raetia was a province north of Rome, which would correspond today to parts of Italy, Germany, Austria, Switzerland and Liechtenstein. Its wine was thought to rival any that was produced in Italy.

19 A reference to sumptuary laws, which, beginning in the second century BCE, sought to place limits on ostentatious public display and extravagant banquets. It is not clear which law or laws are referred to here.

20 The name was derived from Atella, a town in Campania (a fertile region south of Rome) where farces of this type supposedly originated.

21 Aricia was on the Via Appia about 20 miles from Rome. Since the incline slowed traffic, it was a natural place for beggars to gather.

22 The dole (*sportula*) is the amount paid by patrons to their clients. The complaint suggests that this amount would not have gone very far in an expensive resort town like Baiae.

23 Used for sanitary purposes at the latrine.

24 Used as a urinal.

25 Such as the parties of the emperor Domitian at his Alban villa.

26 The Capitoline banquets were celebrated twice a year in honor of Jupiter, Juno, and Minerva, while the dinners of the College of Pontiffs, a group of aristocratic priests, were proverbial for their luxury.

27 Queen of Carthage and lover of Aeneas, who commits suicide when the latter leaves her behind in Book 4 of Vergil's *Aeneid*.

28 The meaning is that extravagance and display are all the more reprehensible when these cheap necessities of cleanliness are missing.

29 This is the only instance in Martial of a female dinner host. Naevia might be the corrupted form of a male name, perhaps Naevole.

30 The epigram plays on the double meaning in Latin of *crudus*, meaning undercooked and indigestible.

31 Hesiod, *Works and Days*, 26.

32 According to Greek mythology, as punishment for his part in a revolt, Atlas was compelled to support the heavens with his head and hands.

33 Chian marbe came from the Greek island of Chios, which was famous for its wine and marble.

34 Carystian marble was distinguished by veins of pale green running through it, hence its comparison to the sea.

35 See 5.40.

36 The Romans regarded dormice as a delicacy, although they were not especially rare. Varro (*On Agriculture*, 3.15) describes how to raise and fatten them up.

37 The *pallium* was a Greek cloak considered by the Romans to be the typical dress of Greek philosophers, who are satirized in this passage.

38 Likely a slave name.

39 The spring perhaps served as a handy source of water for cutting the wine. See Davidson, 55–6.

40 A famous spring near the Acropolis in Athens. First known as Callirhoe ("fair flowing"), it was later called the Fountain of Nine Spouts after it had been enclosed and embellished by the tyrant Pisistratus in the sixth century BCE.

41 The meaning here is uncertain. Perhaps the sausage lies between two berries that garnish the dish. Lupus, the addressee, was a rhetorician from Perigueux in modern-day southwestern France.

42 Usually in the Latin plural (Camenae, i.e. "foretellers"), these were water nymphs with the power of prophecy and identified with the Greek Muses.

43 Roman emperor, 161–180 CE.

44 Elsewhere in the text, we learn Zeno set up an endowment of 10,000 sesterces for feasting in memory of his brother, while Marcellina donated a structure for banqueting and an endowent of 60,000 sesterces for feasting.

45 Gifts exchanged on the New Year.

46 The feast day of the family, also known as the love feast.

47 Day to commemorate the dead, marked by sprinkling violets at the gravesite.

48 The same as at note 47.

49 Aphrodite, the Greek goddess of love, was also known as Cytherea, after Cythera, a cult site that claimed to be her place of birth.

50 The herms (*hermae*) were quadrangular pillars surmounted by a bust of the god Hermes with a phallus below this; some contained moral precepts. These were set up in Athens and elsewhere on street corners, roads, etc. for the protection of travelers and to ward off evil.

51 A choinix was a dry measure equivalent to about a quart, or a daily ration for one person. Barley was considered inferior to wheat (see Chapter 3) but was widely consumed in Greece.

52 Officials elected by the popular assembly who provided oversight of the kings. Herodotus claims that Lycurgus created this institution but Plutarch considers it a later innovation.

Chapter 6

1 A river in Sparta; hence, the broth can only be enjoyed by Spartans.

2 Perhaps hazelnuts or filberts.

3 This entire work is translated from an Armenian version. This particular passage does not appear in all the full-length Armenian versions but is attested by other ancient Armenian sources. For more, see Wolshojian, note 122.2.

4 A maniple was a sub-unit of the Roman army.

5 According to Pliny's *Natural History* (25.83), *hippace* was a plant that shared the same properties as a cheese made by the Scythians from the milk of mares.

6 Thrasybalus was ruler of Miletus, which was involved in a long struggle in the late seventh century BCE with the Lydians, led by king Alyattes; cf. Herodotus 1.21–2; Polyaenus 6.47.

7 390 BCE.

8 A great Roman statesman and general, who flourished in the early part of the fourth century BCE.

9 This incident dates to c. 595 BCE. Pausanias (10.37.5) credited Solon with this stratagem.

10 266–263 BCE. This is Alexander, king of Molossia.

11 Instead of the much preferred rations of wheat.

Chapter 7

1 A measure (in Latin, a *modius*) was perhaps equivalent to one peck.

2 This suggests that chained slaves ate bread while the unchained received grain, which they had to grind to make their own bread or porridge.

3 In the summer.

4 Relishes (*pulmentaria* in Latin), meant anything eaten with porridge or bread. Porridge and bread were common foodstuffs for both slaves and free Romans.

5 In Latin, *alec* (sc. also *allec, halec*); this was the undesirable sediment left over after making fish sauce (*garum*).

6 Terebinth resin, a product of the turpentine tree, was rich in tannin and utilized for its medicinal and aromatic properties and also for preserving wine.

7 A slave who worked at the imperial palace in any number of capacities, e.g. secretary, cook, and dining-room attendant.

8 See Chapter 5, "Community Feasts."

9 See 3.74, note 69.

10 See Chapter 5, note 9.

11 About 260 liters (69 gallons), evidently, the total amount available for distribution among the beneficiaries.

12 I.e. "this year's."

13 I.e. the white part at the end of the rose petals by which they are attached to the stalk.

14 The use here is as a dusting powder, to fight perspiration since it contracts the pores, and as a deodorant.

15 Antigonus Gonatas, (319 BCE–239 BCE) was a powerful ruler who established the Antigonid dynasty in Macedonia.

16 The speaker is Elpenor, who admits from Hades that heavy drinking played a role in his fatal plunge from the roof of Circe, the enchantress.

17 The Centaurs were fantastical beings with the head and neck of a man but the body of a horse. Invited by the neighboring Laphithae to a feast celebrating the wedding of their king, Pirithous, to Hippodamia, the Centaurs attempted to carry off the bride and other women in a drunken frenzy. They were defeated in the ensuing battle and driven from their home.

18 "committing every folly:" the meaning here is not certain

19 Darius, King of the Persians, was defeated by Alexander but kill by Bessus, a Persian nobleman who succeeded to the Kingship.

Works Cited

Authors

Aeneas (Aineias) Tacticus, fourth century BCE. Most likely a general of the Arcadian League, Aeneas was the earliest surviving and most historically interesting of the ancient military writers (*tactici*). Only his *Siegecraft* (*Poliorcetica*), which emphasizes defense against siege warfare and the stresses of war upon smaller communities, survives.

Alcaeus, seventh–sixth century BCE. Born at Mytilene in Lesbos, he was a lyric poet and contemporary of Sappho. His poems, which survive only in fragments, treat politics and personal themes, including wine, love, and hatreds. He invented or adopted the Alcaic stanza, a metre utilized by Horace.

Alciphron, c. 200 CE. A Greek author of fictitious letters, supposedly written by Athenian non-elites of the fourth century BCE, including fishermen, farmers, courtesans, and parasites, Alciphron displays a wide reading in classical literature, especially of Greek New Comedy.

Ammianus Marcellinus, fourth century CE. A Roman soldier and historian born in Antioch (Syria), Ammianus wrote the *Res Gestae,* which extends from the death of the emperor Domitian in 96 CE to the death of the emperor Valens in 378 CE. Books 15–31 have survived.

Anacreon, sixth century BCE. A native of Teos (Teo, Turkey), he was a lyric poet who wrote on the light and playful themes of love and wine. Although his poetry survives only in short fragments, it was much imitated in all periods.

Anacreontea, a collection of Greek poems referring to Anacreon or adopting his persona and treating themes of wine and love in metres derived from the poet. Now thought to have been composed between the first century BCE and fifth or sixth century CE, these poems exercised extensive influence on European lyric poetry.

Apicius, the proverbial name of several Roman connoisseurs, especially of food, most notably M. Gavius Apicius of the early first century CE, who wrote on sauces. The collection of recipes bearing his name (*De re coquinaria*), however, dates to the fourth century CE.

Appian, second century CE. Born in Alexandria, he was a Greek historian who wrote a history of Rome, partially extant, from the arrival of Aeneas in Italy to the Battle of Actium in 31 CE. Conservative in outlook and an ardent supporter of Rome, he preserves more social and economic information than most historiographers.

Apuleius, second century CE. Roman writer and orator born in Madaurus (Algeria). He wrote speeches and a novel, the *Metamorphoses*, an epic and sensationalist account of the adventures of Lucius, who is turned into an ass through witchcraft.

Archestratus, of Gela (Sicily), mid-fourth century BCE poet. Athenaeus has preserved some 340 hexameters from the *Hedupatheia*, a culinary tour of the Mediterranean, which imitates in the choice of addressee, tone, and phraseology the *Works and Days* of Hesiod.

Aristophanes, c. 450–c. 385 BCE. A native of Athens and the greatest poet of Old Attic Comedy, he is the author of some 40 plays, 11 of which are preserved. He is especially known for his vivid dialogue, lyric beauty and outspoken political views on Athens during the Peloponnesian War with Sparta in the fifth century BCE.

Aristotle, 384–322 BCE. Born in Stagirs in Chalcidice (Greece), he was a pupil of Plato and a prolific and influential Greek scientist and philosopher. His surviving works cover a broad range of fields, including biology, physics, logic, ethics, and literature.

Arrian (Lucius Flavius Arrianus) c. 86–160 CE. Born in Nicomedia in Bithynia, he was a successful Roman general and senator before retiring to Athens. One of the most distinguished writers of his day, he is especially known for his *Anabasis* of Alexander the Great, which treats the general and his exploits in seven books, from his accession to his death.

Athenaeus, early third century CE writer from Naucratis (Egypt). He wrote the *Deipnosophistae* (*Sophists at Dinner*) in Greek, a fictitious account of a banquet at which 23 learned men (some bearing the names of real persons) discuss food in all its aspects as well as a variety of other topics. The work is a memorable example of symposium literature and is especially valuable for preserving many excerpts and anecdotes from Greek literature and for illustrating Greek manners of earlier times.

Augustan History (*Scriptores Historiae Augustae***),** fourth century CE? A collection of unreliable biographies of Roman emperors (*Augusti*), heirs to the throne (*Caesares*) and pretenders (*tyranni)*, it has traditionally been ascribed to six authors.

Caesar (Gaius Julius Caesar), 100–44 BCE. Born at Rome, Caesar was a legendary statesman and general. His political measures were conceived on a popular basis but implemented with a disregard for republican institutions, which was in part the cause of his assassination. He wrote commentaries on his Gallic campaigns and the *Civil Wars*, his only extant works.

Catullus (Gaius Valerius Catullus), c. 84–c. 54 BCE. Born in Verona of a well-to-do family, he wrote poetry (elegies and epigrams), including love poetry, tracing his relationship with Lesbia. His light, witty, and elegant poetry provided a new form of literature and exerted a wide influence on his Roman successors.

Dio Cocceianus Chrysostom, c. 40/50–110/120 CE. Born in Prusa in Bithynia (Bitinya, Turkey), Dio was a philosopher and orator with an international reputation in antiquity; hence, he became known as Chrysostom ("golden-mouthed"). He has left a collection of discourses in Greek on political, literary, and philosophical topics that provide much insight into the culture of his times.

Cassius Dio (Cassius Dio Cocceianus), c. 155–235 CE. A Greek senator, consul, and historian from Bithynia (Bitinya, Turkey), he wrote a Roman history in 80 books from the arrival of Aeneas to 229 CE. The work is only partially extant.

Cato, (Marcus Porcius Cato [the Censor]), 234–149 BCE. A Roman statesman from Tusculum (Italy), he held the office of censor in 184 BCE, a post that made him famous as a vigorous defender of traditional values. Among his most important works is a handbook on agriculture (*De agri cultura*), the oldest extant literary prose work in Latin.

Cicero (Marcus Tullius Cicero), 106–43 BCE. Roman orator and statesman, he was born at Arpinum (Italy) and killed in the proscriptions of Marc Antony in 43 BCE. One of the most prolific authors of antiquity, Cicero has left 58 speeches, important philosophical, rhetorical, and scientific works, and more than 900 letters.

Columella (Lucius Iunius Moderatus Columella), first century CE. Born at Gades (Cadiz, Spain), he is the author of *On Agriculture* (*De re rustica*), a 12-book work that is the most systematic extant Roman agricultural manual. His simple but stylish prose and his admiration for Vergil were meant to give credibility to his work among literate landowners of his day.

Quintus Curtius Rufus, first-second cent. CE. A rhetorician and historian, he wrote a history of Alexander the Great in ten books, of which the first two are lost. The work is highly rhetorical and is especially concerned with the romantic side of Alexander's career.

Demosthenes, 384–322 BCE. Born at Athens, he was a prominent Greek orator and statesman. Sixty-one orations, six letters and a book of 54 poems are attributed to him. Generally considered the greatest of Greek orators, Demosthenes combined great eloquence and rhetorical skill with simplicity of language.

Diodorus of Agyrium, Sicily (hence, Diodorus Siculus), first-century-BCE Greek historian who wrote a history of the Mediterranean world in 40 volumes, of which only 15 are fully extant. Few of the sources he cites survive outside of his own work, making it difficult to assess his historical reliability. Diodorus shows a strong interest in the legends of mythology.

Diogenes Laertius, c. 200–250 CE, from Cilicia, (Kilikya, Turkey). There is little known about his life. Diogenes is the author in Greek of *Lives and Opinions of Eminent Philosophers* in ten books, which contains highly anecdotal accounts of the lives of the great thinkers of ancient Greece, from Thales to Epicurus. The portraits vary in quality and are designed to bring out the character of the philosopher concerned.

Dionysius of Halicarnassus, first century BCE. A teacher of rhetoric in Rome in the time of Augustus, he was a literary critic and historian who wrote a 20-book history of Rome (in Greek) down to the outbreak of the First Punic War. The work, only partially extant, is valuable for the Roman annalistic tradition that it preserves.

Euripides, 480–406 BCE. Born at Salamis (Greece), he is the latest of the three great Attic tragedians of the fifth century BCE. From some 90 plays, 19 survive under his name. More skeptical of traditional religion and morality than his predecessors, he was a sharp critic of contemporary society while giving great prominence to female characters and to dramatic effect.

Felix (Marcus Minucius Felix), second-third cent. CE. An early Latin Christian apologist and contemporary of Tertullian, he wrote the *Octavius*, a dialogue between the Christian Octavius and a pagan, Caecilus Natalis of Cirta, Numidia (Algeria). His defense of Christianity focuses less on specific dogma than on the moral and philosophic side of Christianity.

Frontinus (Sextus Iulius Frontinus), first-second century CE. Perhaps from southern Gaul, he was a consul and governor and was hailed as one of the most distinguished men of his day. He has left us a work on military strategy, *Stratagems* (*Strategemata*) and a treatise on the history, administration and maintenance of the aqueducts at Rome (*De aquis urbis Romae*).

Fronto (Marcus Cornelius Fronto), c. 95–c. 166 CE. Born at Cirta, Numidia (Algeria), he was a tutor to Marcus Aurelius and Lucius Verus. Although famed for his oratory in antiquity, he is best known today for his letters to members of the imperial family. He advocated a return to the style and language of older Romans like Cato, Ennius and Varro.

Galen of Pergamum (Bergama, Turkey), 129–216 CE. One of the most famous physicians of antiquity, he authored some 350 medical writings of limited literary value but of great importance to the history of medicine; many of these works have been lost. He also wrote on philosophy, grammar, and literature, of which only some fragments survive.

Greek Anthology (*Anthologia Graeca*). A collection of poems, mostly epigrams from the classical and Byzantine periods of Greek literature. This work mostly derives from two manuscripts of the tenth and fourteenth centuries, respectively.

Hadrian, Roman emperor from 117–138 CE. Of restless spirit and active mind, he took a genuine interest in literature. A small amount of mediocre verse ascribed to him has survived.

Herodian, third century CE. Perhaps from Syrian Antioch (Antakya, Turkey), he wrote in Greek a *History of the Empire after Marcus* in eight books from Marcus Aurelius to Gordian III (180–238 CE). Often unreliable, the work is more valuable the closer it approaches to the author's own times.

Herodotus, c. 484–420 BCE. Greek historian born in Asia Minor. He wrote in nine books a history of the struggle between Asia and Europe, culminating in the Persian Wars of the fifth century BCE. Known as the "father of history" in antiquity, he was the first ancient author to subject the events of the past to research and verification.

Hesiod, 700 BCE? Greek poet from Boeotia. He wrote the didactic poem *Works and Days* and the *Theogony*, a verse account of the origins of the world and the genealogy of the gods.

Homer, most likely eighth century BCE. Although there is doubt about the date and birthplace of the poet, the epic poems attributed to him, the *Iliad* and the *Odyssey*, remain works of astonishing quality, with the result that Homer was the object of deep reverence in antiquity and beyond.

Homeric Apocrypha, a term of convenience to cover a group of non-serious or burlesque poems popular during or after the classical period under Homer's name.

Horace (Quintus Horatius Flaccus), 65–8 BCE. Born at Venusia (Venosa, Italy), he fought with Brutus in the Civil Wars, losing his property as a result. Under the patronage of Maecenas, he was a master of lyric poetry in Latin, most notably his *Odes* in four books. His perfection of form, honesty, and gentle sense of humor combined to make him one of the greatest of Roman poets.

Isaeus, fifth–fourth century BCE. An Athenian orator about whose life little is known, he was a professional speech writer for litigants. Eleven of his speeches survive in full, all of them dealing with cases of inheritance. They provide important insight into Athenian testamentary law.

Isocrates, 436–388 BCE. A renowned Athenian orator and teacher, he claims 60 orations under his name in Roman times, with 21 surviving today. His speeches, written in a fluid and luxurious style, provide important insight into the great political issues of the fourth century BCE.

Josephus (Flavius Josephus), 37–c. 100 CE. Jewish historian born in Jerusalem. Captured by the Romans, he became sympathetic to their cause and took up a literary career during which he produced in Greek his best-known works, the *Jewish War* and *Jewish Antiquities*.

Juvenal (Decimus Iunius Iuvenalis), c. 65–130 CE. While few details of his life are known for certain, he wrote his *Satires*, a series of poems in the early second century CE that explore the decadence and immorality of Rome through the use of an indignant persona.

Justin (Marcus Iunianus Iustinus), second-third century CE. He wrote in Latin an abridged version of an earlier universal history of the ancient world. Although it contains some striking descriptions, the work is generally considered as tedious.

Livy (Titus Livius), c. 59 BCE–17 CE. Roman historian born at Patavium (Padua, Italy). His talents won the interest of the emperor Augustus, under whose reign he produced the *Ab urbe condita libri* (*Books from the Founding of the City*), a history of Rome in 142 books from the foundation of the city to 9 BCE. The work is only partially extant.

Longus, second-sixth century CE. Creator of the pastoral romance in Greek, he is best known for *Daphnis and Chloe*, the story of two foundlings raised by shepherds who fall in love and eventually marry. The work, known for its psychological analysis and impressive style, helped to give shape to the ancient prose romance, or novel.

Lucian, c. 115–180 CE. A Greek writer from Syria about whom little is known, he wrote a variety of rhetorical works including dialogues, which often combined popular philosophy and comedy. Many of Lucian's works display a satirical point of view.

Lucilius (Gaius Lucilius), 180–102 BCE. Born at Suessa Aurunca (Sessa Aurunca, Italy), he is famous as the creator of the purely Roman literary genre known as satire. Lucilius wrote 30 books of *Sermones*, on everyday themes and incidents from his own life. His satires, marked by pointed criticism of individuals, gluttony and greed, served as a model for the later satires of Horace.

Lucretius (Titus Lucretius Carus), first century BCE. Almost nothing is known for certain about his life. He is famed for his poem *On the Nature of Things* (*De rerum natura*), an Epicurean work that seeks to dispel human fears about the gods and death while also presenting an atomic theory of natural phenomena and the place of man in the world.

Luke, the Evangelist, first century CE. A native of Antioch in Syria, he was one of the Four Evangelists or authors of the canonical Gospels of Jesus Christ. Luke was understood by the early church fathers as the author of both the *Gospel according to Luke* and the book of *Acts of the Apostles*, which originally formed a single literary work.

Lysias, c. 459–380 BCE. A famed Attic orator from Athens, he wrote over 200 speeches, of which 35 survive. He is best known for his pure style and his ability to put himself in his client's place in order to persuade the jury.

Macrobius (Macrobius Theodosius), fourth century CE. A distinguished Roman writer and philosopher, he is best known for his *Saturnalia* in seven books, a dialogue chiefly devoted to the works of Vergil, and his *Dream of Scipio* (*Somnium Scipionis*), from the sixth book of Cicero's *De republica*, an analysis of the soul, especially its divinity and immortality, in the context of Neoplatonist doctrines.

Martial (Marcus Valerius Martialis), c. 40–c. 103 CE. Born in Bilbilis (Spain), he was a celebrated poet during the time of the emperor Domitian. Famed for his *Epigrams*, short, witty poems on various themes in 12 books, he returned to Spain from Rome in 98 CE.

Matthew the Evangelist, first century CE. One of the 12 apostles of Jesus and one of the four Evangelists (see Luke above). A tax collector from Galilee (Israel), he witnessed the Resurrection and Ascension of Christ according to the *New Testament.*

Menander (Menandros), c. 342–c. 293/89 BCE. As the most famous poet of Greek New Comedy, he wrote about 100 plays, of which only fragments survive. The plays, which generally focus on the entanglements of love, provide insight into the Athens of his day and deeply influenced Plautus, Terence, and modern comedy, especially the works of Molière.

Cornelius Nepos, c. 100–c. 25 BCE. Most likely a native of Gaul, he devoted himself to a literary career at Rome. He is best known for his 24 *Lives of Famous Men* (*De viris illustribus*), which focuses on the character of each subject rather than the historical events of his life. The work is marred by inaccuracies, omissions, and lack of historical perspective, although some of the lives (e.g. Alcibiades and Atticus) are well done and valuable for their insight.

Onasander, a Platonic philosopher according to tradition, whose only surviving work, the *Strategikos* (first century CE), treats the duties of a commander and commonplace military principles. It was very popular during the Renaissance.

Ovid (Publius Ovidius Naso), 43 BCE–17 CE. Born at Sulmo (Sulmona, Italy), he was educated at Rome and became a leading poet under the emperor Augustus. His best-known work, the *Metamorphoses*, is an epic poem of 15 books on tales from Near Eastern myth and legend. Banished to the Black Sea by the emperor for an unknown offense in 8 CE, he remained there until his death.

Pausanias, second century CE. A Greek traveler, geographer and author of *A Description of Greece*, he was familiar with Palestine, Italy, Egypt, and especially Greece. His work is valuable for its sketches of important cities and their mythology and history as well as for historic battlefields, monuments, and memorials. Existing remains have confirmed much of his accuracy.

Persius (Aulus Persius Flaccus), 34–62 CE. A wealthy and well-connected Etruscan knight, he has left a book of *Satires* written from a Stoic viewpoint, which focuses on virtue and the rejection of sloth and luxury. At one time out of favor due to his obscure language and contorted thought, he has enjoyed renewed interest in recent years.

Petronius (Gaius Petronius Arbiter), first century CE. Author of the *Satyrica* (known as the *Satyricon*) a picaresque and satirical novel set in southern Italy of the first century CE, much of which is lost. The most complete section is the famous feast of Trimalchio (*Cena Trimalchionis*). Petronius may have been connected with the court of Nero.

Philon, commonly known as **Philo Judaeus**, c. 30 BCE–45 CE. A life-long resident of his native Alexandria and leader of its Jewish community, he wrote numerous works, including principally commentaries on the *Old Testament*, which he interpreted allegorically and as the source of the main tenets of Plato, Aristotle, and other Greek philosophers.

Philon of Byzantium, probably late third century BCE. He produced a work on technology, perhaps in nine books, of which is preserved information on war catapults, siphons, and siege works. He was generally more interested in mechanics and engineering than in theory.

Plato, c. 429–347 BCE. Born at Athens, he was a famous Greek philosopher, the founder of idealism in Greek philosophy, and one of the finest of Greek prose writers. His ideas survive in 26 philosophical dialogues and 13 letters. His thinking has exercised an immense influence on religious and philosophical thought from antiquity to the present day.

Plautus (Titus Maccius Plautus) c. 250–184 BCE. Born in Umbria (Italy), he was a writer of comedies in Latin. As adaptations of Greek New Comedy, his 21 surviving plays, which are especially known for their imagination and wit, are the earliest Latin works that are preserved completely.

Pliny the Elder (Gaius Plinius Secundus), c. 23–79 CE. A Roman equestrian from Novum Comum (Como, Italy), Pliny pursued a public career, only to perish while attempting to rescue victims from the eruption of Mount Vesuvius. He wrote an encyclopedic work, the *Natural History*, in 37 books, which surveys aspects of scientific knowledge across a wide spectrum.

Pliny the Younger (Gaius Plinius Caecilius Secundus), c. 61–after 112 CE. Born at Comum, he was adopted by the elder Pliny. A wealthy lawyer and statesman, he wrote nine books of carefully crafted letters and a tenth book containing his correspondence with the emperor Trajan while serving as governor of Bithynia in the Black Sea region.

Plutarch (Lucius Mestrius Plutarchus), c. 50–120 CE. Born at Chaeronea (Greece), where he spent most of his life, Plutrach did travel to Rome during his lifetime. He wrote in Greek popular philosophical essays, including biographies of famous Greeks and Romans with a moral emphasis, which was much admired in later times.

Polybius, c. 200–c. 120 BCE. A Greek aristocrat who was held hostage by Rome for many years, he wrote a history of the Mediterranean world in 40 books from 266–144 BCE, with an emphasis on the supremacy of Rome. The work is only partially extant.

Porphyry 232/3–c. 305 CE. Born at Tyre (or Batanea in Palestine), he was a scholar, philosopher, and student of religions and one of the chief advocates of Neoplatonism. His writings, numerous and varied, included a biography of Plotinus, his teacher, and a *History of Philosophy*. Although an unoriginal thinker, he was a true polymath who has preserved much older learning.

Propertius (Sextus Propertius), c. 50–15 BCE. Born at Asisium (Assisi, Italy), he became a leading poet at Rome under the patronage of Maecenas. Propertius wrote elegies on various themes and is best known for his love poems celebrating his devotion to Cynthia.

Pseudo-Callisthenes. The so-called *Alexander Romance*, incorrectly attributed to Callisthenes in antiquity and dated to about 100 BCE, this work belongs to the genre of 'fabulous historiography' developed in Alexandrian times.

Sallust (Gaius Sallustius Crispus), 86–35 BCE. Born at Amiternum (Italy) to a wealthy family, Sallust became a follower of Julius Caesar and eventually withdrew from public life. He wrote two historical monographs that emphasized moral decline. His other works survive only partially.

Seneca (Lucius Annaeus Seneca), c. 4 BCE–65 CE. Born at Corduba (Spain), he became a distinguished statesman, writer, orator, and Stoic philosopher. Tutor to the emperor Nero, he eventually fell out of imperial favor and was forced to commit suicide. Seneca's extant works include ethical treatises, moral letters, satires, and tragic plays.

Shepherd of Hermas, first or second century CE. A highly allegorical work comprised of a series of mandates, parables and visions granted to Hermas, a former slave, the *Shepherd* was first produced at Rome in Greek. While the author remains unknown, many early Christians considered the work valuable.

Sidonius Apollinaris (Gaius Sollius Modestus Apollinaris Sidonius), c. 430–c. 490 CE. Born at Lugdunum (Lyons, France), Sidonius was well educated and became bishop of Clermont in 470 CE. He wrote panegyrics and letters.

Statius (Publius Papinius Statius), c. 45–96 CE. Born at Naples, he became a popular poet during the reign of the emperor Domitian. He wrote the *Silvae*, 32 poems on everyday topics, and the *Thebaid*, an epic poem about the mythical struggle for the throne of Thebes.

Strabo, 64 BCE–c. 21 CE. Born at Amaseia (Amasya) in Pontus, he traveled widely. Strabo wrote (in Greek) a history (a continuation of Polybius), which is lost, and the *Geography* (*Geographia*), an encyclopedia of geographic knowledge of the Mediterranean world, in 17 books.

Suetonius (Gaius Suetonius Tranquillus), c. 70–after 121 CE. Suetonius held posts in the imperial administration under the emperor Hadrian and is best known for a series of 12 biographies from Julius Caesar through the emperor Domitian. The biographies show little historical insight but are valuable and entertaining.

Tacitus (Publius (?) Cornelius Tacitus), c. 56–c. 116 CE. Probably born in Narbonese or Cisalpine Gaul, Tacitus pursued a distinguished political career, including the consulship, and he also wrote biography, ethnography, dialogues, and history. He is best known for the *Histories*, an account of the years 69–96 CE, and the *Annales* on the reigns of the Julio-Claudian emperors. Although neither work survives in full, both demonstrate a penetrating insight into character and contemporary issues and an antipathy toward the imperial system.

Tertullian (Quintus Septimius Florens Tertullianus), c. 160–240 CE. Born in the vicinity of Carthage, he converted to Christianity and utilized his literary talents to defend the Christian faith and elucidate Christian doctrine in several works, all of which display great rhetorical skill and a rich vocabulary that helped to shape theological Latin.

Theophrastus, c. 372–c. 288 BCE. Born in Lesbos (Greece), he was a Greek philosopher and a pupil and friend of Aristotle. He wrote in Greek on a variety of subjects but is best known for his *Plant-researches* (*Historia Plantarum*) and *Characters*, in which he describes various types of contemporary character.

Thucydides, c. 460/55–399 BCE. A Greek general and historian, he wrote in eight books a history of the Peloponnesian War between Athens and Sparta in the fifth century BCE. One of the greatest historians of all time, he is known for his compressed style, his reasoning on political issues, and his deep interest in the causal connection between events.

Varro (Marcus Terentius Varro), 116–27 BCE. Born at Reate (Rieti, Italy), he studied in Rome and Athens, supported Pompey in the civil war, and was proscribed by Antony, only to escape assassination and spend the rest of his life in scholarly pursuits. Varro wrote on a wide range of subjects, including history, law, rhetoric, philosophy, medicine, language, and architecture. Only two of his works survive substantially.

Vegetius (Flavius Vegetius Renatus), c. 400 CE. He is the author of a manual in four books written under the emperor Theodosius I (379–395 CE), which is important as a source of information on the Roman military.

Vergil (Publius Vergilius Maro), 70–19 BCE. Born near Mantua (Mantova, Italy), Vergil became the leading poet of his age at Rome in the literary circle of Maecenas and Augustus. Although he wrote extensively, he is best known for the *Aeneid*, an epic poem that made him the Roman Homer. The work traces the flight of Aeneas from Troy to the founding of Rome.

Vitruvius Pollio (or **Mamurra**), end of first century BCE. He wrote a ten-book work, *On Architecture* (*De architectura*), which treats architecture and building in general (both public and domestic building) in many aspects from a largely Hellenistic point of view. His rules on proportion are especially valuable.

Xenophon, c. 430–354 BCE. An Athenian, he wrote on various subjects according to his many interests and experiences, most notably as an admirer of

Socrates, as a military commander, and as an observer of the political events in many countries. His most significant works are the *Anabasis* and the *Hellenica*.

Inscriptions and Fragments

Bertier, J. Bertier. 1972. *Mnésithée et Dieuchès*. Bertier, Leiden.

CIL, T. Mommsen et al., (1863–). *Corpus Inscriptionum Latinarum*. Berlin.

CMG, *(1927–)*. *Corpus Medicorum Graecorum*. Leipzig.

FGr Hist, F. Jacoby. (1923–1958; 1994–). *Fragments of the Greek Historians*. Berlin and Leiden.

Hansen, P. A., 1983. *Carmina Epigraphica Graeca Saeculorum VIII–V A. Chr. N., Text und Kommentare* 12. Berlin.

IC, M. Guarducci, F. Halbherr, eds. (1935–50). *Inscriptiones Creticae*. Rome.

IG, A. Böckh et al., eds. (1873–). *Inscriptiones Graecae*. Berlin.

ILS, H. Dessau. (1892–1916). *Inscriptiones Latinae Selectae*. Berlin.

LSCG, F. Sokolowski. 1969. *Lois sacrées des cités grecques*. Paris.

LSS, F. Sokolowski. 1962. *Lois sacrées: supplément*. Paris.

Res Gestae, P. A. Brunt and J. M. Moore. 1967. *Res Gestae Divi Augusti*. Oxford.

Rhodes-Osborne, P. J. Rhodes and R. G. Osborne, eds. 2003. *Greek Historical Inscriptions 404-323 BC*. Oxford.

SIG[3], W. Dittenberger. (1915–24). *Sylloge Inscriptionum Graecarum*, 3rd edn. Hildesheim.

Papyri

P. Mich., *Michigan Papyri*. 1931–. Ann Arbor, MI.

PSI, *Papiri greci e latini*. 1912–. Florence.

PGM, K. Preisendanz et al., eds. 1973–4. *Papyri Graecae Magicae: Die griechischen Zauberpapyri*, 2 vols, 2nd edn. Stuttgart.

Select Papyri, A. S. Hunt and C. C. Edgar, eds. 1932–41. Loeb Classical Library, Cambridge, MA.

Suppl. Mag., R. W. Daniel and F. Maltomini, eds. 1990–2. *Supplementum Magicum*, Papyrologica Coloniensia 16/1–2, 2 vols. Opladen.

Vindolanda Papyri, A. K. Bowman, and J. D. Thomas. 1994. *The Vindolanda Writing Tablets*. London.

Legal Sources

Theodosian Code, C. Pharr, ed. 1952. *The Theodosian Code and Novels, and the Sirmondian Constitutions*. Princeton. The first systematic compilation of Roman imperial legislation, assembled in 438 CE at the instigation of Emperor Theodosius II.

Index

Page references in italic denote a figure